Spoiled Distinctions

Spoiled Distinctions

AESTHETICS AND THE ORDINARY
IN FRENCH MODERNISM

Hannah Freed-Thall

OXFORD
UNIVERSITY PRESS

OXFORD
UNIVERSITY PRESS

Oxford University Press is a department of the University of Oxford.
It furthers the University's objective of excellence in research, scholarship,
and education by publishing worldwide. Oxford is a registered trade mark
of Oxford University Press in the UK and in certain other countries

Published in the United States of America by
Oxford University Press
198 Madison Avenue, New York, NY 10016,
United States of America

© Oxford University Press 2015

Library of Congress Cataloging-in-Publication Data
Freed-Thall, Hannah.
Spoiled distinctions : aesthetics and the ordinary in French modernism / Hannah Freed-Thall.
p. cm.
Includes bibliographical references and index.
ISBN 978-0-19-020102-9 (cloth) — ISBN 978-0-19-020103-6 (updf) 1. French literature—
20th century—History and criticism. 2. Modernism (Literature)—France. 3. Modernism
(Aesthetics)—France. 4. Life in literature. I. Title.
PQ307.M63F74 2015
840.9'112—dc23
2015001732

1 3 5 7 9 8 6 4 2

Printed in the United States of America on acid-free paper

{ CONTENTS }

{ ACKNOWLEDGMENTS }

It is a pleasure to acknowledge those whose support has made this book possible.

UC Berkeley's Comparative Literature Department was the ideal place to gather my thoughts about aesthetics and the ordinary. I was very fortunate to work with Michael Lucey, Ann Smock, and Barbara Spackman—wonderful advisors who supported this project from its earliest stages, and who helped me to think more rigorously and creatively about the topics that matter most to me. I also benefited from the guidance of Professors Anne-Lise François, Eric Naiman, David Miller, Rob Kaufman, Suzanne Guerlac, Karl Britto, Tim Hampton, and Vicky Kahn. And I was inspired by my brilliant fellow graduate students, too numerous to name here. I will mention only my dear friend Sarah Ann Wells, who generously read drafts of this project (along with nearly everything else I've written over the past several years) with a keen critical eye.

The project took new shape and direction during my time at the Princeton Society of Fellows. I am deeply grateful to Susan Stewart and Mary Harper, whose generosity, tact, and intelligence made this a dream fellowship. I also wish to express my gratitude to Carol Rigolot and Molly Greene, who helped me to find my way at Princeton. I was fortunate to be affiliated with the Princeton French Department, and wish to thank François Rigolot, André Benhaïm, Effie Rentzou, and Eliza Zingesser in particular for going out of their way to make me feel at home. In the Society of Fellows, I learned a great deal from all of my fellow postdoctoral and faculty fellows. I especially thank Ellen Lockhart, whose well-lit kitchen table became a favorite writing station, and whose friendship made the fellowship years more lively and hilarious. I was lucky to have met Dora Zhang during my time at Princeton; I am grateful to her for reading the manuscript and offering valuable suggestions. That this book exists at all is thanks to Anne Cheng, mentor extraordinaire, who stepped in at just the right moment to help me find a publisher.

The book was completed at Brown University, where I was happy to be supported by the Department of Comparative Literature, and by a postdoctoral fellowship in the Pembroke Seminar, "Aesthetics and the Question of Beauty." I am grateful for the vibrant intellectual community that I have found at Brown. Members of the Pembroke Seminar, members of the Brown French department, Leela Gandhi's Human Sciences seminar, and Thomas Schestag all offered insightful feedback on chapters of the manuscript. Marc Redfield provided encouragement and guidance as department chair and seminar leader. Tamara Chin and the Environmental Humanities Reading Group gave me the opportunity to think about the ecological resonances of my project. I am especially indebted to Thangam Ravindranathan, who read sections of the book with extraordinary generosity and critical acumen.

It has been a pleasure to work with Brendan O'Neill at Oxford University Press. I wish to thank him, as well as three anonymous reviewers for their helpful and encouraging suggestions on the manuscript. I am also thankful for the attentiveness and professionalism of my production editor, Manikandan Kuppan, and the entire production team. Earlier versions of chapters 1 and 2 appeared in *New Literary History* and *Modern Language Notes*. I thank Johns Hopkins University Press for permission to publish this material in revised form.

I have sought permission to reprint several translated poems. Thanks to Lee Fahnestock for permission to cite from her *Mute Objects of Expression* (New York: Archipelago Books, 2008); to Wake Forest University Press for permission to cite lines from "The Butterfly" by Francis Ponge, first published in *Francis Ponge: Selected Poems*, ed. Margaret Guiton, trans. C.K. Williams, John Montague, and Margaret Guiton (Winston-Salem: Wake Forest University Press, 1994); and to Peter Manson and Miami University Press for permission to reprint "Little Tune" ("Petit Air"), first published in *Stéphane Mallarmé: The Poems in Verse*, translated by Peter Manson (Oxford, OH: Miami University Press, 2012).

Finally, I wish to thank my family, especially Michael, Patricia, and Aaron Freed-Thall, Marvin and Harriet Thall, and Jeanette and Lewis Freed. It is difficult to adequately express my gratitude for all that they have taught me, and all that they have given me, except to say that their love and support have made everything possible. I am also grateful to Julie and Bob Porter, whose guest room ("Quail Run") served as my writing retreat on many occasions, and whose enthusiasm turned the occasion of submitting the manuscript into an event. Above all, I thank Jillian Porter, who has read and reread every page of this book. To share the everyday with her is the greatest of gifts.

Spoiled Distinctions

Introduction

This is a book about French modernism's love affair with the ordinary, unso-phisticated side of aesthetic experience. The protagonists of this study—Marcel Proust, Francis Ponge, Nathalie Sarraute, and Yasmina Reza—experiment with the limits of aesthetic perception, staging scenes in which the ordinariness of things confounds critical appraisal. These authors are less interested in the pleasing and harmonious beautiful than in beauty's weird progeny, from the nebulous drift of "nuance" to the cloying, sticky "douceâtre" (sickly sweet). They invite us to behold objects too evanescent or ubiquitous to be masterfully displayed: not the monumental statue, but the squat coffee table statuette; not the classical fountain, but the modest glass of tap water. This book thus investigates modernism's alternatives to the beautiful—its ca-pacity to treasure the botched, the flawed, and the imperfect.

One of the main arguments developed here is that French modernists expose the underside of cultural distinction. To cultivate distinguished taste is to rehearse the separation between "sophisticated" and "vulgar" ways of looking, and between "refined" and "ordinary" objects. And yet intensified attention to the phenomenal qualities of things can be disorienting, and the signs of distinction are often difficult to manage. Deeply concerned with questions of prestige and sophistication, Proust, Ponge, Sarraute, and Reza hone in on everyday processes of value-production. They investigate how dis-tinction is made and unmade: how the invaluable can short-circuit into the valueless; how, in the absence of any determining aesthetic rule or standard, the realm of precious objects becomes indistinguishable from the world of ordinary things.

Above all, these authors are fascinated by the volatility of value and the problem of inestimable worth. A defining feature of modernism, I argue, is the way it foregrounds the wavering line between the utterly particular—*thisness*—and the common. As an emblem of such radiant indeterminacy, consider the painting featured on the cover of this book. Manet presented his limp, iridescent *Asparagus* (1880) as an ambiguous conjunction of gift and leftover when he sent it to the buyer of his previously executed still life, *A Bunch of Asparagus*. "Your bunch was missing one" ("Il en manquait une à votre botte"), the artist declared in an accompanying note.[1] An index pointing toward nothing in particular, the single asparagus stalk is both a singular condensation of preciosity and a forgotten or abandoned thing. Many modernist texts draw our attention to objects that similarly blur the lines between the poetic and the prosaic. One might think, for example, of Baudelaire's bedraggled swan amidst the bric-a-brac of modern Paris—at once a mythical allegory of exile and an image representing "anyone at all" ("quiconque") who has lost whatever cannot be recovered.[2] Or of Flaubert's story, "A Simple Heart," which ends with the spectacle of a shabby and resplendent stuffed parrot rising dubiously to the heavens. Just as difficult to evaluate is Lily Briscoe's amateur painting in Woolf's *To the Lighthouse*—a possibly visionary work that will be stashed in an attic or "rolled up and stuffed under a sofa."[3] Proust famously equates aesthetic value with a "precious" fragment of yellow wall in a Vermeer painting—perfectly self-sufficient, yet ambiguously bound up with some indigestible yellow potatoes. He is drawn to objects that shimmer with uncertain worth, like the questionable diamond that materializes as if by magic in his "Lemoine Affair" pastiches, or Venice, the long-dreamed-of city that shines like a mirage in the penultimate volume of *À la recherche du temps perdu* before crumbling into "whatever place," strange in its utter commonness.[4]

Ponge, Sarraute, and Reza present equally captivating case studies of baffled judgment. Each draws our critical gaze away from dignified and untouchable forms, disengaging art and aesthetic attention from the museum space of high culture. Ponge serves up objects that resist display—such as soap (which expends itself in the course of the poem), blackberries (prickly and suspiciously excremental), or a packing crate (already used up, still gleaming new but transforming into trash before our eyes). Sarraute examines the process by which the singular thing becomes a cliché. She foregrounds her characters' struggle to possess objects that are already too significant, too saturated with other people's evaluations: a pre-Columbian sculpture exhibited in the bourgeois home, a passed-around postcard reproduction of a Courbet painting, a much-debated antique chair. Representing aesthetic judgment as a ritual at once meaningful and absurd, Reza structures her play, *"Art,"* around a scene in which a painting is desecrated and then washed clean again. Each of these writers invites us to pay attention to things that hover on the border between worth and worthlessness. Alternately precious and unremarkable, such inestimable objects cast the aesthetic subject out of the navigable universe of taste.

In rethinking the relation between art and the ordinary in twentieth-century France, this book skirts the old division between high modernism and the avant-garde. According to Peter Bürger's classic account, modernism can best be understood as a fundamentally defensive reaction to cultural modernity. In this view, modernist texts like Proust's *Recherche* are unable to call into question their own alleged autonomy—their institutional status as art—because this is precisely what defends them against consumption by the masses. Not wanting to be legible to just anyone, modernism cultivates difficulty, but it also mystifies this practice, encouraging its devotees to imagine that their enjoyment reflects an innate gift, a superior sensitivity. To put Pierre Bourdieu's terminology in service to this theory, we could say that high modernism fosters an ideology of charisma, whereby the artwork is imagined to have "a magical power of conversion capable of awakening the potentialities latent in a few of the elect."[5] The avant-garde, on the other hand, works to demystify and denaturalize institutionalized privilege by smashing the divide between art and the everyday, demanding, as Bürger puts it, that art "be integrated into the praxis of life."[6] In this account, modernism aestheticizes the ordinary and closes itself off from the logic of capitalist consumption, while the avant-garde contests the logic of aesthetic autonomy, drawing on the energies of vernacular culture in order to imagine an artistic practice potentially available to all.

Proust in particular has long been read as the "high priest" of high modernism: he is famous for championing an aesthetics of redemption, wherein a gifted perceiver can extract enduring worth from the merely phenomenal world by elevating it into the sacred realm of art.[7] According to this view, the *Recherche* valorizes the ordinary only to the extent that it can be mined for lasting, private aesthetic wealth. In my reading, however, Proust's novel looks less like a heroic monument to high art and more like a guide to commonplace, modest modes of enjoyment. I argue that Proust teaches us to value the formal and material vibrancy of inestimably ordinary things: splotches of light on a toolshed, pond, or painting; nebulous, shape-shifting blossoms that turn into girls, clouds, and shadows; precious diamonds that anyone might cook up in the oven. Ponge and Sarraute—experimental writers who loosely and briefly associated with avant-garde groups—follow Proust in developing alternatives to both avant-garde subversion and high-modernist sublimation. Each explores the far edges of distinction, the zone where the aesthetic beholder can only gape, point, or stammer in astonishment (or embarrassment).

Rei Terada has compellingly described "phenomenophilia" (attention to "aberrant appearance"—"looking away at the colored shadow on the wall, or keeping the head turned to the angle at which the sunspot stays in view") as a way of saying "no" to a shared, commonplace world, and hence as a way of escaping from other people.[8] Persuasive though this argument is, I would suggest that in Proust, occasions of intensified attention to the ephemeral textures of the everyday are not expressions of what Terada calls "dissatisfaction with the given,"[9] but rather, instances when the aesthetic subject's quest to prove himself better than other people is temporarily suspended. Because they are available to all, such perceptions do not shore up the perceiver's solipsistic mastery. In gazing at a chicken on a roof, a hedge in bloom, or a bouquet of moving steeples, the astonished beholder suddenly finds that he has become part of the composition, rather than standing above it to judge. At such moments, character and reader alike enjoy a small break from the teleological drive toward epistemological (aesthetic or erotic) revelation that often dominates the narrative.

Each of my chapters is organized around a scene of beholding—an encounter with the ordinary. Each identifies a particular critical quandary or instance of theoretical discomfiture. In these moments of non-domination (or failed domination), instead of assimilating a perception into a powerful summary, the perceiver is moved simply to point at the object, touch it, or mimic it. Rather than affirming her solitude and superior refinement, the aesthetically disoriented subject finds herself drawn into the orbit of others. I contend that such occasions of befuddled beholding are not failures at all, even when they are explicitly presented as such. Rather, taken together, these scenes of awkward judgment tell a new story about French modernism. Setting aside notions of prestige and aesthetic heroism, my narrative highlights the ordinariness of aesthetic perception, and the unexamined intensities of the ordinary.

Ordinary, Everyday, Quelconque

The everyday escapes, that's its definition.
−MAURICE BLANCHOT, "EVERYDAY SPEECH"

Although the terms "aesthetic" and "ordinary" might not immediately appear to belong together, this book makes a case for their intimate alliance. The authors examined here multiply strategies for reading and valuing the ordinary—or rather, *ordinaries*—since ordinariness, I argue, cannot be reduced to a single concept, and must instead be approached as a rhetorical knot, or constellation of figures and signifying practices.

The ordinary is a crucial concept in modernism, although its meaning is not fixed—in fact, it might be defined precisely as the featureless or the unqualifiable. The ordinary is that which always eludes set categories of apprehension; like its sister term, the "everyday," the ordinary is what escapes. Existing scholarship on the ordinary underscores the slipperiness of the concept. Critics emphasize the uncertainty inherent in what appears most given, whether they conceptualize ordinariness narratologically—as a departure from type that stimulates narrative desire (Gallagher); linguistically—as a region of speech beyond affirmation or negation (Blanchot); in literary-ecological terms—as a happening that leaves no trace, receding even as it appears (François); or in relation to material culture—ordinary objects being "intimate" but undomesticated, impossible to display (Brown).[10]

I approach this elusive topic by focusing, chapter by chapter, on particular modalities of ordinariness: *prestige* (the semi-magical production of everyday cultural value); the *quelconque*, or *whatever* (an overlap of singularity and banality); *nuance* (shimmering, minimal variation); the *awkward* (the exposed labor of poetic making); and the *douceâtre* (a minor, quotidian form of disgust). "The ordinary" therefore takes numerous forms here. Sometimes it appears as the given, the world *as such*—luminous, textured, mutable, finite, forgettable. Alternatively, it appears as the ubiquitous, the object that "grows on trees" (or "runs the streets"—"court les rues" in the French idiom). In other circumstances, the ordinary is the broken-down, wasted, or abandoned, the leftovers and scraps of value-production, including overused or worn-out language: cliché, platitude, the limp or "sleeping" metaphor. In each case, we are challenged to imagine forms of value based neither in durability nor in scarcity.

By exploring a variety of unclassifiable objects and affects, modernist literature heightens our awareness of what we normally overlook. For Proust and other twentieth-century experimenters, attending to the ordinary is a matter of fine-tuning our sensibilities, our capacity for close listening and subtle, transient forms of attention. Such experiments involve a recalibration of scale and speed. Early critics were abashed by the unprecedented indolence of Proust's prose and by his penchant for extremely close up, hyper-nuanced descriptions of phenomena. Ponge also ushers us into a state of suspended motion. He invites us, for example, to slow down and look at the world from the vantage point of a lowly snail, or to enter the miniature landscape of a loaf of bread. Playing with scale in a different way, Sarraute makes us cognizant of what she terms the "tropism": a micrological, unquantifiable sensory quality suffusing every ordinary social situation. Sarraute's literary language is designed to be super-sensible to these minute quotidian quakings, these tiny floods of social feeling.

Modernism is not only oriented toward the phenomenology of minor aesthetic objects and affects. It also foregrounds the everyday language of aesthetic encounter. Modernists—and Proust above all—are famous for flaunting the inimitable singularity of their style. But Proust, Ponge, and Sarraute are also fascinated by inarticulacy. Their works stage flummoxed scenes of enjoyment: occasions in which a perceiver's masterful appraisal morphs into a variety of new expressive forms. Different object-encounters invite different styles of aesthetic response. Thus the specter of a fabricated diamond inspires the playful ventriloquism of Proustian pastiche, while the smallness of Ponge's chosen objects—a pebble, a shrimp, a fig—calls for a humble and unpretentious tone. The many limp, soft objects central to Sarraute's fiction find their stylistic reflection in a rich lexicon of clichés and platitudes.

A number of recent studies have explored modernism's commitment to the common, developing alternatives to the theory that this literature aims to transcend, transvalue, or sublimate the everyday.[11] *Spoiled Distinctions* expands on this critical turn toward a pragmatic, public, everyday modernism. The originality of this book, however, lies in the way it engages the ordinary from the vantage point of aesthetic theory. By focusing on scenes of aesthetic beholding, I am able to identify figurations of the ordinary that are not entirely reducible to humdrum and routine. While Liesl Olson defines the modernist ordinary in terms of "experiences that are *not* heightened," I argue that Proust and his literary heirs teach us to see the incomparable *thisness* inherent in the most ordinary objects and in the least sophisticated modes of enjoyment.[12] They pose the question: What kind of "heightened" or singular perception is truly common—not an index of personal refinement, but available to all?

Consider the case of the "quelconque," a modality of the ordinary that underwent a semantic permutation in the late nineteenth century. In its most basic sense, *quelconque* is a gender-neutral adjective that designates an object as neither specific nor generic, but indeterminate in quality or identity. *Quelconque* is a strange adjective. A marker of unmarkedness, rather than qualifying its object, it un-qualifies. In the last decades of the nineteenth century, *quelconque* acquired a pejorative connotation, and began to signify an object's lack of distinction, making it possible for the first time to declare something "très quelconque," or "very whatever." By the turn of the century, then, *quelconque* indicates an ambiguous overlap of tones. Alternatively neutral and dismissive, it signifies indeterminacy, on the one hand, and insignificance, on the other.

In an 1888 essay on Maupassant, Henry James highlights the aesthetic potentiality of the *quelconque*. James argues that Maupassant's short fiction is organized as a "series of observations upon an épisode quelconque"—an ordinary episode, any episode whatsoever. Maupassant does not arrange his narratives according to plot, James contends. Rather, inspired by Flaubert, "his effort has been to give the uncomposed, unrounded look of life, with its accidents, its broken rhythm, its queer resemblance to a compound of trains that start but don't arrive, and trains that arrive but don't start."[13] The unqualifiable, the featureless, and the inestimable are central to Maupassant's proto-modernist prose, organized like a *fait divers* (minor news item) around unexpected everyday incidents and encounters. In his discussion of the "épisode quelconque," James points us toward a new, complex understanding of the ordinary. In its open-ended indeterminacy, James suggests, the fin-de-siècle *quelconque* is an instigator of fiction, a blank spot of thought, a placeholder or open space from which new concepts and new genres might emerge.

Allied with both semantic freedom and flatness, with both the unknowable and the overused, the *quelconque* belongs to the era of mechanical reproduction. Lithographer Hermann-Paul underscored this association when he titled his 1895 lithography series about the lives of ordinary men and women *La Vie de Monsieur Quelconque* and *La Vie de Madame Quelconque* (*The Life of Monsieur Whatever* and *The Life of Madame Whatever*).[14] In these albums, Hermann-Paul plays at the limits of typicality. Each series presents ten typical views of its typical subject. Hence we see "Madame Quelconque" moving from childhood to adolescence, marriage, maternity, adultery, grandmotherhood, and death. "Monsieur Quelconque" progresses through the predictable benchmarks of bourgeois masculine personhood: scholarly exams, a visit to the brothel, military service, and a variety of official ceremonies, including, finally, his own funeral.[15] These prints tend to show Monsieur or Madame in absence, from the back, or indistinguishable among an identical (or nearly identical) set of figures. What is most interesting about these images is that rather than definitively capturing Monsieur and Madame Quelconque in visual form, the effect of such intense typification is instead to release the subject from view. For example, the first print of the *Vie de Madame Quelconque* series is an image titled "Her childhood is happy" ("Son enfance est heureuse"). The happy child—the miniature Madame Quelconque—appears only by not appearing: instead of the girl, we see two identical women, a man in the background hidden behind a newspaper (perhaps the girl's father, or merely a random stranger, included in the frame as if by accident), and, in the foreground, some conventional props of childhood play: buckets and a jump rope (Figure 0.1). Throughout the *Monsieur* and *Madame Quelconque* series, Hermann-Paul exploits the aesthetic qualities of lithography itself: *quelconquerie* (whateverness) is allied here with superficiality, seriality, turned backs, and inscrutable faces. These series give visual form to a new crystallization of ordinariness—an abstraction and generalization that simultaneously constrains and unfixes. Even as they are flattened into utter typicality, Monsieur and Madame Quelconque are granted a certain measure of inscrutability. Impressed upon the page, they nonetheless evade our gaze.

Nearly a century after Hermann-Paul first allied this term with the mechanically reproducible image, Roland Barthes linked the *quelconque* to photography's strange mix of contingency and seriality. In *Camera Lucida*, Barthes cites this peculiar adjective several times, always placing it in quotation marks, but never specifying the source of the citation. The vagueness and imprecision of an unattributable citation is precisely what *quelconque* suggests: something is *quelconque* because it is familiar to everyone; it belongs to the doxa ("what everyone sees and knows").[16] Yet the *quelconque* is also a space where opposing edges meet, where "banality" shades into

FIGURE O.1 Hermann-Paul, *La Vie de Madame Quelconque.*
Source: *Typ 915.00.4505, Houghton Library, Harvard University.*

"contingency, singularity, risk."[17] Qualifying the vacuous mood bordering
a sudden flash or "fulguration," the *quelconque* suggests a field that appears
alternately commonplace or singular, depending on one's point of view.
Hence the photograph Barthes prizes above all others, the most indescrib-
ably beloved (the Winter Garden photograph) is for us "nothing but an indifferent picture, one of the thousand manifestations of the 'quelconque.'"[18]
Elsewhere Barthes uses the term "neutral" ("neutre") to speak of something that is incomparable and yet not unique, and this paradoxical singularity is also at stake in the *quelconque.*[19]

In bundling together the obvious and the unknowable, both Hermann-Paul's *Quelconque* series and Barthes's meditation on photography explore tensions within the concept of the everyday. The everyday is a radically ambiguous concept. It signifies a fully captured and quantified level of existence, and at the same time implies an escape from all coherence and regularity. As Maurice Blanchot suggests in his 1962 essay, "Everyday Speech" ("La Parole quotidienne"), the everyday is a zone where the stagnant and tedious ("what lags and falls back, the residual life with which our trash cans and cemeteries are filled") meet the spontaneous and unfinished.[20] If the everyday ultimately eludes final reckoning, it is because modernity's regime of heightened typification and quantification paradoxically grants its subjects a new kind of anonymity. Hence Blanchot indicates that the everyday is not the site of the individual, but of the contradictory being he terms the "homme quelconque" ("whatever man"). "In the everyday," according to Blanchot, "we have no name, little personal reality, scarcely a face. [. . .] [W]hen I live the everyday, it is anyone, anyone whatsoever, who does so."[21]

In 1894, the same year that Hermann-Paul introduced his *Quelconque* series, Mallarmé composed a sonnet titled "Petit Air" ("Little Tune" in Peter Manson's translation, or in E. H. and A. M. Blackmore's rendering, "Little Ditty").[22] The first of three identically titled poems, this sonnet, like Hermann-Paul's lithography, is also part of a series of sorts. Mallarmé, too, plays on the contradictions of the *quelconque*. The sonnet disorients by throwing an untethered "quelconque" at us in its very first line. An initial suggestion of indeterminacy and ordinariness hangs suspended, modifying nothing in particular and yet casting a shadow—or "little air"—over the entire poem:

Petit Air

Quelconque une solitude
Sans le cygne ni le quai
Mire sa désuétude
Au regard que j'abdiquai

Ici de la gloriole
Haute à ne la pas toucher
Dont maint ciel se bariole
Avec les ors de coucher

Mais langoureusement longe
Comme de blanc linge ôté
Tel fugace oiseau si plonge
Exultatrice à côté

Dans l'onde toi devenue
Ta jubilation nue.[23]

Little Tune

Any given solitude
with neither swan nor quayside
mirrors its obsolescence
in the gaze I abdicated

here from the vain glory
too high to be touched
in which many a dappled sky
puts on sunset gold

but languorously follows
like white linen cast off
some ephemeral bird if plunges
adjacent exultatrix

into the wave become you
your nude jubilation[24]

The English phrase, "any given solitude," aptly conveys the sonnet's evasion of specificity. Yet this translation also somewhat tames the strangeness of that unfixed and ungrammatical initial "quelconque," an adjective not syntactically attached to anything. More literally—and awkwardly—we might translate that opening line as "Whatever a solitude," or "Any a solitude." Mallarmé is laying the accent here on an undefinable "something or other," and on a kind of indifference or insignificance that, with a slight shift of emphasis, becomes surprising. He subtly rearranges elements in order to open a channel between what Blanchot identifies as the everyday's two conflicting modalities: insignificance as deficiency of meaning and insignificance as potentiality— the site of all signification.[25] Indeed, the entire sonnet, which ends with the suggestion of a bather leaping into the water, works to bring exultation into proximity with the *quelconque*. In its floating, sketch-like quality, the poem illustrates Henry James's definition of the "épisode quelconque," with its plotless "accidents," its "broken rhythm," and its effect of minimal arrangement, as if certain words and phrases had been jumbled in a bag and tossed onto the page. And yet the *quelconque* in "Petit Air" is also the jumping off point for poetic jubilation.

At this same historical juncture, Paul Valéry was exploring the possibilities of the *quelconque* in his experimental narrative, *La soirée avec Monsieur Teste* (*An Evening with Monsieur Teste*), first published in 1896. Although Teste is described as an "extraordinary" and "singular" man, his spare dwelling—adorned only with a few pieces of furniture, some newspapers, a dozen *cartes de visites*, and a pharmaceutical flask—is singularly unremarkable: "I've never had a stronger impression of the *quelconque*" ("Je n'ai jamais eu plus fortement l'impression du *quelconque*") the narrator declares upon entering Teste's home for the first time (Valéry's emphasis).[26] The narrator goes on to tell us that this "*quelconque* lodging" is analogous to the "*quelconque* point of theorems." Valéry is drawing here on the mathematical meaning of "quelconque," which is not a negative concept, but simply designates an element as generic or unmarked, sharing the properties of every other element of its class.[27] By placing his exceptional hero in a setting as unexceptional as possible, Valéry experiments—like Hermann-Paul and Mallarmé—with the distinction between singularity and generality. He explores the narrative potential of indeterminacy: Is it possible to create a character who is at once extraordinary and utterly anonymous? What can occur in a space with no qualities, a space identical to any other?

A contradictory modernist structure of feeling, the *quelconque* marks the flip side of durable, lasting aesthetic worth.[28] In Proust, the *quelconque* is linked to ephemerality and to minor, quotidian objects and events. What is noteworthy about the Proustian *quelconque* is that it is not negatively cast, as one might expect, but presented as a richly indeterminate semantic field. A signifier of the unspecifiable, the *quelconque* in Proust incites both boredom and curiosity, and it appears in particular proximity to scenes of reading and interpretation. Tracing the *quelconque* through Proust reveals a non-redemptive, non-subversive economy of aesthetic interest. This flexible and open mode of attention particularly suits the modernist reader, Proust suggests: when his narrator encounters a piece of the *Recherche* in the newspaper, he is thrilled to disappear into the ranks of the "lecteur quelconque"— a reader without qualities, any reader at all.

A number of twentieth-century philosophers have followed Proust in wresting the *quelconque* from its pejorative signification and orienting it toward more promising ends. Deleuze, Agamben, and Jean-Luc Nancy all understand the *quelconque* as a paradigm-thwarting concept that blurs the distinction between the particular and the general. For these philosophers, *quelconque* invokes a new way of conceiving of community and the commonplace. Deleuze uses the term *espace quelconque* ("any-space-whatever") to describe a cinematic space in which singularity is multiplied, made virtual: "it's a perfectly particular space which has merely lost its homogeneity, that is to say the principle of its numeric relations or the connection amongst its proper parts, so well that the interrelations amongst them may be made in an infinite number of ways."[29] Agamben also associates the *quelconque* with the potentiality of the singular, or "tel quel." In *The Coming Community*, he turns in circles around the "whatever" (*qualunque, quodlibet*) as the notion of an unnameable exteriority—a thing without attributes, without archetype—thinkable only as pure limit or threshold. "Whatever singularity," Agamben explains, is "freed from the false dilemma that obliges knowledge to choose between the ineffability of the individual and the intelligibility of the universal." Reclaimed from having a certain property, or belonging to a certain set or class, whatever singularity is allied for Agamben with the *lovable*—with the lover's desire for the loved one "with all of its predicates, its being such as it is."[30] Similarly, in "The Heart of Things," Nancy attempts to elaborate a non-privative sense of *quelconque. Quelconque* for him indicates a paradoxical singularity: a singular existence that is "posited and exposed" as simultaneously determined and indeterminate.[31] *Quelconque* is a difficult concept for us to think through, Nancy notes, because it requires that we leave behind what thinking usually means, abandoning "all our determining, identifying, destining thoughts" in order to see the world as comprised of the permutability of all things.[32]

Complex and mutable as it is, the *quelconque* is only one of various forms that ordinariness takes in modernity. Each of the four other aesthetic concepts that this book explores is similarly generative. Each emerges in scenes of everyday aesthetic judgment—occasions when particular objects or sensory details appear to float free of encompassing category, inviting the perceiver's intensified attention without yielding any final truth.

Aesthetic Indistinction

Of all the various strains of modernist thought, French modernism is particularly concerned with relations among art, social distinction, and everyday life. Tensions among these concepts have fueled French literature and theory since the mid–nineteenth century, from Baudelaire's lyrical experiments with bad taste and Flaubert's narrativization of insignificance, to the more recent interventions of Roland Barthes, Pierre Bourdieu, Jean-Luc Nancy, and Jacques Rancière. By focusing on the work of these and other French thinkers, this book offers a perspective on the aesthetics of the ordinary that is often neglected in modernist studies, with its dominant focus on Anglo-American literature.

In France, thinkers otherwise very different in their convictions converge around the problem of art's ordinariness. Instructive in this regard are the examples of philosopher Jacques Rancière and sociologist Pierre Bourdieu, arguably the two most important theorists of the relation between aesthetics and everyday life. Despite their fundamental methodological differences, Bourdieu and Rancière agree on one thing: a major shift in practices of aesthetic production and perception took place in Europe during the nineteenth century.[33] For Rancière, this "aesthetic revolution" involves a movement away from the "representative" or "mimetic" regime of art—a hierarchical system of norms and rules determining which genre should correspond to which objects, and clearly separating the "poetical" from the "prosaic," or art from life.[34] This division of "noble" and "ignoble" subjects gives way in modernity to an "aesthetic regime" marked by a fundamental indifference with regard to subject matter. Instead of dividing art from non-art, the aesthetic regime both emphasizes art's autonomy—its freedom from any specific rule or hierarchy—and underscores its embrace of the ordinary. As Rancière points out, the advent of the aesthetic regime corresponds to "the triumph of the *quelconque*."[35] There is a paradox inherent in the aesthetic regime's intimacy with the everyday: art will no longer be determined by any criteria of perfection, but will henceforth be recognizable "by its lack of any distinguishing characteristics—by its indistinction."[36] Concerned with the social consequences of this shift, Rancière questions what happens when artworks no longer celebrate the glory of those who commissioned them, but instead, offer themselves "to the gaze of anyone at all."[37]

Rancière finds in Flaubert a compelling illustration of this problem. In *Madame Bovary*, Flaubert elevates description to the plane of action, and refuses to prefer one character or one type of object to any other. Observed at the level of the "microevent," everything becomes equal for him: the ambitions of a farmer's daughter are no less poetic than the deeds of an aristocrat; a swirling dust cloud is as stylistically interesting as a racing carriage. Rancière notes that while this "equality" of subjects in literature is independent of a political stance in favor of democracy, it is nonetheless historically linked to a general "redistribution of the sensible," whereby the grand actions of noble men are no longer intrinsically superior (or more aesthetically valuable) than the everyday lives of working men and women. The problem for Flaubert, Rancière notes, is how "Art" will remain special or distinctive if it no longer has any particular distinguishing features. In fact, Emma Bovary's "practical" sentimentality—her desire to consume art, chairs, and dresses without regard to the distinctions between them—makes her Flaubert's inverted double: both character and writer dissolve the separation between art and life.[38] Hence Rancière contends that Flaubert "kills" Emma in a gesture of defense against her kitsch aesthetics, an attempt to preserve some margin of distinction for art, to protect it from the everyday appetites of ordinary people.

Bourdieu explores the same problem—the indistinction of art—from a different point of view. We should not pose the ontological question, "what is art," he declares. Instead, we have to examine what "art" *does* and how this particular mode of value is continuously made, remade, and put into circulation. While Rancière is concerned with the ways in which the emergence of the aesthetic regime relates more broadly to ideals of equality and democracy, Bourdieu analyzes how the nineteenth-century rise of a market for cultural goods corresponds to the consolidation of a relatively autonomous literary and artistic field.[39] This new sphere of literature is no longer subservient to the powerful. Because it deals in new forms of credit, it can afford to mock both the bourgeoisie and the *Académie française*—that traditional "central bank" of cultural capital and institutional "monopoly holder" of cultural prestige, which had previously assured the definition of "art" and the "artist."[40] Eschewing traditional modes of consecration, the newly autonomous literary field will henceforth be based in "free competition among creator-prophets freely asserting the extraordinary and singular *nomos*, without precedent or equivalent, which properly defines them."[41] Subject matter will no longer be important; art will no longer be limited to a particular category of privileged objects. From now on, nothing is too insignificant or too vulgar to appear in a poem or a painting, Bourdieu contends. What counts is the way these things are represented, how they are filtered through the singular vision of a historically unprecedented social personage: the modern artist.[42]

Freed from academic rules and expectations, materializing the fantasies of the outcast "prophet" who created it, the artwork itself now attains a status at once sacred and profane. Hence Flaubert proclaims that a work of art is priceless, beyond appraisal, "inappréciable," and Baudelaire denounces the ignorance of critics who try to measure "l'oeuvre singulière" against formal and universal rules.[43] Academic criteria such as the dignity of the work's conception, the superiority of its technique, and the *savoir-faire* inherent in its execution will no longer be the operative standards of judgment. Instead, Bourdieu notes, the critic will simply have to "submit" to the work itself in some undefined way.[44] In a transformation exemplified by Manet's redistribution of light on the canvas—such that there is no longer any single privileged place for light, which now appears "everywhere on the surface of things"—"art" is no longer a "closed world of predetermined possibles," but becomes "an infinite universe of possibles."[45]

What does this historical shift toward aesthetic autonomy (and indeterminacy) mean for the aesthetic beholder, who is henceforth required to "submit in some way" to a work that obeys no laws except to break with all precedents? Proust, Ponge, Sarraute, and Reza explore the consequences of this aesthetic revolution—this "triumph of the *quelconque*"—which makes any ordinary thing an aesthetic object and potentially endows any ordinary person with an aesthetic gaze. From one point of view, these writers struggle (like Flaubert) to maintain the distinction of art—to protect it from the leveling force of the market and prevent it from becoming a consumable commodity like all others. At the same time, they show us just how untenable the line is between the concept-blurring realm known as "the aesthetic" and the everyday, phenomenal world.

Beauty's Afterlives

One of the ultimate objectives of this book, then, is to demonstrate that the aesthetic is nothing special. This may seem counterintuitive, especially when we consider aesthetics from the standpoint of "taste"—a concept that brings to mind highly codified scenes of evaluation, organized around lingering pre-capitalist ideals of prestige. Yet even if, following Bourdieu, we regard taste as a force of social classification and an index of status, to contemplate taste is to consider the everydayness of aesthetic encounter. Understood pragmatically, taste is about the imbrication of subject and world.

As a sociological concept, taste implies the presentation of a social face: as Antoine Hennion points out, in the objects of our taste, we tender an image of ourselves to others.[46] "Taste classifies, and it classifies the classifier," Bourdieu more acidly declares in the opening pages of *Distinction*.[47] Yet taste suggests not just a relation of reflexive classification, but what Hennion terms a "perplexed," unsettled, and unsettling relation to objects.[48] As Claudio Benzecry has noted in his ethnography of opera fanatics, taste sometimes takes the form of an affective intensity irreducible to the desire for class status or cultural domination.[49] As a manifestation of what Marielle Macé terms "aesthetic conduct," akin to a performer's "phrasing" of a musical line, taste is both an active stylization of the given and a surrender to the materials at hand.[50] In our everyday engagement with the things that we find pleasing or displeasing, collectable or disposable, objects solicit our attention, and we open our senses to the encounter. To taste is to attune oneself to things.

French modernism is centrally animated by the contradictions of aesthetic taste. The authors featured in this study teach us to understand taste pragmatically: like Bourdieu, they demonstrate that the ability to enjoy objects "without interest" requires initiation, an investment of time, and a great deal of practice. They examine the ways in which subjects instrumentalize aesthetic pleasure (and displeasure) in order to accumulate social prestige or distinction. But unlike Bourdieu, they also play with the very notion of distinction, testing out its grounds and its limits. In their works, aesthetic experience—allied with infelicitous speech acts rather than with eloquent judgments—cannot be reduced to name recognition or to the exercise of worldly erudition. Even as they demystify the scene of sophisticated judgment, these authors explore forms of worth that challenge the logic of acquisition and display.

In its orientation toward unsettling particularity, French modernism implicitly draws on Kantian aesthetic thought. This tradition names a practice of non-domination, a way of experiencing the particular without subsuming it under the general. Readers familiar with the *Critique of the Power of Judgment* will recognize that the styles of critical attention theorized throughout this book are variations on what Kant terms "reflecting" or "reflective" judgment ("reflektierende Urteilskraft"). Reflecting judgments—which is to say, aesthetic judgments—do not simply subsume particulars under pregiven universals, as determining judgments do, but actively explore the *thisness* of things.[51] In this regard, Kant's aesthetic philosophy turns out to be a surprisingly productive site for thinking about the ordinary. Emerging in the eighteenth century as an offshoot of the then more rule-bound discourse of taste, philosophical aesthetics addresses the problem of how we can value the ordinary without instrumentalizing it—without seeking to consume it or fix a price tag to it.[52] Is it possible in modernity to treasure a flower, a stone, or a patch of sky as something other than raw material or potential profit? "Aesthetic" names the worth that adheres to those objects or perceptions that are precisely *not* immediately or obviously exchangeable or sellable. It indicates a different, stranger form of value—one based in feeling rather than verifiable knowledge. As Adorno puts it, the aesthetic requires us to ponder that which is "incommensurable with the empirical measure of all things."[53]

What I most want to wrest from the Kantian tradition of thinking about feeling-based judgment is the value of letting go, rather than appropriating or incorporating objects and perceptions. This is a value particularly aligned with the Kantian beautiful. Kant partitioned disinterested (profitless) perceptual pleasure into two categories: the beautiful and the sublime. Minimal and harmonious, beauty as a mode of representation elicits an affirmative response from the subject. The sublime, by contrast, is awesome and formless. Threatening to overwhelm the mind's classificatory schemes altogether, the sublime incites the subject to cognitive battle. While the sublime stages a drama of mastery lost and regained, the beautiful privileges sharable, non-monumentalizing perceptual attitudes. One way of understanding the Kantian beautiful, then, is as the very opposite of Baudelaire's evocation of beauty as a "dream of stone."[54] The beautiful does not necessarily name a relation of austerity and coldness, but might be read as a feeling of gentle non-appropriation—a way of treasuring what is merely there, without much emphasis or fanfare. This unspectacular mode of attention finds its twentieth-century echo in the myriad forms of the modernist ordinary.

Modernists have reconstrued the beautiful/sublime opposition in diverse ways, identifying many consonant and dissonant, manageable and unmanageable varieties of aesthetic response. Witness, for example, Baudelaire's "spleen" (a mixture of boredom and disgust); Freud's familiarly unfamiliar "uncanny"; the state of visual indifference that Marcel Duchamp termed "anesthesia"; Woolf's quotidian "ecstasy"; surrealism's violent and erotic "convulsive beauty"; the Kafkaesque or Beckettian clowning Adorno calls "second naiveté"; and the many explicitly unremarkable states and unproductive feelings that Roland Barthes spent his last years cataloguing— especially those compellingly subtle refractions of the Kantian beautiful that go under the rubric of the "neutral," including weariness, benevolence, silence, sleep, and tact.

Today, a number of critics are revitalizing aesthetic discourse by retooling its categories. In doing so, they are following the model already set by modernists themselves. A short list of such critical engagements with minor or experimental aesthetic concepts would include Joseph Litvak's study of the perversity of sophistication; Renu Bora and Eve Kosofsky Sedgwick on the overlooked, queer concept of "texture"; Judith Brown on the smoky forms of modernist "glamour"; Anne Anlin Cheng on the "shine" of racialized celebrity in the early twentieth century; and Sianne Ngai on a whole gamut of unprestigious aesthetic concepts that reveal the marginal, powerless status of art in modernity—concepts ranging from "irritation" and "stuplimity" to the "cute" and the "zany."[55] *Spoiled Distinctions* builds on the iconoclastic energies of this contemporary critical reorientation of aesthetic thought. I argue that aesthetic perception—dreamy attention to the formal, textural, "useless" qualities of things—is not necessarily dominating (as Bourdieu would have it), nor necessarily antisocial (as Terada has argued), but can make possible a reconfiguration of expected ways of seeing and feeling.

Road Map

Thinking the ordinary in a non-pejorative way is one of the challenges of modernism. If we make too much of it, it ceases to be what it is: the unnoticed, the unremarked-upon. To conceptualize such smallness and minorness, we will need small or weak concepts—concepts sympathetic to insignificance. The present work charts this conceptual terrain, exploring particular conjunctions of wonderment and banality in each chapter. The book is divided into two sections. Part 1 theorizes an unexamined counterplot in Proust's novel of aesthetic education, while part 2 surveys the post-Proustian landscape, identifying experimental taste concepts in key mid-century works of fiction and poetry.

Chapter 1, "Prestige," presents a case study in the volatility of aesthetic value in early twentieth-century France. The chapter investigates Proust's involvement in the Lemoine Affair, a diamond-fabrication scandal that captured the French popular imagination in 1908, just before Proust began drafting his novel. An engineer claimed to have invented a method of manufacturing diamonds, and upon performing a carefully choreographed trick (he cooked up diamonds, in the nude, for an astonished executive), he managed to defraud the De Beers diamond corporation out of a large sum of money. When the scam was made public, it inspired Proust to publish a series of pastiches in *Le Figaro*. Enthralled by the volatility of the diamond—the preciousness of which had suddenly been revealed as a fiction of controlled scarcity and investor confidence—Proust undertook his own virtuosic exercise in fraud, writing fictional accounts of the affair in the styles of Balzac, Flaubert, Michelet, Sainte-Beuve, and Edmond de Goncourt, among others. My argument is that these experimental pieces highlight modernism's fascination with inestimable worth. Organized around the specter of the massproduced diamond—the ultimate luxury good suddenly transformed into a commodity like any other—the pastiches expose the thin margin that divides signs of preciosity from signs of ordinariness in modernity. They also help us to recognize the central part that the newspaper played in the genesis and development of Proust's novel.

Chapter 2, "Babble," theorizes inarticulacy as central to Proust's aesthetics of the unqualifiable, or "whatever" ("quelconque"). Proust is famous for attributing monumental powers to art and aesthetic attention. Yet *In Search of Lost Time* sometimes calls our attention to objects so unexceptional that they halt and reorient the act of judgment, spoiling the profits of distinction. Early in the novel, the narrator utters his first aesthetic judgment—an enthusiastic, umbrella-waving "zut, zut, zut, zut"—when he sees an assemblage of objects that appears at once wondrous and banal: a chicken strutting on a roof and a pinkish glimmer of light on a pond. Rather than standing at a distance to judge, the perceiver is drawn into the ordinary scene. Tracing echoes of that initial "zut" throughout the *Recherche*, I argue that at such moments of ineloquent astonishment, the Proustian beholder enjoys the world in its commonplace singularity, rather than as a mineable source of private wealth.

One of my aims throughout this book is to disjoin notions of polish and refinement from the idea of subtlety—to show how ordinary subtlety can be. I undertake this challenge most explicitly in chapter 3, "Nuance," which develops a theory of modernist nuance through readings of Proust and several of his admirers, including Roland Barthes, Walter Benjamin, and Maurice Merleau-Ponty. These writers read nuance against the grain, conceiving of it not as the province of an elite or sophisticated sensorium, but merely as everyday, minimal variation. The very fabric of form, nuance is accessible only to a theoretical and perceptual mode weak enough to recognize micronetworks of graduated difference, or what Proust terms "dégradation." Proust's ordinary aesthetics of nuance opens up a formalism not governed by the profit-oriented thrust of human desire. It is based, rather, in the lateral transformations of natural objects (the blossoming of flowers, the drift and transmutation of clouds) that catch the human observer up in their movement.

The second half of the book focuses on authors for whom the spoiling of distinction is no longer a minor or occasional mode (as it is in Proust), but the very substance of aesthetic experience. Chapter 4, "Profanation in Ponge," identifies a logic of reverse sacrifice at the heart of prose poet Francis Ponge's "congested" and botched lyricism. Ponge ruins the sophistication of art, I argue, by privileging scenes of work, and by exposing the lexical waste matter that poetic labor produces. I focus on two radically ineloquent prose poems written in the 1940s. In the first, *La Mounine, Or Note Struck in Afterthought on a Provence Sky*, Ponge deconstructs an epiphanic perception, taking it down to size, one desacralizing analogy after another. In the second, *The Glass of Water*, Ponge labors to let us glimpse an unconventional sort of "perfection": a sufficiency and simplicity open to all. The link between Ponge and Proust is not obvious, as Ponge undoes pretention at every turn, while Proust has a reputation for preciousness. Yet both theorize the afterlife of beauty—its ghostly survival in the guise of the banal. And both permit their reader to behold objects that are at once (as Ponge puts it) "generally unremarkable" and "almost incomparably remarkable."[56]

Proust and Ponge's ethos of unsophisticated wonderment is foreclosed in the work of Nathalie Sarraute, a writer uniquely attuned to the awkward margins of conventional aesthetic perception and response. Sarraute is best known for her association with the gleaming lines and surfaces of the mid-century structuralist "nouveau roman." In fact, as I argue in chapter 5, "Sarraute's Bad Taste," she should be read as the heir to Proust's experiments with the sociology of distinction. By amplifying the performative infelicity that lurks in speech acts of aesthetic judgment, Sarraute concocts strange affective potions. Adding "tenderness to rancor, vindictiveness to generosity," her fictions serve up compositions of pleasure and displeasure that we cannot easily consume.[57] I focus on the "douceâtre"—the toned-down mode of disgust that Sarraute allies with art appreciation in an era of ubiquitous cliché, when it is impossible to distinguish between everyday ordinariness and aesthetic ordinariness, between platitude "mastered" in a work of art and "platitude in the raw." Stickier than beauty, too trivial to be sublime, the *douceâtre* is the mood of cultural consumption in mid-twentieth-century France. Unable to manage the codes of distinction, to judge and classify the objects socially designated as works of art, Sarraute's characters are perpetually discomfited by their inability to take the right amount of pleasure in appropriate objects in an appropriate way.

Finally, the Afterword identifies a contemporary successor to this experimental aesthetic plot: playwright Yasmina Reza, who has made the crisis of distinction into an international spectacle in plays such as *"Art"* and *God of Carnage*. Reza structures her work around scenes of aesthetic bewilderment. She asks what it means to be "moved" by an unqualifiable object, and whether it is possible to make a judgment about art that is not simply an attempt to prove one's own superior refinement. The much-disputed minimalist painting that features centrally in *"Art"* fittingly concludes my study of luminous spots, clouds, glasses of water, and coffee table statuettes. An index of sophistication and a mere stage prop, this blankly inexpressive object flickers in and out of view, inciting both passionate attachment and revulsion in the characters that attempt to evaluate it. Reza's lesson is ultimately also that of Proust, Ponge, and Sarraute: artworks are inappropriate to the task that culture has assigned them. Volatile and uncertain signs of prestige, they signify in unpredictable ways.

This book presents the aesthetic as an experimental site in modernity—a site for the production and circulation of a variety of objects, affects, and signifying practices. I argue that if, according to Bourdieu, aesthetic taste functions as an internalized sense of direction ("sens de l'orientation sociale"), orienting subjects toward their proper "place" in the social hierarchy, aesthetic experiences nonetheless also *dis*orient, inviting us to imagine other means of partitioning the visible and the invisible, the thinkable and the unthinkable.[58] By fabricating ever new and different ways of dividing up and sharing out the perceptible world, French modernism does not simply reinforce the high-low, distinguished-vulgar codes of taste, but makes us aware of the classification-thwarting margins of both aesthetic experience and literary critique.

{ PART 1 }

Aesthetic Disorientation in Proust

{ 1 }

Prestige

In 1908, a diamond-fabrication scam captured the French popular imagination. The story featured a con artist named Henri Lemoine who claimed to
have invented a "secret process" for manufacturing diamonds.[1] Lemoine
managed to defraud the De Beers diamond company out of one and a half
million francs by performing a carefully choreographed trick: he invited
company executives to observe as he made a show of cooking up diamonds in
an electric furnace, in the nude, with the aid—unbeknownst to De Beers—of
a false-bottomed crucible. De Beers paid Lemoine to keep his "formula" secret
(he stashed it in an English bank), and the company also invested in the diamond factory that Lemoine pretended to build in the Pyrenees.[2] The hoax
only became public knowledge when De Beers grew suspicious and pressed
charges for fraud, effectively calling Lemoine's bluff.[3] The story was soon reported in a wide range of newspapers—from the elite, literary *Le Figaro* to the
popular *Le Petit Parisien*—with sensationalizing titles like "The Diamond
Affair," "The Alchemist's Diamonds," and "Lemoine's Secret." Throughout
the highly publicized trial that ensued, Lemoine continued to play the part of
the great inventor, insisting that he really could fabricate diamonds and
pleading for the opportunity to perform the experiment again.[4] For several
weeks, a public debate raged over whether Lemoine was a clever impostor or
a misunderstood inventor: "un imposteur de génie ou un grand inventeur
méconnu."[5] Despite Lemoine's unfaltering performance, his trial revealed
that the diamonds he claimed to have created had jewelers' marks on them—
proving they had been bought in Paris and originated in De Beers's own
South African mines.[6] In other words, Lemoine had passed off "real" precious
stones as fake ones: his genuine synthetic diamond turned out to be just an
ordinary diamond.

If people know about the Lemoine Affair today, it is largely thanks to
Proust, who was so intrigued by what he termed "the prestige of a momentary

diamond" that he made the affair the subject and guiding thread of a series of pastiches published in the *Figaro*'s literary supplement in February and March of 1908. In the year before he began drafting *In Search of Lost Time*, Proust composed accounts of Lemoine's hoax in the styles of Balzac, Flaubert, Sainte-Beuve, Michelet, Renan, Goncourt, and the literary critic Émile Faguet. In March of 1909, after Lemoine had skipped bail and fled to Eastern Europe (he would be recaptured in April), Proust published a Lemoine Affair pastiche of the symbolist poet Henri de Régnier. In the summer of 1909, Proust planned to publish pastiches of Chateaubriand and Maeterlinck, as well as a second pastiche of Sainte-Beuve, but he missed his deadline at the *Figaro*, so these did not appear in print at the time.[7]

While a wealth of recent criticism investigates convergences between high modernism and mass cultural forms, Proust's participation in public life and his interest in modernist material culture remain largely unexplored in Proust scholarship.[8] Few critics have written about Proust's journalistic and pastiching activities; those who have tend to take the position that the practice of strategically counterfeiting the styles of celebrated authors enabled Proust to purge external influences and find his own voice.[9] I propose that we might, instead, view the Lemoine Affair pastiches as modernist experiments in the production of value—test cases exploring the phenomenology of "convulsive" and "unstable" preciosity.[10] These ventriloquistic exercises highlight Proust's fascination with the volatility of value and with the peculiar status of the aesthetic object in modernity. Casting himself in the role of the performance artist alternately described in the papers as an "alchemist," an "illusionist," and an "ingenious swindler," Proust simultaneously flaunts and mocks his own cultivation of sophisticated discourses. As he delves into the shimmering substance of Lemoine's real/fake diamond, he plays on the conceptual kinship between precious stones and pure art, demonstrating high modernism's capacity to ironize and deconstruct its own claim to aesthetic autonomy. These outrageous imitations also reveal a Proust whose habits of perception and of composition were conditioned by the spatial and temporal rhythms and textures of the daily newspaper. "Prestidigitator," journalist, stock-market speculator, and literary ventriloquist, the Proust of the Lemoine Affair pastiches is unabashedly connected to the worldly networks of his day.

This chapter approaches Proust's experiments with aesthetic value and au-thorial prestige from three points of view. The first section investigates what Proust's enthusiastic participation in the Lemoine Affair can tell us about the conjunction of trickery and enchantment at the heart of modernist aesthetics. In these pastiches, Proust simultaneously dismantles the fantasy of aesthetic autonomy and luxuriates in it. He exposes—and enjoys—the magical thinking inherent in the production of authorial distinction, reminding us of the conceptual link between "prestige" and notions of artifice and illusion.[11] The second section explores the phenomenology of newspaper reading and writing in Proust, and makes a case for the importance of this medium to the genesis and structure of *In Search of Lost Time*. Finally, I conclude by examining the only explicit embedded pastiche in the novel—the Goncourt pastiche in *Time Regained*. Investigating the reparative role this pastiche plays in the narrative, I explore the centrality of verbal mimicry to Proust's aesthetic imagination more broadly. In his Lemoine Affair pastiches and in the newspapers that both inspired and disseminated them, Proust reveals the cultivation of distinction and the fabrication of art as banal, non-auratic, everyday exercises, and as enchanted practices of absorption and self-loss.

Synthetic Diamonds

Proust is famous for championing an economy of aesthetic redemption. According to this logic, the most mundane objects conceal secret aesthetic riches that can be mined by those endowed with special powers of perception. The Proustian narrator calls this trick "translation," "deciphering," or "conversion," and suggests that by mastering the magic of "involuntary memory," one can conjure treasures out of the "waste product of experience." The true meaning of things lies hidden from most people, but the exceptional perceiver can learn to convert visible "hieroglyphics" into their "spiritual equivalent," distilling lasting subjective "truth" from mere materiality.[12]

Proustian involuntary memory is a trick that pays off in the *Recherche*: in a series of mnemonic feats, the narrator manages to pull his entire childhood out of a cup of tea, the beach at Balbec out of a starched napkin, and the city of Venice out of a cobblestone. The Lemoine Affair pastiches operate according to a different logic, however, revealing a Proust who is less interested in the redemptive or sublimatory power of art than in discredited performances of sophistication and spoiled economies of distinction. In his Lemoine Affair pastiches, Proust is enchanted not so much by alchemy and miraculous transformations, but by the failed bluff—the conjuring trick that falls flat, humiliating the credulous executive even more than the would-be magician. (Lemoine's main line of defense was that his procedure had to be legitimate, because if it were a hoax, it would mean that the world's great diamond experts were idiots for having believed him.[13])

In 1919, when Proust had become a literary celebrity, he published his Lemoine Affair pastiches as a volume. He contended at this time that the affair had been an insignificant subject chosen at random. The few critics who write about the pastiches have been quick to take him at his word—no one is interested in the Lemoine Affair itself. This is probably because it is difficult to reconcile Proust's fascination with the hoax—which he spent months writing and rewriting from various points of view—with his reputation as the highest of high modernists. While his novel has been mythologized as the paragon of cultural sophistication, Proust himself is often imagined as a sickly esthete walled up in a cork-lined room. This mythology is undercut by the image of Proust as an avid newspaper reader and journalist, as a speculator, and a scandal- and gossip-monger who followed every detail of Lemoine's trial as it played out in the paper—and then brought the affair back to the front page by publishing his own lovingly mocking accounts.

Proust embeds Lemoine's fantasmatic artificial diamond differently in each pastiche: it appears as one more piece of gossip passed around in a Balzacian salon; as the collective dream of a dusty courtroom crowd in a Flaubertian trial scene; as the perfect theatrical subject for Edmond de Goncourt; and even as a glistening bit of snot hanging from Lemoine's collar in a pastiche of the symbolist poet Henri de Régnier:

> One could make out just the one single succulent, quivering mass, transparent and hardening, and in the ephemeral brilliance with which it decorated Lemoine's attire, it seemed to have fixed the prestige of a momentary diamond there, still hot, so to speak, from the oven from which it had emerged, and for which this unstable jelly, corrosive and alive as it was for one more instant, seemed at once, by its deceitful, fascinating beauty, to present both a mockery and a symbol.[14]

> On ne distinguait plus qu'une seule masse juteuse, convulsive, transparente et durcie; et dans l'éphémère éclat dont elle décorait l'habit de Lemoine, elle semblait y avoir immobilisé le prestige d'un diamant momentané, encore chaud, si l'on peut dire, du four dont il était sorti, et dont cette gelée instable, corrosive et vivante qu'elle était pour un instant encore, semblait à la fois, par sa beauté menteuse et fascinatrice, présenter la moquerie et l'emblème.[15]

In this deliciously revolting pastiche, the diamond is presented as a sign of distinction that "quivers" precariously on the border between the delectable and the disgusting. Pairing Régnier's rarefied syntax with the image of Lemoine's leaking body, Proust dares his reader to relish this conjunction of refinement and vulgarity.

Proust said that he composed his pastiches by setting an "internal metronome," and indeed, we can sense him practicing his act in these pieces.[16] He tests out the limits of different generic norms, alternating between fiction and criticism, presenting the affair as a vaudevillian tragedy that "abounds with improbabilities" ("fourmille d'invraisemblances")—but also as a historical topic that gives Michelet a headache.[17] The pastiches are joyfully anachronistic: representing his contemporary moment as a present bristling with temporal contradictions and overlaps, Proust revels in inserting Lemoine's fabricated diamond into incongruous epochs. In a particularly outrageous example of this, Proust imagines Ruskin traveling by airplane (a feat not yet possible in

Ruskin's lifetime) in order to look at Giotto's medieval Lemoine Affair fres-
coes.[18] Experimenting with narrative conventions, Proust repeatedly over-
steps the border between diegetic and extra-diegetic worlds: he blurs the line
between the fictional and the real by introducing his own friends and ac-
quaintances into established literary frames, or by confounding novelistic and
historical personages. In the Balzac pastiche, for example, Proust describes
Lemoine as "one of those extraordinary men" who could either be celebrated,
like Ivan the Terrible or Peter the Great, or disgraced, like Balthazar Claës or
Vautrin.[19] Several of the pastiches are constructed as critiques of other pastiches. Proust plays on the fictionality of the entire exercise, for example, when
he ventriloquizes Sainte-Beuve in order to critique his own invented Flaubert
(Sainte-Beuve quibbles with Flaubert's lack of verisimilitude), and when he
ventriloquizes the critic Émile Faguet in order to "cite" lines from a play of his
own invention—a vaudevillian tragedy about Lemoine's hoax by the playwright Henri Bernstein. Proust even writes himself into the affair as a character: Edmond de Goncourt happily receives the news of Lemoine's discovery
along with news of Marcel Proust's suicide—he has allegedly killed himself
due to the devaluation of his stock portfolio. (Goncourt is disappointed to
learn the next day that Lemoine is a fraud and Proust is still alive).[20]

According to one familiar critical view, pastiche was for Proust merely a
"preliminary exercise" to personal creation: in composing his Lemoine Affair
pastiches, Proust was working to forge a stylistic instrument that would "owe
nothing" to its illustrious models.[21] Yet what could be less Proustian than this
ideal of self-sufficient debtlessness? I propose, instead, that in writing his pastiches Proust sought to multiply his connections and attachments. Proust
flaunts his debt to the past in these exercises. Even more perversely, he imagines that the debt goes both ways. In a March 1915 letter to Georges de Lauris,
Proust notes that the overt practice of pastiche enables him to avoid accidentally stealing the goods of others. But he also claims that his pastiches are not
thefts, but gifts bestowed upon past authors. It's a peculiarity of his character,
he notes, to spend his best lines on others, rather than saving them for himself: "not trying to 'shine,' I generally deposit into a pastiche things that a
better property manager would prefer to keep, for the sake of signature and
personal honor."[22]

In a 1919 review of the pastiches (collected in *Pastiches et mélanges*), Louis
Aragon praises Proust's skill, but notes that "the game ran the risk of being
vulgar" ("le jeu risquait d'être vulgaire"). He also admits that he does not
really have the stomach for such a medley: "à vrai dire, mon estomac supporte
mal les mélanges."[23] Aragon is gesturing here to the etymology of "pastiche,"
which derives from the Italian "pasticcio," a pie made of various ingredients.
Proust exploits this etymology as well, returning in several of the pastiches to
the image of the diamond being cooked in the oven. His Renan dramatically
exclaims, for example: "Rekindle tomorrow the furnace that has already gone

out a thousand times whence the diamond might one day emerge!" ("Ral-
lume encore demain le four éteint mille fois déjà d'où sortira peut-être un
jour le diamant!")[24] In the unpublished pastiche of Ruskin, the baked diamond as aesthetic object is replaced by a tuber: Giotto's painting technique is
analogized as a procedure of drawing perspective lines on a potato fresh out
of the oven.[25] In the Régnier pastiche, as we have seen, the special diamond
oven is actually Lemoine's nose. Anticipating the conjunction of high art and
everyday culinary arts so central to his novel, Proust is playing on Lemoine's
flagrantly down-home "scientific" experiment. In response to the prosecu-
tor's query as to why no one else had been able to manufacture diamonds
using his method, Lemoine cheekily responded that perhaps they simply
failed to cook their diamonds long enough: "La cuisson n'avait pas dû être
suffisante."[26]

My wager is that Proust's Lemoine Affair pastiches reveal something crucial about the precarious distinction between art and the ordinary in modernity. The diamond, after all, suggests a certain fantasy of aesthetic autonomy.
The ultimate luxury item, an object Adam Smith described as "the greatest of
all superfluities," the diamond is a gleaming chunk of pure form. Its dazzle
obscures its material origins, the labor that drew it from the earth, and the
economic networks that maintain the illusion of its rarity.

The diamond has been described as a "super-commodity": a commodity
without planned obsolescence.[27] The same might be said of the work of art
in modernity. Bourdieu describes the work of art as a "fetish": an object
that exists only by virtue of the collective belief—or rather, "collective
misrecognition"—that acknowledges it as a work of art.[28] Metaphorizing the
artist as an illusionist, Bourdieu notes that works of art exist as symbolic
objects only if they are received by spectators capable of legitimating them
as such. According to Marcel Mauss's 1903 analysis of the social basis of
magic, the magician's "legitimate imposture" is dependent on the "magic
group." Similarly, the production of the work of art as a "sacred and consecrated object" involves, as Bourdieu puts it, an "immense enterprise of *symbolic alchemy* involving the collaboration [. . .] of a whole set of agents
engaged in the field of production."[29] Hence the avant-garde artist who
offers up a "ready-made" object as his own original artwork is effectively
testing the power of the spell.[30] When Lemoine tries to pass off De Beers's
diamonds as his own creation (claiming "je reconstitue le diamant tel que le
fait la nature"), he is performing a Duchampian experiment on the limits of
modernist magical thinking (in this case, the collective investment of belief
that enables the gross overvaluation of certain shiny rocks). Just as Lemoine's hoax tested the elasticity of the system that produces and maintains
faith in the diamond's uniqueness, Proust's pastiches are experiments in the
production and circulation of aesthetic value. In his ventriloquist's act, we
see Proust practicing his tonal and generic flexibility as he investigates the

mixture of lucidity and magical thinking that shores up the fantasy of the aesthetic object's inherent worth. As he tries out various points of view on Lemoine's manufactured diamond, Proust plays at the limits between enchantment and disenchantment, illusion and disillusion, knowledge and belief. This capacity to shuttle back and forth between a position of sociological demystification and an attitude of aesthetic captivation becomes one of the most striking features of *In Search of Lost Time*.[31]

A January 31, 1908, cartoon in *Le Figaro* shows a wealthy couple luring a lady to their salon by boasting that their guest list includes a countess, an "unheard-of cinematographer," "two fakirs," and the "prestidigitateur Lemoine." "We'll make cash and diamonds!" ("on fera du blé et des diamants!"), the couple exclaims. As a number of recent accounts have shown, belle-époque illusionists ("prestidigitators") fostered in their audiences a state of "lucid self-delusion."[32] With his mixture of science, performance skills, and rhetorical dazzle, Lemoine played on the appeal of the modernist prestidigitator. Just as trick cinema and magic-show audiences enjoyed cultivating a special mixture of credulous incredulity, the public knew Lemoine was a fraud and took great pleasure in believing in his act all the same. As a January 13, 1908, editorial in the socialist daily, *L'Humanité*, puts it (speaking of the diamond recipe that Lemoine had placed in a safe-deposit box in a London bank, in order to keep it safe from the prying hands of De Beers executives): "we know perfectly well that the envelope deposited in a London Bank contains nothing, or that if it does contain a formula, it is worth nothing, we know this . . . and nonetheless we love to hear ourselves repeat that perhaps there could be something in it . . ." (original ellipses).[33] It was precisely the excitement of investing belief in an obvious fiction that made the Lemoine Affair so compelling.

The Lemoine Affair was an event that both demystified and remystified the diamond. First the diamond's uniqueness is threatened when it is imagined to be artificially reproducible. Then, it turns out not to be reproducible, and De Beers stockholders everywhere breathe a sigh of relief.[34] Nonetheless, the diamond emerges from the Lemoine Affair looking like an unstable apparition: a fiction of investor confidence and controlled scarcity. Lemoine's trick of cooking up synthetic diamonds, after all, offered the paradoxical lure of a preciosity so easy to reproduce that it wouldn't be worth much at all.[35] Proust's pastiches experiment with the wavering prestige of Lemoine's "momentary" synthetic diamond, which appears in the pastiches as miraculous and abject, precious and banal.

Proust is famously interested in sublimatory economies that transform unremarkable everyday things into rare treasures. But he is also fascinated by objects that are simultaneously invaluable and valueless—at once incomparable and perfectly forgettable. He is drawn, for example, to characters that seem to oscillate between the poles of originality and banality, appearing alternately singular and utterly typified. His novel simultaneously celebrates and denigrates Odette (a demi-mondaine with a Botticelli face), Rachel (a "femme quelconque" who is also a "femme d'un grand prix"), Charlus (a prince so distinguished that he prefers to go by the lowly title of "baron"), and Albertine (an incomparably desirable lover who is also just an ordinary-looking middle-class girl). In a draft of *The Fugitive*, the narrator describes a woman (Madame de Putbus's maid) whom he desperately desires but has never met. He imagines her as singularly ordinary: her smile suggests the most common of all commonplaces; her expression is paradoxically more banal than any other ("la plus banale et la plus commune du monde").[36] This paradox of superlative ordinariness is precisely what interests Proust about the fantasy of mass-produced diamonds.[37]

Such conjunctions of the remarkable and the insignificant recall the strange union, in Kant's "Analytic of the Beautiful," of the "pure" or "disinterested" aesthetic gaze with the random assemblage of objects cited as especially appropriate to it: flowers, certain birds, "a host of marine crustaceans," and "foliage for borders or on wallpaper."[38] Exploring the tension between the incomparable and the unspecifiable inherent to aesthetic judgment, modernist writers hone in on similarly singular/ordinary signs. The momentary snot-diamond that Proust tenderly serves up in his pastiche of Henri de Régnier is something like Woolf's "solid object"—an inestimable "drop of solid matter" that washes up on shore, a mere "large irregular lump" that is "nothing but glass" but appears nonetheless to be "almost a precious stone."[39] Similarly, Woolf's "mark on the wall" resembles a jewel lying about "at the roots of turnips," and sparks innumerable fantasies before it turns out to be a mere snail.[40] Proust's conjunction of preciosity and worthlessness is also reminiscent of James's "figure in the carpet," a hyper-meaningful and yet meaningless metatextual index that vaguely signifies "something or other," and is metaphorized, variously, as a "little point," a "foot in a shoe," a "piece of cheese in a mouse-trap," a "little trick," an "exquisite scheme," a "silver lining," a "buried treasure," or simply "*that!*"[41]

These authors, like Proust, are attuned to the empty-fullness of the aesthetic sign. In the pastiches and throughout *In Search of Lost Time*, Proust explores the instability intrinsic to the prestige of aesthetic production and reception alike: in his work, performances of distinction tend to get out of hand. Art is thus a source of both enchantment and embarrassment in Proust. His characters are perpetually making fools of themselves when they try to derive cultural capital from displays of "disinterested" aesthetic pleasure. They froth at the mouth while waxing poetic about Chopin, make absurdly exaggerated claims to musical sensitivity, mispronounce names, knock objects off the table, lose track of time gazing at a painting and hold up a fancy dinner party for forty-five minutes, and so on. This may be because they lack the training and rhetorical skills necessary to manipulate complex and shifting aesthetic discourses: like Lemoine's, their bluff is not quite practiced enough. Or it may be that there is something inherently discomfiting about art in modernity. It's the ultimate luxury item, reflecting the good taste of the select few who know how to enjoy it, but it's also troublingly unremarkable— an object defined by its explicit lack of established criteria, set content, or precise purpose, and which is supposed to incite not intelligence or wittiness, but states of unthinkingness. This dazzling emptiness makes the artwork in modernity a risky investment—like the diamond, circa 1908.

Proust's Newspaper

The Lemoine Affair pastiches present a case study in modernist value production. These pastiches also enable us to see Proust not as a singular figure whose genius transcends markets and history, but as an artist whose writing practices and habits of perception and interpretation were bound up in the circuits and rhythms of early twentieth-century material culture—especially those of the daily newspaper. Indeed, as this section of the chapter will demonstrate, the newspaper appears in Proust as a miniature version of the novel: at once a social compass and a heterogeneous text capable of provoking multiple overlapping modes of feeling and attention. At stake here is not the compensatory, self-aggrandizing aesthetics of involuntary memory, but a distinction-spoiling valorization of the most ordinary of literary objects.

The Lemoine Affair was for Proust entirely mediated by the newspaper: Proust followed the developments of the Affair in early 1908 as it played out in the pages of *Le Figaro*. The pastiches he then published in that paper are performances that not only riff on the styles of a particular set of authors but also play on the articles that ran throughout the month of January. The *Figaro* articles about what it dramatically calls "The Diamond Affair" include a hodgepodge of voices and opinions: the articles already read like a set of pastiches. They shift from one point of view to the next, quoting Lemoine's supporters and detractors at length, citing scientists, jewelers, lawyers, Lemoine's wife, amateur chemists, gem enthusiasts, and even letters that were sent to Lemoine in prison from enthusiastic fans hopeful that he might be willing to cook them up a diamond or two. Like Proust, the *Figaro* journalists are enchanted by the details of Lemoine's performance; they want to know everything about the mysterious "substance" he allegedly transformed into diamonds: "What did it look like, what was its size, what was its consistency? Was it hard or soft, powdery or sticky, amorphous or crystalline, heavy or light?"[42] Along with this excitement, some fret that Lemoine's trick, if genuine, could destroy not only the diamond industry, but also the "divine prestige" of the stone itself. At least pearls will never be industrialized, one journalist consoles his readers in a January 17, 1908, front-page article titled "If We Made Diamonds . . ." ("Si on faisait du diamant . . .") (Figure 1.1).

FIGURE 1.1 *Le Figaro* (January 17, 1908), page 1.

Source: Bibliothèque nationale de France.

Roland Barthes has suggested that Proust only began serious work on his novel after his critical essay, *Against Sainte-Beuve* (*Contre Sainte-Beuve*), was rejected by *Le Figaro* in 1909. This rejection, according to Barthes, was the force that propelled Proust out of journalistic, episodic writing and into an entirely different rhythm of prose—"une écriture longue."[43] It is tempting to think of Proust's monumental novel, launched in response to a journalistic failure, as the ultimate anti-newspaper. The newspaper, after all, deals in daily humdrum; it is composed of disconnected information bound together only by the idea of "today"—information rendered obsolete by the mere act of reading it. *In Search of Lost Time*, on the other hand, is famous for celebrating what Deleuze calls the "true signs" of art.[44] Proust's novel supposedly demonstrates the power of art to overcome the passing of time; it valorizes the cultivation of a perceptual disposition capable of transforming merely ephemeral apparitions into lasting aesthetic riches.

Yet, as the following chapters will demonstrate in depth, Proust's novel valorizes not only redeemed time, but also the contingent and episodic, the forgettable and forgotten. The Proustian narrator describes the newspaper as precisely the medium in which these temporal modes coexist: as he puts it, the newspaper presents "the incalculable proportions of absence and presence of mind, of recollection and forgetfulness, of which the human mind is composed" ("les proportions inattendues de distraction et de présence d'esprit, de mémoire et d'oubli dont est fait l'esprit humain").[45] Two opposing temporal orders exist within the newspaper—one privileging continuity, the other obsolescence:

> In the same newspaper in which the moralist of the leader column says to us of an event, of a work of art, *a fortiori* of a singer who has enjoyed her "hour of fame": "Who will remember this in ten years' time?," does not the report of the Académie des Inscriptions overleaf speak often of a fact in itself of smaller importance, of a poem of little merit, which dates from the epoch of the Pharoahs and is still known in its entirety?[46]

> Dans le même journal où le moraliste du "premier Paris" nous dit d'un événement, d'un chef-d'oeuvre, à plus forte raison d'une chanteuse qui eut son heure de Célébrité: "qui se souviendra de tout cela dans dix ans?," à la troisième page, le compte rendu de l'académie des inscriptions ne parle-t-il pas souvent d'un fait par lui-même moins important, d'un poème de peu de valeur, qui date de l'époque des Pharaons et qu'on connaît encore intégralement?[47]

In the pages of the mass daily, the "philosophy of the serial novelist" ("philosophie du feuilletoniste") according to which "all is doomed to oblivion," is on equal footing with its opposite: "a contrary philosophy which would predict the conservation of all things."[48]

One way to understand the distinction between high-culture and mass-culture literary production and consumption is in terms of two opposing temporal regimes. As Bourdieu points out, so-called "pure art" privileges production and slow time, while the literary industry privileges dissemination and temporal immediacy. The prestige that adheres to high-brow art requires a delay in publishing success. The work must be imagined as a priceless "symbolic offering," a gift met with the most precious counter-gift: authorial name recognition.[49] Essential to this symbolic economy is the "time lag" between offering and counter-offering. The economic logic of literary and artistic industries, by contrast, privileges immediate and temporary success, measured by sales, and adjusted according to client demand. What I want to show here is that Proust does not simply dismiss the instantaneity of diffusion in favor of the longue durée—the "time regained"—of elite literary production: he explores the interstice between these two economies, and is as intrigued by the possibility of an instantly disseminated "high" literature as he is by the possibility of a mass-produced precious gem.

In Search of Lost Time is a novel about someone who wants to write a novel, but it began as a newspaper article about someone who wants to write a newspaper article. In late 1908, when Proust began working on the project that would become his novel, he conceived of it as a newspaper piece. It would open with a man tossing and turning in bed, wondering what happened to the article he submitted so long ago; then in the morning, thrilled to find that his article has finally been published on the front page of *Le Figaro*, he has a conversation with his mother about another newspaper article he plans to write.[50] This newspaper frame, I argue, didn't really drop out of Proust's *Recherche* but was absorbed into and scattered through the three-thousand-page novel.

Open the first volume of the *Recherche*, and you get a sense of Proust's affinity for the press right way, since this volume is dedicated to Gaston Calmette, editor in chief of *Le Figaro*.[51] When you turn the page, however, you might be jarred by the apparent contrast between that publication-world dedication, and the elaboration of the time-and space-expanding, metamorphic force of reading with which the novel begins. In the celebrated first paragraph, the narrator's literary reflections take a "rather peculiar turn" when he falls asleep perusing an anonymous "volume" and imagines himself absorbed into the text he has been reading. The narrator-reader's personality and will are scattered as he *becomes* the heterogeneous subjects of his book:

> For a long time, I would go to bed early. Sometimes, the candle barely out, my eyes closed so quickly that I did not have time to tell myself: "I'm falling asleep." And half an hour later the thought that it was time to look for sleep would awaken me; I would make as if to put away the book which I imagined was still in my hands, and to blow out the light; I had gone on thinking, while I was asleep, about what I had just been reading, but these thoughts had taken a rather peculiar turn; it seemed to me that I myself was the immediate subject of my book: a church, a quartet, the rivalry between François I and Charles V.[52]

> Longtemps, je me suis couché de bonne heure. Parfois, à peine ma bougie éteinte, mes yeux se fermaient si vite que je n'avais pas le temps de me dire: "Je m'endors." Et, une demi-heure après, la pensée qu'il était temps de

chercher le sommeil m'éveillait; je voulais poser le volume que je croyais avoir encore dans les mains et souffler ma lumière; je n'avais pas cessé en dormant de faire des réflexions sur ce que je venais de lire, mais ces réflexions avaient pris un tour un peu particulier; il me semblait que j'étais moi-même ce dont parlait l'ouvrage: une église, un quatuor, la rivalité de François Ier et de Charles-Quint.[53]

Strangely enough, in drafts, this potent, liminal state is sparked not by a "volume," but by the newspaper that the narrator is reading:

~~I thought that I was still reading the newspaper and I told myself that~~ an hour had passed, and thus the thought that it was time to go to sleep woke me | I ~~woke without realizing that I had just been asleep~~ + | wanted to toss away the newspaper that I thought I still held in my hands

~~je me croyais encore en train de lire le journal et je me disais qu'il était~~ une heure après, et donc la pensée qu'il était temps de m'endormir m'éveillait | Je ~~je m'éveillais sans me rendre compte que je venais de dormir~~ + | voulais jeter le journal que je croyais avoir encore en mains[54]

This initial newspaper disappears in the published version of the *Recherche*, but remains a phantom presence throughout the novel's overture. It surfaces surreptitiously several pages later, when the narrator evokes his habit of falling asleep by weaving a nest out of the "most disparate things," including bits of pillow, blanket, and shawl; the edge of the bed; and a newspaper ("un numéro des *Débats roses*").[55] The newspaper is therefore intimately allied for Proust with threshold states of consciousness and with the scattering and dispersal of attention. It is not just a record of daily events, but a generator of dreams, a matrix of fiction.[56]

Belle-époque newspapers were more abundant and miscellaneous than to-day's well-ordered grids, and they left it to the reader to make sense of their inexhaustible variation.[57] Juxtaposing literary compositions, weather reports, jokes, advertisements, pastiches, musical scores, obituaries, war news, and society gossip, the newspaper's multi-directional reading pathways and endlessly renewed and annulled present orient us away from the dynamics of temporal redemption for which Proust is so well known. In Proustian involuntary memory, the force of analogy conquers the passage of time, as lasting aesthetic profit is drawn from spent quotidian experience. Involuntary memory takes place on a vertical axis, and it permits the perceiving subject to cast away the outside world and retreat into the sphere of his imagination. The experience of newspaper reading, on the other hand, is heterogeneous, and involves perpetual reorientation in relation to the outside world and its multiple overlapping circuits. Hence Philip Fisher has described the newspaper as an "open" or "torn space" that provokes readers to "look *around*" rather than "looking directly *at* objects."[58] And in a brilliant essay historicizing the news-paper's capacity to provoke such unspecifiable modes of attention, Kevis Goodman suggests that the rise of "the news" in the eighteenth century ush-ered in a new structure of feeling that preceded and laid the groundwork for Romantic (Kantian) aesthetic "free play." The news, Goodman argues, gener-ates a "globally telescopic eye" allied with what she terms a "paradoxically full but non-ideational vacuity"—a "permeable, open circuit of awareness."[59]

As an illustration of the newspaper as portal or "open circuit," consider Édouard Vuillard's 1898 painting, *Madame Vuillard Reading the Newspaper* (Figure 1.2)—a work first exhibited in Paris in 1908. Here the newspaper is a prop in the dramaturgy of everyday domestic life, but it is also a window onto the outside world. In this scene of readerly absorption—an example of what Garrett Stewart calls "reverse ekphrasis"—we cannot read the newspaper along with Madame Vuillard, and yet its visual energy is mobilized and dis-persed throughout the room.[60] The newspaper nearly merges with the decora-tive wallpaper, but it also echoes that large centrally featured window, which, like the paper, grids space into columns. The reader has her back to this window, but only because she is absorbed into a different aperture. As she slouches in her armchair, drawn into the paper's world, her individuality is dissolved: she could be anyone, any reader of the news. As we will see in chap-ter 2, this is an apt image of the Proustian newspaper reader—a figure he calls the "lecteur quelconque" ("whatever reader").

In Search of Lost Time is not only a celebration of the death-defying essence of art. It is also a semiotic laboratory that multiplies and accumulates inter-pretive and phenomenological possibilities. This patchwork novel orients us

FIGURE 1.2 Édouard Vuillard, *Madame Vuillard Reading the Newspaper.*
Source: The Phillips Collection, Washington, D.C. © 2014 Artists Rights Society, New York.

toward numerous points of view and modalities of attention, oscillating between gossip and philosophy, melancholia and euphoria, sleepiness and wakefulness, solipsism and schizophrenic multi-voicedness. From this point of
view, the newspaper—and especially *Le Figaro*, circa 1908—is quite possibly
the most significant and critically overlooked intertext in the novel. With a
largely upper-class readership, *Le Figaro* was known for its society news, literary columns, and theater reviews.[61] But it was also a space for aesthetic experi-
mentation and published various avant-garde manifestos: Baudelaire's "Painter
of Modern Life" appeared in 1863, Jean Moréas's symbolist manifesto in 1886,
and Marinetti's futurist manifesto in 1909. Moreover, like the *Recherche*, *Le
Figaro* was from the start a space for the mixing and cross-pollination of
genres. In its very first issue, published in 1826, *Le Figaro* calls itself a literary
paper with a satirical bent, and declares that it will investigate "theatre, criticism, science, art, customs, news, scandals, domestic economy, biography, bib-
liography, fashion, etc., etc." This wild thematic and generic heterogeneity will
find its literary reflection in Proust's novel. In fact, Proust was so associated
with the newspaper medium—and with the elite, gossipy *Figaro* in particular—that when André Gide apologized in a January 11, 1914, letter for having
refused to publish *Swann's Way*, he explained that the mistake was due to his
perception of Proust as "the one who writes in *Le Figaro*."[62]

Proust evidently did not mind the association: he was eager to continue
writing for *Le Figaro* even after he had become a celebrated author. In May 1914
he wrote to his friend Robert de Flers, an editor at the paper, admitting that he
was "more or less ruined," and requesting a regular column. Proust suggests in
this letter that he would be especially delighted to write the weather column,
or the "run-over-dogs" column, or perhaps music, theater, stock markets, or
the society pages. "You would see that I'm capable of abstaining from literature, of being brief and practical" ("tu verrais que je suis capable de m'abstenir
de littérature, d'être bref et pratique"), Proust insisted. Not surprisingly, this
job never panned out.[63] Later, in 1918, Proust vied to become the literary critic
for *Le Figaro*, but to his disappointment, was passed over for the position.[64]

Elisa Tamarkin has persuasively argued that by the nineteenth century, the
newspaper offered a lesson in presentism, training its readers to "keep pace
with the progress of the current moment."[65] Yet Proust allies the practice of
reading the news with diverse relations to mood and time. Everyone reads the
newspaper in the *Recherche*, from aristocrats to cooks, but characters cultivate a variety of different habits of newspaper reading. The Duc and Duchesse
de Guermantes maintain two separate subscriptions to *Le Figaro*, so that they
will not have to share: "nous avons chacun notre *Figaro*," as the duc puts it.[66]
(Neither seems to read it very thoroughly, however, since both overlook the
narrator's front-page article, much to his disappointment.) The Baron de
Charlus claims to read newspapers the way he washes his hands—habitually
and without the slightest care. "Je ne fais aucune attention aux journaux" he

declares, "je les lis comme je me lave les mains, sans trouver que cela vaille la peine de m'intéresser."[67] Charles Swann, however, is not only a newspaper enthusiast but a gifted and attentive reader of the newspaper, such that "if he read in a newspaper the names of the people who had been at a dinner-party, could tell at once its exact degree of smartness, just as a man of letters, simply by reading a sentence, can estimate exactly the literary merit of its author."[68] In contrast to Charlus's practiced nonchalance and Swann's analytics, the cook, Françoise, reads passionately and with deep investment, weeping "torrents" of tears over newspaper calamities that would leave her unmoved if they happened to the people she knew in her everyday life.[69]

Françoise is not alone in her susceptibility to such newspaper-provoked passion. Proust highlights a different side of the newspaper's capacity to incite strong feeling in a scene from *Swann in Love*. Swann is reading the paper "mechanically" ("machinalement"), when he suddenly leaps back, startled by a word that seems to morph before his eyes: he reads the name Beuzeval, which reminds him of the name Beuzeville, which in turn bleeds into the name Bréauté, which is the name of a man who may have been Odette's lover.[70] In this papery inversion of involuntary memory, the newspaper appears less as a signifier of reality than as the instigator of fiction, and as the site par excellence of graphic instability and semantic transformations. The narrator will experience the same phenomenon volumes later. When he reads in a newspaper the name of a Fauré melody, it sparks a convoluted set of associations, leading from Fauré to the duc de Broglie, to Chaumont, to the Buttes-Chaumont, where Albertine used to go with Andrée. Here the narrator allies newspaper-reading with thoughts that diverge "as from a crossroads in a forest."[71]

Newspapers, allied with mobile, metonymic habits of thought, and with the cultivation of multiple habits of reading, circulate throughout Proust's novel. They mark parties, deaths, wars, theatrical performances, and art exhibitions, and even allow the narrator to track his lover's movements without leaving his bed. The narrator suggests that seeing one's name printed in the newspaper is equivalent to seeing oneself in a mirror, and indeed, the newspaper does function as a mirror in Proust: or rather, it is both a miniature version of the novel and a supplement, filling in information to which the not-quite-omniscient first-person narrator does not have access. Hence, in *Sodom and Gomorrah*, the narrator treats the newspaper as a narrative prosthesis, borrowing from the newspaper account of a party he has attended in order to add details missing from his own limited account.[72]

Adding to its function as a narrative supplement, sometimes in Proust the newspaper works as a sort of mask or social shield. The sociologist Erving Goffman has highlighted this protective function of the paper, noting that one "deprivation" caused by the 1954 newspaper strike in Britain was that commuters in the Underground suddenly had "nothing to hide behind,

nothing into which they could properly withdraw." Without their habitual
paper, they found themselves disorientingly exposed, in a state of what Goffman calls "over-presence."[73] Moreover, citing the account of an "ex-bum,"
Goffman notes that although it looks suspicious to loiter in a public place at
night reading a book, "newspaper readers never seem to attract attention and
even the seediest vagrant can sit in Grand Central all night without being
molested if he continues to read a paper."[74] In *The Captive*, Proust's narrator
employs the newspaper in precisely this way—as a shield or cover, a tool for
saving face. Having become flustered while attempting to flirt with a milk-
maid he has invited into his bedroom, he turns to the newspaper in order to
regain his composure:

> I tried to spring back again; her cheeks, which I had not noticed in the shop,
> appeared to me so pretty that I was abashed, and to recover my composure
> said to the young dairymaid: "Would you be so kind as to hand me the
> *Figaro* which is lying there. I must make sure of the address to which I am
> going to send you." [. . .] "Are you quite sure it won't be giving you too much
> trouble," I said, while I pretended to be searching the columns of the *Figaro*,
> "if I send you rather a long way?"[75]

> je tâchai de rebondir; les joues, non aperçues dans la boutique, me parurent
> si jolies que j'en fus intimidé, et pour me donner une contenance, je dis à la
> petite crémière: "seriez-vous assez bonne pour me passer *le figaro* qui est là,
> il faut que je regarde le nom de l'endroit où je veux vous envoyer." [. . .] "Ça
> ne vous gênerait vraiment pas trop, dis-je en faisant semblant de chercher
> dans *le figaro*, que je vous envoie même un peu loin?"[76]

The newspaper gives the narrator a "countenance"; it is not only an emblem of
his ideal social self, but an extension of his body, a second skin. Both a shield
and a conduit, the newspaper plugs its reader into multiple narrative trajectories and social worlds: even as the narrator pretends to skim the paper in
order to cover his embarrassment, he cannot help but read it, and his attention is soon oriented away from the flirtation at hand and toward an alternate
intrigue.[77]

Walter Benjamin famously disparaged the press for privileging random
bits of information over more integrated experiential modes. In essays on
Leskov and on Baudelaire, Benjamin associates the press with the "atrophy"
of experience, arguing that the newspaper "paralyzes" readers' imaginations,
damaging our capacity to perceive external events as anything other than
"issueless" and "private."[78] In a lesser-known essay, however, Benjamin presents the newspaper in a different light. He acknowledges the desire that binds
the newspaper reader to the newspaper, and suggests that in the act of
newspaper reading, a flickering "dialectical moment" lies concealed. The
newspaper reader, excluded from the sphere of cultural production, smolders

with impatience to see his interests represented. Benjamin concludes that "the decline of writing in the press turns out to be the formula for its restoration," since the reader is "at all times ready to become a writer."[79] In the newspaper, Benjamin contends, experience is not simply privatized; rather, the newspaper makes "public property" of literary competence.[80]

If the newspaper erodes the divide between readers and writers, it also calls into question the opposition between the trivial and the esteemed. Early in the novel, Swann advocates a reversal of the "essential" and the "insignificant," whereby newspapers would publish philosophy, and salon gossip would only appear in a gold-embossed volume published once a decade.[81] Proust ultimately shows us that the newspaper's eclectic form is what makes such evaluative leaps and reversals imaginable. Reading the newspaper in Proust elucidates a different side of *In Search of Lost Time*: this is not a nostalgic monument to aesthetic distinction, but an experimental text that explores the unredeemable open-endedness of the ordinary.

Pastiche

I will conclude this chapter by offering a third perspective on Proust's play with economies of prestige. I have suggested that the Lemoine Affair pastiches test the line dividing signs of distinction from signs of ordinariness. These pastiches explore the enchanted disenchantment fueling fantasies of autonomous aesthetic value. They also highlight Proust's love of the newspaper, with its heterogeneous assemblage of temporalities, voices, and attitudes. In this final section of the chapter, I want to look closely at the only explicit embedded pastiche in the novel—the Goncourt pastiche in *Time Regained*. This pastiche scrambles all the codes of Proust's novel. It revisits a familiar scene and turns it inside out, reviving the exhausted narrator's interest in and attachment to the fictional world he inhabits.[82]

The term "pastiche" is often used to refer to the characteristic style (or stylelessness) of postmodernity. Jameson famously defined postmodern pastiche as "blank parody"—a depthless, ahistorical, random cannibalization of all the styles of the past.[83] Modernist pastiche, on the other hand, was a particular practice of writing, popular in France around the turn of the century, which required its practitioners to give themselves up to the rhythm and *feel* of another writer's voice.[84] Anticipating surrealist automatic writing, the belle-époque fad for pastiche can also be tied to modernism's broader interest in travesty, masks, animal mimicry, and emotional contagion, from Gabriel Tarde's fin-de-siècle theory of imitation as the foundation of social cohesion, to Marcel Mauss's 1934 theory of "habitus" as "a prestigious imitation" whereby the individual "borrows" his corporeal dispositions.[85] Walter Benjamin, Roger Caillois, and Jacques Lacan were all taken by the notion that

identity might be fundamentally imitative, based in a sort of mimetic com-
pulsion to "become other."[86]

Pastiche was a widely practiced school exercise during the French Third
Republic, and by the early twentieth century there was a market for pastiche
compilations, like the multi-volume series, *À la manière de . . .*, edited by
Reboux and Müller and published in five installments between 1908 and 1950.
Pastiche as practiced by Reboux and Müller is caricatural in tone: it mocks
the very concept of stylistic novelty, and denigrates the authors it pastiches
instead of celebrating them.[87] But Proustian pastiche is not simply parodic—
it's not just about surpassing more powerful authors or becoming free from
literary influence. Rather, Proustian pastiche is a rehearsal of tonal flexibility
and plasticity, a practice of intimacy with a variety of styles and generic
norms. It makes hallowed works of literature accessible and inhabitable, turning them into objects to be played with rather than revered. Bourdieu has
suggested that Proustian pastiche is not caricature or parody—it does not
simply reproduce the most salient characteristics of a style. Rather, Proust's
pastiches reproduce the *habitus* of other writers—Proust gets inside those
writers' tastes, reproducing their dispositions, their habits of perception and
interpretation, the quasi-corporeal rhythms they cultivate, their manner of
orienting the reader through time and space.[88]

In the overture of the *Recherche*, the narrator describes the experience of
being stripped of all memory and identity and then returning to selfhood
from the very outer limits of imaginable consciousness.[89] This interplay of
anaesthesis and revivification recurs at other points in the novel as Proust
shuts down his textual world and then builds it back up again. As if the
narrative had momentarily lost interest in itself, the space of the text is
sometimes divested of color and vibrancy, only to appear once again radiant and alive. A particularly memorable instance of this occurs in the final
pages of *Within a Budding Grove*, where the fictional world quietly dissolves as the narrator's vacation at the beach in Balbec draws to a close. The
novel gently ushers us out of the luminous oceanside world, making the
departure from Balbec less abrupt by allowing us to linger with the narrator in his shrouded hotel room, where there is nothing to see but a small
patch of light playing on the floor and walls, and nothing to hear but the
faint sound of an oceanside orchestra concert wafting up from below. This
diminution of perceptual and affective intensity prepares us to be trans-
ported into the unknown spaces and moods of *The Guermantes Way*. Involuntary memory is the most noted Proustian method for suspending and
renewing excitement about the world, but many other experiences do this
as well. A short list would include: drinking champagne; riding in a train,
a carriage, or an automobile; looking at clouds or paintings; listening to
music or street noise; going to sleep; waking up; smelling flowers; eating
asparagus; and on and on.

For Proust, writing pastiche is another activity that renews curiosity, awareness, and vitality, rekindling the pasticheur's interest in the world around him. In *Within a Budding Grove*, for example, pastiche is explicitly allied with seduction and flirtation: one afternoon in an impromptu study session by the sea, Albertine pulls out her friend Gisèle's exam pastiche (a letter from Sophocles to Racine). Thrilled by the fabrication, Albertine reads Gisèle's pastiche aloud with sparkling eyes. In nearly the same gesture, she passes a note to the narrator declaring her feelings for him ("je vous aime bien").[90] The spatial and temporal proximity of the two epistles indicates, on the one hand, that Albertine's amatory declaration is just as practiced and put-on as her own exam pastiche will be. On the other hand, the crossing of Albertine's and "Sophocles's" compositions suggests that pastiche itself is a sort of love letter, a practice of affection and affinity that pulls the loved one close.[91]

Albertine's love note will single her out and individualize her as the object of the narrator's previously wandering desire: while the girls are discussing the pastiche, he decides that it is with Albertine that he will have his "novel." Nevertheless, as if the mere proximity to pastiche undermines any claim to propriety and self-possession, "je vous aime bien" is a composition to which all three girls contribute: Albertine drafts her confession with the help of her entourage, borrowing Andrée's pencil and Rosamonde's paper.

Paralleling this collectively composed love note, the exam pastiche brings together multiple voices and points of view. As we saw in the Lemoine Affair pastiches, Proust loves to complicate his imitations by layering mimicry upon mimicry. Just as the Lemoine Affair pastiche of Sainte-Beuve critiques the pastiche of Flaubert, here Proust not only composes a pastiche of Sophocles written in the voice of a teenage girl, but also doubles back and repeats the act—this time in the mocking tones of Andrée, who appraises Gisèle's essay and points out how she herself would have written it. (Sophocles ought to have addressed Racine as "Monsieur," and not as "My dear friend," she admonishes Albertine.)[92]

Contra the critical tendency to separate the desacralizing, playful force of mimicry (a mere "preliminary exercise") from the sacred realm of the *Recherche*, I contend that nothing—not even the much vaunted Proustian metaphor—is more essential to Proust's style than pastiche. *In Search of Lost Time* often reads like a catalogue of verbal tics: Proust invites us to enjoy Odette's anglicisms, Swann's ironic emphases, Legrandin's symbolist vagaries, Norpois's diplomatic formulas, and Albertine's slang, not to mention the particular malapropisms of Françoise, the Balbec hotel manager, the lift-boy, and many others. Describing this proliferation of eccentric speech forms as "imaginary pastiche," Gérard Genette argues that "no one else, either before [Proust] or after, and to my knowledge not in any language, has so nailed down the 'objectivation' [. . .] of the characters' style."[93] Proust's characters are first and foremost *voices*, and each speaks with idiosyncratic flair. In his pastiche-studded novel, Proust flaunts his stylistic versatility, testing and stretching his own vocal range and freeing up authoritative forms for playful reuse. We see this profaning and reinvigorating effect most explicitly in the Goncourt pastiche.

Proust injects the Goncourt pastiche into the *Recherche* at the precise moment that the narrative has hit a lull. At the beginning of the final volume, the narrator has returned to Combray, where everything seems insignificant, small, and flat.[94] The return to Combray is introduced in a tone of boredom: the narrator informs us that he almost abstained altogether from telling us about the visit. The narrative itself is exhausted; the world that has been so lovingly built around us for thousands of pages seems like a shoddy set. The narrator complains that his imagination and sensibility must have "weakened": "I was distressed to see how little I relived my early years" ("j'étais désolé de voir combien peu je revivais mes années d'autrefois"). The river Vivonne, once described as "flowing crystal" full of minnows and tadpoles and waterlilies and framed by buttercups, is now "narrow and ugly" ("mince et laide"). Even Gilberte, whom the narrator had once found so lovely, "was no longer beautiful at all."[95]

It is into this dead world that Proust inserts the Goncourt pastiche. In an echo of the very first scene of the novel, the narrator reads several pages of the Goncourt *Journal* before falling asleep one night. Uncharacteristically, he "cites" at length from this work—which is, of course, not really a quotation from Goncourt, but Proust's own invention. In this pastiche, we're invited to imagine the nineteenth-century novelist and esthete as a guest in the *Recherche*: Goncourt details the Verdurin salon—a social world with which any reader who had read all the way to Proust's final volume would be quite familiar. In other words, in this pastiche the novel doubles back on itself, presenting one of its privileged spaces from an entirely new point of view.

Why would Proust have selected the Goncourt *Journal* in particular, when, as the Lemoine Affair pastiches demonstrate, he could have ventriloquized any number of other texts? Perhaps, as Jean Milly suggests, Proust wanted to index a publication intrigue of the day: the final volumes of the Goncourt *Journal* were due to appear in 1916, but their publication was delayed because the Académie Goncourt feared being sued for libel.[96] Yet Proust also lets us know that the choice of Edmond de Goncourt is more or less arbitrary: he could have given us the same scene in a radically different generic and tonal register, as a pastiche of Balzac's *The Girl With the Golden Eyes*. What sort of queer, sadomasochistic dinner party could Proust have served up in place of the hyper-refined salon portrait he filters through the perspective of Goncourt? We will never know: the narrator claims that Gilberte was engrossed in Balzac's novella that night, and he did not want to take it from her.[97]

The Goncourt pastiche turns Proust's novel inside out, shuffling and rearranging its elements. Indeed, Goncourt's Cottard could be diagnosing the novel itself when he describes a case of dual personality ("de véritables dé-doublements de la personalité") whereby a patient can simply be touched and awakened to a second life.[98] The pastiche is full of Proustian elements: a reference to *One Thousand and One Nights*, to Venice, to Japanese chrysanthemums. But now we focus on Monsieur, rather than Madame Verdurin, and on the material details of the dinner (the plates, the food, the décor) rather than the conversation. And instead of presenting the Verdurins as the novel has up until now—as a couple of wealthy, faux-bohemian social climbers—Goncourt describes them as the epitome of refinement, insisting on the rarity, the remarkable quality, and the "genuine" distinction of their salon.

Like the Lemoine Affair pastiches, the Goncourt pastiche highlights the volatility of signs of distinction. Focalized through Goncourt's more decisive and distanced point of view, all the work and desire that characters invest in their social performance of self vanishes. All we are given to see are felicitous signs of sophistication. Proust therefore highlights the disjunction between a perspective (Goncourt's) that pays homage to distinction, and a perspective (the narrator's) that deconstructs and denaturalizes it—while enjoying it all the same. In the pastiche, it is as if we are suddenly offered a vision of things that has been repressed until now—although this depth metaphor does not quite work, since the narrator suggests that Goncourt records the "copiable" surface of things, while he himself has X-ray eyes, and attends, like a surgeon, to all the laws and causes hidden beneath them.[99] Or, as he puts it in a second analogy, Goncourt is like a painter who transcribes "a thousand" details, while his own portraits privilege "volume, light, movement."[100] A number of critics who discuss this pastiche argue that it is included in the volume in order to elevate the narrator's own accomplishment: according to this view, Proust is disparaging Goncourt's vision in order to make his own style and point of view seem smarter.[101] Instead, one could say that this occasion of narrative redoubling reveals Proust's love of perspectival variety, and interest in the invigorating multiplicity of the perceptual world.

Indeed, the pastiche energizes and revives the tired narrative: the narrator tells us that reading the episode fills him with the desire to see those places and people again: "by an odd contradiction, now that they were being spoken of in this book I had a desire to see them."[102] When he begins describing his stay at Tansonville, the narrator claims to have become disinterested in the world around him—he says that Combray now leaves him "incurious"—and yet the words "curious," "curiosity," and "surprise" recur repeatedly in the pages just before the pastiche is introduced. The inclusion of the Goncourt pastiche at the end of the *Recherche* thus remaps the novel's synapses, stretching its generic limits and multiplying its points of view. This pastiche rearranges the coordinates of the novelistic universe that has been constructed for us over thousands of pages, revealing how extremely different everything could look.

My aim throughout this chapter has been to demonstrate that Proust is not exclusively interested in the cultivation of aesthetic sophistication. Rather, he is attuned to the circuits of investment—and the suspension of belief— necessary to the production and maintenance of literary authority and prestige. In his pastiches, in his newspaper articles, and in the pages of his novel, Proust takes us behind the curtain of the magic show, while still permitting us to cherish the illusion. "Prestige" in Proust is therefore nothing innate, but a matter of practice, a carefully rehearsed (and not always successful) sleight-of-hand. Sometimes the show is all the more enchanting when it doesn't quite come off—when the prestidigitator shows his hand, or when a vaunted diamond turns out to be mere snot on a trickster's collar. In 1908, when he wrote his Lemoine Affair pastiches, Proust was not exorcising influences: he was rehearsing the various styles and perceptual modes that he would activate throughout his novel. These pastiches help us to recognize the affective, sensory, and epistemological heterogeneity of the *Recherche* itself, showing us just how elastic, expansive, and variegated Proust's fictional world can be.

{ 2 }

Babble

In a rare moment of garbled speech, Proust's narrator issues his first aesthetic
judgment as a stutter of delight ("ravissement"). What is most striking about
this arrested or "ravished" judgment is the ordinariness of the scene that provokes it. Stopping to gaze at a chicken fluffing its feathers in the wind and a
red toolshed roof reflected in a pond, the nascent aesthetic theorist can only
point inarticulately with his umbrella as he exclaims in astonishment, "zut,
zut, zut, zut." This peculiar conjunction of wonder and banality recurs at key
moments of the *Recherche*, as Proust directs our attention to objects so stun-
ningly unremarkable that they resist critical hold.

According to Bourdieu, the judgment of aesthetic taste is always an expression of class position. It is therefore fundamentally combative, acquisitive, and
self-interested—a means of establishing one's "proper place" in relation to
others and of asserting one's "sense of social value."[1] Bourdieu frequently cites
the *Recherche* as a prime illustration of the theory that taste functions as an
internalized "sense of direction" or social orienting device ("une sorte de sens
de l'orientation sociale"), maintaining subjects' attachments to particular positions in social space.[2] In Bourdieu's view, Proust is the author best able to
expose the hidden "social relationship[s] of membership and exclusion" that
distinguished, seemingly "disinterested" practices of taste simultaneously activate and deny.[3] Indeed, it is only a slight exaggeration to say that *La Distinction*

is a book about Proust; in this work, Bourdieu refers more frequently to Proust than to any other literary author, noting in particular Proust's capacity to "cultivate and also analyze cultivated pleasure."[4]

Proust's engagement with aesthetics is stranger than Bourdieu's analysis would suggest, however. Chapter 1 examined elements of this strangeness, focusing on Proust's penchant for newspapers, public hoaxes, and ventriloquistic imitation. The present chapter turns back to the *Recherche* in order to explore an even more unsophisticated side of the novel. I argue that what Bourdieu terms the "aesthetic disposition"—the capacity to garner cultural profit, or distinction from judgments of taste—is entangled in Proust with what this disposition allegedly rejects: the facile, the creaturely, the infantile. Defining the aesthetic disposition as "the only socially accepted 'right' way of approaching the objects socially designated as works of art," Bourdieu suggests that a distinguished aesthetic orientation is founded on a denunciation of "naive" reactions.[5] "A generalized capacity to neutralize ordinary urgencies," the aesthetic disposition implies distance from all that is "*common*, i.e., easy and immediately accessible, starting with everything that reduces the aesthetic animal to pure and simple animality."[6] In what follows, I examine scenes in which Proust valorizes precisely such commonplace urgencies, foregrounding distinction-shattering, immediate pleasure in his representation of aesthetic experience. The *Recherche* sometimes calls attention to an object so ordinary—simply *there*—that it defies eloquent appraisal: a toolshed roof reflected in a pond, a blossoming hedge, some steeples, a bit of yellow wall. Provoking an impasse for critical judgment, these unqualifiable objects generate a childish or creaturely state of wonder, marked by nonsensical interjections or singsong babble.

In Search of Lost Time might be read as the ultimate celebration of aesthetic distinction—or even as a "monumental expression" of "supersophistication."[7] Yet Proust has no interest in flawless exhibitions of cultivated taste. He is drawn, instead, to the edges of distinction, the zone where the aesthetic and the ordinary intersect or shade into one another. He writes in *Contre Sainte-Beuve* that he is out to upset the conventional notion of the aesthetic disposition: his novel will ruminate on objects and events that break with traditional hierarchies of value, and which men of taste ("les gens de goût") may consider tasteless. In Proust, the everyday, the overlooked, and the minor become potential sources of aesthetic wealth. Instead of a celebrated opera, an ultra-elegant soirée, or a philosophical oeuvre, the Proustian aesthete prefers ordinary events, finding inestimable value in provincial musical performances, silly balls, the names of northern train stations, and insipid books.[8] An aesthetic value system oriented toward such everyday objects, Proust readily admits, will seem stupid to intelligent people. Deriving aesthetic worth from the apparently worthless is a dangerous game, as people might read your interest in the undistinguished as a sign of your own lack of distinction. As Proust acknowledges, a writer's taste for the unrefined prompts distinguished people to remark that for a man of talent, he has very poor taste ("pour un homme de talent il a des goûts très bêtes").[9] Indeed, Proust's fascination with the unintelligent—ordinary objects, gossip, states of stupor or unthinkingness—has struck some readers as stupid. Rejecting *Swann's Way* for publication, a reader for the Ollendorf publishing house proclaimed: "I might be obtuse, but I don't see the point of reading thirty pages about the way some fellow tosses in bed before falling asleep."[10]

The consequences of a taste for indistinction are significant. Proust's flagrant disregard for the hierarchies of taste opens up radically democratic possibilities. If any ordinary thing is a potential aesthetic object, what is to distinguish art from what it is not, and the aesthetically disposed perceiver from everyone else? As Jacques Rancière queries in his reading of *Madame Bovary*, if *anything* can be made into art, what is to keep *anyone* from becoming an aesthetic subject?[11]

Proust defends against the destabilizing threat of an everyday aesthetics by claiming to value in the ordinary not its ordinariness, but rather its potential transformation: the secret value it reveals to those endowed with special powers of perception. If the vulgar and mundane (silly balls, inane books, provincial train stations) interest him, it is because Proustian aesthetics generally works on the principle of sublimation, or "translation."[12] According to this logic, the merely phenomenal world—composed of what Proust's narrator sometimes calls the "waste product" of experience—is valuable because it is a source of subjective truth.[13] As the narrator puts it in "Combray," the task of the writer consists in replacing the "opaque" impenetrability of real things ("a dead weight which our sensibilities have not the strength to lift") with an assimilable immateriality "which the soul can assimilate."[14] As Leo Bersani has shown, in this act of translation, the subject quells the world's strangeness by swallowing it up with metaphor and making it into an extension of his own mind.[15] When the perceiver finds a "metaphoric equivalent" in the object for himself, he rescues the thing from the realm of the commonplace, that wasteland in which reality is "more or less identical for each one of us."[16] The most complete elaboration of this theory occurs in *Time Regained*, when the narrator discovers that his task is to translate the material into the spiritual, to decipher the truth hidden beneath clouds, triangles, church spires, flowers, and stones.[17] According to this view, humble, ordinary things are valuable only if they can be converted into signs of the perceiver's interpretive authority.[18]

Indeed, the *Recherche* presents an assemblage of insignificant, everyday objects—cookies, paving stones, napkins, and so on—which are valuable because they can be assimilated into general laws and made to reflect the subject's totalizing power. Yet alongside this assemblage of decipherable objects, a secondary, shadow constellation is perceptible. This constellation consists of ordinary things that are moving—even ravishing—not because they are recuperable to theory, but because they are simply *there*. Because neither special skill nor training is required to appreciate such objects, they erase distinctions, rather than upholding them. The writer Bergotte's stupefied recognition of a yellow patch of wall in a Vermeer painting—a luminous spot that asks nothing and reflects nothing of the perceiver—is one example of this alternative, non-appropriative aesthetics. A pinkish splotch of light that flashes from a roof to a pond—halting the narrator in his tracks and provoking his inarticulate cry of pleasure—is another. Like the ungraspable "neutral glimmer" the narrator glimpses while waiting for involuntary memory to divulge its secrets,[19] these perceptions tend to surprise the perceiver while he is on the path to somewhere else. Unlike the novel's collection of theoretically profitable, involuntary-memory-provoking objects, these ordinary things function not as arrival points, but as minor impasses. At such moments, rather than sublimating or "translating" the ordinary object into a general theory, the perceiver simply points back at it. In fact, in this aesthetic paradigm, the aesthetic subject tends to imitate the object, rather than compelling it to mimic him.[20] Tracing such instances of aesthetic disorientation reveals a different side of the *Recherche*. In the margins of its celebration of desirous appropriation ("the conquest of truth"), we find a modest affirmation of the world's inassimilable, everyday appearance. This is not the celebrated paradigm of time regained, but a more humble aesthetics of things glimpsed along the way.

"Zut, zut, zut, zut"

This alternative aesthetic plot begins with an episode evoked at the outset of the present chapter, in which the narrator is thrilled, or "ravished" by the wind in a chicken's feathers and the reflection of light on a tool-shed and a pond. Tired from reading all morning, he is taking a walk in order to allow his long-immobile body to discharge its accumulated energies "in all directions" like a spinning top. Cheerfully ("avec allégresse"), he spins himself into a scene that is simultaneously radiant and unremarkable. At the edge of a pond, sunlight is shining on a gardener's hut and on the hen that struts along its red-tiled roof:

> The wind tugged at the wild grass growing from cracks in the wall and at the hen's downy feathers, which floated out horizontally to their full extent with the unresisting submissiveness of light and lifeless things. The tiled roof cast upon the pond, translucent again in the sunlight, a dappled pink reflection which I had never observed before. And, seeing upon the water, and on the surface of the wall, a pallid smile responding to the smiling sky,

I cried aloud in my enthusiasm, brandishing my furled umbrella: 'Gosh, gosh, gosh, gosh!'[21]

Le vent qui soufflait tirait horizontalement les herbes folles qui avaient poussé dans la paroi du mur, et les plumes de duvet de la poule, qui, les unes et les autres se laissaient filer au gré de son souffle jusqu'à l'extrémité de leur longueur, avec l'abandon de choses inertes et légères. Le toit de tuile faisait dans la mare, que le soleil rendait de nouveau réfléchissante, une marbrure rose, à laquelle je n'avais encore jamais fait attention. Et voyant sur l'eau et à la face du mur un pâle sourire répondre au sourire du ciel, je m'écriai dans mon enthousiasme en brandissant mon parapluie refermé: 'Zut, zut, zut, zut.'[22]

In this scene, the aesthetic subject is disoriented by an assemblage of ordinary, theoretically profitless objects. Here, the material world does not hide truths that the theorist must penetrate and reveal: the passage foregrounds horizontality, contiguity, immediacy, in-distinction. The perceiver does not stand above the scene (if anyone does, it's the chicken). He does not "translate" or extract essences from things, but simply sees the passing correspondence between them: a "smile" of light binding a wall to a pond. The scene does not privilege any single object, but draws our attention to a zigzagging reflection that tenuously and momentarily joins roof, water, wall, and sky. It is hard to say where this composition begins and ends, whether it extends to include the downy feathers or the wild grass poking up through the wall. The dappled reflection ("marbrure") that the shed's roof makes on the pond's surface suggests the variegated surface of a book cover or of skin—emphasizing the flatness of the scene and extending its composition to include the reader, whose eyes skim along the surface of the book she is holding.

It is important, too, that this "humble discovery" takes place in the enthusiastic top-spinning mood of post-reading—what occurs here is not a scene of "translation" (like the redemptive translation or abstraction of ordinary things into lasting signs the narrator advocates elsewhere). The narrator is not consuming the world, making it his own. Rather, he's simply spinning through it—discharging the energies stored up in his body. The chicken is the narrator's double: just another sentient being out for a walk (note that the narrator's "promenade" is echoed by the image of the hen that struts—"se promenait"—along the toolshed roof). Not unlike a chicken's clucks or squawks, the narrator's *zut*s are word-objects—"mots opaques"—sounds or corporeal gestures that draw the speaker into the scene rather than permitting him to stand without to judge it.[23] Just as the narrator's body is not consuming objects but rather, expending its wild, spinning energies in all directions, "zut, zut, zut, zut" is neither descriptive nor analogical, but indexical. "Zut" is an exclamation, meaning that it has a performative function, and only vague propositional content.[24] This utterance does not capture and replace its object, but simply binds the speaker to the world. Similarly, instead of insulating the narrator against the elements, the closed umbrella functions as a pointer, extending a line from the narrator's body to the objects around him, expanding the indexical force of his enthusiastic exclamation. Following Paul Fry, we might call this an "ostensive moment"—an instance of "a-theologic astonishment" that "temporarily releases consciousness from its dependence on the signifying process."[25] The narrator's joyful, "indistinct" vocalization is not a failure, but the model for a non-recuperative encounter between the speaking subject and the world.[26]

The narrator seems to dismiss his own undignified response, indicating that he has failed to see clearly into the source of his rapture and suggesting that his "unilluminating" cries are merely manifestations of confused, unelucidated ideas.[27] Yet the scene itself, which culminates in the description of sunlight embracing the surface of things, is nothing if not luminescent. This lustrous, dehierarchized visual composition will find its reflection later in a painting by Elstir, in which a "hospital with no style" or a "slightly vulgar lady" are bound together by a shimmer of light, and appear no more or less precious than a more conventionally valorized object, such as a cathedral. The narrator will take a surprising lesson from this reorganization of the perceptual field. Time passes; it cannot be regained: "One felt that the lady would presently go home, the boats drift away, the shadow change place, night begin to fall; that pleasure comes to an end, that life passes and that instants, illuminated by the convergence at one and the same time of so many lights, cannot be recaptured."[28]

If this recognition is largely engulfed by the redemptive theory that the narrator preaches to us at the end of the novel, it is because perceptions of this sort are not ultimately memorable. Six volumes later, when the narrator recalls the Montjouvain pond scene in the context of disparaging the incompleteness of his response—his failure to translate his feeling into more essential language—he actually misattributes the perception, suggesting that he was provoked to cry out "zut alors!" upon seeing the shadow of a cloud on the river Vivonne.[29] This misattribution and slight misquotation indicate the contingency and forgettability of the scene; ravishing as it is, the novel cannot derive any lasting aesthetic wealth from it.[30]

In a draft version of "Combray," the string of "zuts" is attached to what is now one of the most well-known and oft-discussed scenes of the novel. This is the famous bedtime drama ("drame du coucher"), the scene in which the unhappy narrator is sent to bed without his mother's kiss. Critics have interpreted this scene as the point of origin for the Proustian "law" that desire is jealous, insatiable, and grounded in loss.[31] So it is surprising that a draft version of this episode demonstrates a striking resemblance to the chicken/toolshed/pond scene of the published novel. Having just decided to wait up for his mother, the narrator is sitting by his open bedroom window in a state of joy ("allégresse"), enchanted by the insignificant words floating up to him from the garden: "I repeated to myself 'Zut! zut! zut! zut! zut! alors!' with the same intoxicated tone as if these words signified some delicious truth, I leapt alone in my room, I smiled to myself in my mirror, and not knowing where to place my tenderness and joy, I seized my own arm with rapture and planted a kiss on it."[32]

The published version eliminates the exclamations, the reflected smile, and the kiss, presenting in their place a scene of appropriative mastery, whereby the perceiver transforms the external world into a reflection of his inner state. Instead of crying "zut" and kissing his own arm, the narrator, fearful of being heard, silently opens the window and sees a mute, frozen landscape—a tense, circumscribed projection of his own anxiety: "Outside, things too seemed frozen in a mute intentness not to disturb the moonlight."[33] In the draft, however, the narrator opens the window and is "enchanted" by the babble he hears. The logic of reflection, rather than assimilation, structures the passage. Instead of "translating" the world around him, here the narrator simply calls back to it, his meaningless exclamation doubling the "insignificant words" that float up from below. And if the exclamation conveys any truth, it is not lasting and immaterial but "delicious"—sensual and finite. What we find in the draft version of the bedtime drama is not the primal scene for all subsequent jealousy, but the blueprint for a non-totalizing, disorienting aesthetics. Like the narrator's encounter with the luminous pond and toolshed roof, the drafted *drame du coucher* eschews the arrival in favor of the intermediary instant, and prefers the momentary caressing of a surface to the mental assimilation of things.

"Little patch of yellow wall"

If the narrator's response to a zigzag of light on the Montjouvain pond is a senseless exclamation of pleasure, he feels he must henceforth learn to derive theoretical profit from his sensory experiences. He dismisses his enthusiastic "opaque words" as a childish response to aesthetic pleasure, a failure to translate the world's thickness into immaterial concepts. Still, traces of this initial stuttered "zut" are scattered through the novel—instances when the eloquence of aesthetic judgment is replaced by blather or song. The writer Bergotte's astonished perception of a little patch of yellow wall in a Vermeer painting is such a moment of critical impasse. Bergotte's stammer of impossible judgment—"little patch of yellow wall with a sloping roof, little patch of yellow wall"—indicates that aesthetic disorientation is not something one grows out of in the *Recherche*.

In *The Captive*, the narrator reads in the newspaper that a writer he has long admired has died. Bergotte's death is remarkable in that it occurs precisely in the instant that the writer discovers impersonal, disinterested beauty—"une beauté qui se suffirait à elle-même."[34] In a patch of yellow wall in Vermeer's "View of Delft" Bergotte recognizes a beauty that does not require the perceiver's interested gaze in order to exist. Inassimilable, self-sufficient, the "little patch of yellow wall" ("petit pan de mur jaune") is not recuperable to a subject's search for personal meaning, and permits only a deictic gesture of acknowledgment. Suggestive of the dappled pink reflection that flashes from roof to pond at Montjouvain, the "little patch of yellow wall" also recalls the narrator's intermediary, unredeemed image of Combray— before he has resurrected it with involuntary memory—as a "luminous panel" ("pan lumineux").[35] Moreover, the patch of wall seems all the more ungrasp-able when one seeks its referent in Vermeer's painting, which assembles— amidst its many pointy spires—a variety of luminous spots, none definitively more "precious" than the others.[36]

Presented as the most precious object imaginable, the yellow patch is also disorientingly ordinary. Mieke Bal reads the patch as a "dis-figure"—the "visual equivalent of a Freudian denial"—and argues that it presents not a lack of meaning, but a surplus or overdetermination of form.[37] What interests me about the "little patch of yellow wall," however, is the way it appears to hover outside of the dualistic logic of surface and depth, concealment and exposure, overdetermination and insufficiency, failure and success, which governs the teleological plot of aesthetic conversion in Proust. Conjoining the rhetoric of preciosity with the stuff of the everyday, the patch is inestimable in both senses of the word: at once unremarkable and incomparable. In the fol-lowing passage, the ideal aesthetic object is joined in a chain of associations with the most commonplace things—the undercooked yellow potatoes Ber-gotte eats before arriving at the museum and the random news item ("fait divers") he fears becoming as he collapses onto the sofa:

> "All the same," he said to himself, "I shouldn't like to be the headline news of this exhibition for the evening papers." He repeated to himself: "Little patch of yellow wall, with a sloping roof, little patch of yellow wall." Mean-while he sank down on to a circular settee; whereupon he suddenly ceased to think that his life was in jeopardy and, reverting to his natural opti-mism, told himself: "It's nothing, merely a touch of indigestion from those potatoes, which were undercooked."[38]

> "Je ne voudrais pourtant pas, se dit-il, être pour les journaux du soir le fait divers de cette exposition." Il se répétait: "petit pan de mur jaune avec un auvent, petit pan de mur jaune." Cependant il s'abattit sur un canapé circu-laire; aussi brusquement il cessa de penser que sa vie était en jeu et, reve-nant à l'optimisme, se dit: "C'est une simple indigestion que m'ont donnée ces pommes de terre pas assez cuites, ce n'est rien."[39]

Socially incommensurate phenomena (a *fait divers*, a Vermeer masterpiece, potatoes) are bound together in a metonymic chain. The passage blunts the distinction between aesthetic perception and ordinary consumption: Bergotte enters the exhibition and eats the potatoes in adjoining clauses ("Bergotte mangea quelques pommes de terre, sortit et entra à l'exposition").

Stunned by the sight of a painting that is actually less remarkable than he expected (it appears less "dazzling," less "different from all that he knew"), the distinguished writer is suddenly a child reaching for an untenable butterfly: "his dizziness increased; he fixed his gaze, like a child upon a yellow butterfly that it wants to catch, on the precious little patch of wall."[40] Like a creature with a will of its own, the "little patch of wall" resists appropriation and the aesthetic subject can only point in childish "exhilaration" ("étourdissement"). "Étourdissement," a word repeated in the description of Bergotte's crisis, suggests giddiness and euphoria as well as vertigo and disorientation, and also bears connotations of inattention and mindlessness.[41] Rather than confirming his aesthetic disposition, this experience leaves the perceiver disoriented and indisposed.

As he collapses in front of the painting, Bergotte utters a repetitive phrase that points to and doubles the object without containing it in any way: "little patch of yellow wall with a sloping roof, little patch of yellow wall" ("petit pan de mur jaune avec un auvent, petit pan de mur jaune"). Similarly, early in the novel, the narrator is overwhelmed by the "inexhaustible" and incomprehensible joy caused by the sight of a hawthorn hedge in bloom: his mind "did not know what to do with it."[42] At a loss to "descend further" into the object's "secret," he can only look again and again, heart pounding "like that of a traveller who glimpses on some low-lying ground a stranded boat which is being caulked and made sea-worthy, and cries out, although he has not yet caught sight of it, 'The Sea!'"[43] Like the hawthorn hedge and the scene at the Monjouvain pond, Bergotte's yellow patch is an aesthetic object that thwarts theoretical appropriation. Indeed, this is an experience that the perceiver will not even live to tell about.

Following Barthes, we might describe the exclamations that accompany aesthetic disorientation ("zut, zut, zut, zut"; "little patch of yellow wall"; "the sea!") as *punctive*. In *Camera Lucida*, Barthes theorizes the photographic "punctum" as a mark of sheer contingency: "that!" ("ça!"). Not a sign, but an inassimilable detail, the punctum does not signify, but rather, "pricks" the beholder. Similarly, the Proustian stutter of ravishment or exhilaration marks the perception of a joltingly uncodable object or assemblage of objects. This form of language is punctive because it neither describes nor symbolizes, but simply indexes. Pointing toward an unspecifiable particularity, such utterances indicate what the speaker cannot assimilate into theory or translate into art.[44] These punctive interjections are not non-referential—they are hyper-referential, indexing a presence that eludes critical language.

By highlighting the deictic or punctive force of aesthetic perception, Proust is playing on Kant's theory of non-conceptual, non-instrumental, "disinterested" aesthetic pleasure. Kant indicates that there is nothing to say *about* the radical particularity of the aesthetic, defined precisely by its lack of determined content or evaluative criteria. In the face of a perception that does not fit any given concept, the judge of aesthetic beauty is reduced to pointing, able only to reiterate the declaration of pleasure without describing or analyzing the experience any further. According to Vivasvan Soni, because Kantian aesthetic judgment engages only the phenomenality or sensuous immediacy of "this" particular object, it "says nothing except 'Look!' It only points at the object mutely, without reason or argument." Therefore "the only form that a judgment of beauty can take is the monotonous repetition of the sentence 'This object is beautiful.'"[45] By highlighting the babble that aesthetic experience incites, Proust makes explicit a link between aconceptual pleasure and inarticulacy that remains implicit in Kant.

The self-sufficient little patch—contiguously linked to the indigestible yellow potatoes—belongs to a constellation of unqualifiable objects in the *Recherche*, objects that are stunning and yet beclouded by ordinariness, and which provoke the most singsong or commonplace response. If we let Bergotte's yellow patch guide our reading of Proust, a different textual landscape begins to emerge: not a textual space organized around hidden depths to be penetrated and exposed, but rather one composed of luminous surfaces and dazzling points. This intermittent aesthetic mode in the *Recherche*—call it "ravissement" or "étourdissement"—obliterates the distinction between art and non-art, simply affirming (not sublimating or subverting) the ordinariness of things.

"I began to sing my head off"

At the center of this alternative topography we find the Martinville steeples. Reinforcing the narrator's assimilative or digestive relation to the world, Combray often appears as an edible landscape: this is a place of delicious pastries (*brioches, madeleines,* and *chaussons*), a universe saturated with imbibable essences and odors. Yet the town and its environs are also speckled with prickly, indigestible steeples and spires. Poking up between the "finger of God" that opens the second chapter of "Combray," and the "uplifted forefinger of dawn" that closes it, the Martinville steeples are particularly important indexes: they provoke the narrator to begin writing the very text that we are reading. As he speeds past the shimmering, mobile points from his carriage seat above a chicken cage, he is moved to compose a description, and then to punctuate his accomplishment with a joyful squawk.

As it presents the narrator's only embedded piece of writing in the entire novel, critics have accorded much attention to the Martinville passage. Peter Collier and J. D. Whiteley celebrate the passage as the only instance in the *Recherche* "when the protagonist becomes specifically and absolutely the artist," and argue that it presents a mise-en-abîme of the general movement in Proust from ignorance toward enlightenment.[46] Making a similar argument from a critical point of view, Bersani and Dutoit contend that the passage epitomizes the novel's assimilative aesthetics: the narrator sees something that moves him and so he metabolizes it in metaphor, incorporating and taming the threatening unfamiliarity of the perception. Indeed, the narrator initially encourages this reading, introducing his composition by alluding to the loss that the act of writing has prevented. He suggests that had he not been compelled to symbolize his perception in writing, the steeples would have sunk into a forgettable constellation of ordinary, unassimilated stimuli: "those two steeples would have gone to join the medley of trees and roofs and scents and sounds I had noticed and set apart because of the obscure pleasure they had given me which I had never fully explored."[47] We therefore expect the description that follows to penetrate the objects and extract their essence, preventing their fall into the limbo of unredeemed sensation.

Yet the passage, which juxtaposes two descriptions of the same phenomenon (one composed by the juvenile narrator, one by the mature narrator), celebrates shifting surfaces and points, not penetrable depths, and foregrounds a logic of mutability, not monumentality. The continuous addition and subtraction of steeples in the young narrator's composition confounds analogy: the objects will not hold still long enough for a totalizing metaphor to be applied to them. Instead, the steeples are caught and released by one figure after another—likened to birds, then trees, then flowers, then girls. Like the momentarily illuminated assemblage that provokes the narrator's ravished "zut, zut, zut, zut," the conjunction of objects that generates aesthetic pleasure here is fleeting. This passage foregrounds above all a complex "fugue" playing out between the pair of Martinville steeples and the third, distant Vieuxvicq steeple. Continuously changing in number and placement, appearing and disappearing, the steeples are two, then three, then separate into two plus one, then oscillate between three and two, then vanish. In Proust's 1907 *Figaro* article, "Impressions de route en automobile," on which this passage is based, the steeples are compared to the central yet marginal titular edifice in a landscape painting by J. M. W. Turner. Simultaneously remarkable and entirely forgettable, the steeples take up very little space: they are as ephemeral as a rainbow or a glimmer of evening light.[48]

For some critics, the doubled description of the steeples works to highlight the younger narrator's artistic immaturity. Comparing the "opacity" and "uselessness" of this instance of writing to the narrator's earlier "zut," Michel Butor

cites the observer's failure on both occasions to uncover the source of his emotion and forcefully "respond" to phenomena, rather than simply being moved
by them: "We have before our eyes merely a second description [. . .] to which
images have been uselessly added. It is futile to seek in this description the
reason for the young Marcel's emotion, and in this regard [. . .] it remains as
opaque as the 'zut' pronounced on the Méséglise Way."[49] According to this
logic, both the description of the steeples and the "zut" cry are derivative,
secondary; in each case, Butor contends, the narrator fails to place himself at
the center of the scene. Roger Shattuck reads the episode in a similarly dismissive vein, arguing that the Martinville passage is one of the markers of "horizontal" experience, or "limited vision," against which the final "vertical"
experience of aesthetic transcendence is opposed. In Shattuck's reading, the
vision of interwoven steeples lacks any final form or pattern; the steeples are
astonishing and confusing because they can only be "seen at eye level."[50] I
would suggest, however, that the primacy of horizontality here—especially in
juxtaposition to the sharpness of the objects—is precisely what makes the
perception so interesting. Note that the steeples appear both depthless and
pointy—*flèche* also means arrow, pointer, or spear. The passage becomes even
pointier when we consider the name of the doctor in whose carriage the narrator is riding: Doctor Percepied, or "pierce-foot," a name that suggests precisely the kind of pedestrian epiphany, or shocking ordinariness that I am
investigating here.[51]

    Echoing the joyous "zut, zut, zut, zut" that punctuates his perception of a
reflection on the Montjouvain pond, the narrator concludes his first literary
composition with an inarticulate cry. As he finishes his description of the
steeples, he bursts into a joyful, head-splitting, egg-laying song from his seat
next to a cage full of chickens: "as though I myself were a hen and had just laid
an egg, I began to sing my head off."[52] Critics who discuss the Martinville episode rarely address this odd moment. According to Collier and Whiteley, the
"deliberate depoeticization" of the scene (crowned by the "grossly inelegant
assimilation of the fledgling writer to a clucking hen") works to contrast the
"artistic" piece of writing to its nonpoetic, banal ("deliberately sub-Proustian")
surroundings.[53] The last in a series of clichés ("à bride abattue," "comme le
vent," "pris d'une sorte d'ivresse"), the song sung "à tue-tête" is included, Collier and Whitely suggest, in order to "downgrade the linguistic climate" of the
real and hence foreground the superiority of the narrator's piece of writing.
Against the notion that this passage contrasts a "blank, artless view of reality"
to an artistic one, we might say that this scene demonstrates the extent to
which aesthetic experience in Proust is allied with its alleged other. In its
most moving forms, the aesthetic is nothing special—which is to say, it belongs less to the world of essences and ideas than to a material immediacy
that resists appropriation, transforming the writer and would-be theorist into
a squawking hen or a stammering child. The original desire to write is shown

here to be less about incorporating the object's strangeness than it is about calling back to the world.

In a study of impersonality in modernism, Sharon Cameron queries Ralph Waldo Emerson's peculiar penchant for clichéd figurations. Cliché, that strange modern concept of words devalued through overuse, is often described as exhausted or broken metaphor.[54] Flaunting its resistance to propriety, untethered to any original source, cliché seems to speak itself without the speaker's intention or knowledge, much to the dismay of critics like Eric Partridge, whose *Dictionary of Clichés* qualifies cliché as "pointless," "nauseating," "frightening," "half-baked," and "uncultured."[55] But we might understand cliché not simply in terms of a degradation of uniqueness, but as a gestural, non-appropriative iteration. Cameron's essay is useful here because it engages the relation between banal or platitudinous language and an impersonal mood that Emerson, like Proust, calls "ravishment." Cameron notes that despite his remarkable eloquence, Emerson tends to give voice to "propositional banality" in describing the ecstatic erasure of personal identity.[56] In Emerson, Cameron suggests, platitudinous language is not opposed to the "ravishment" of the impersonal. Rather, the voice that is anyone's and no one's is in fact the very voice of ravishment.[57] Cliché marks the obliteration of personal identity and indicates an experience of self-shattering at the heart of Emerson's—and, I would argue, Proust's—conception of the aesthetic.[58] Cliché, after all, is "the voice of no private person."[59] What is so interesting about cliché as a mode of aesthetic response in Proust is that it suggests not an experience so private that it cannot be transmitted, but an experience that could be had by anyone.

And what about the chicken? Bersani and Dutoit interpret it as proof that the narrator has indeed incorporated his vision. The metaphor of laying an egg comically illustrates the narrator's movement from subjective deprivation to plenitude, they argue: the "egg" is the "egg of his own descriptive resources that he has finally expressed, pressed out of himself onto the page."[60] I would suggest, however, that the entire passage, and especially this crowning moment of disarticulation, works to turn the narrator's writerly authority inside out. The desire to write is not unlike the urge to crow or squawk—not a masterful act, but a responsive one, generated from the infantile or creaturely margins of speech.

"Bah!"

Inspired to write by the sight of objects that appear simultaneously piercing and pedestrian, the narrator completes his first literary text by singing (like a chicken) as if to bust his head ("à tue-tête"). The episode in which the article appears in print—a scene Proust originally planned to place in the overture of his novel—is also marked by strikingly undistinguished speech.[61] Highlighting the volatility of distinction in the *Recherche*, this scene heralds the narrator's artistic success even as it foregrounds the disorienting ordinariness of the daily newspaper that transmits his work. As he begins to leaf through the *Figaro* one morning, the narrator suddenly recognizes his essay on the Martinville steeples. Responding to this passage from the very novel we are reading, the narrator places himself in our position, modeling for us a non-appropriative and unsophisticated attitude of reading that oscillates between indifference and fascination. Proust presents the event of becoming an author as a distinction-flattening experience, a fall into the de-individuating space of the "quelconque"—the ordinary, undistinguished, or "whatever."

The newspaper is neither discarded nor redeemed in this scene. Instead, the passage highlights a vertiginous conjunction of oppositions: the newspaper appears simultaneously interesting and uninteresting, boring and miraculous, elite and common. As chapter 1 has demonstrated at length, Proust presents newspaper reading as an experience by turns distracted and concentrated, inviting a glance that is at once diagonal, horizontal, and vertical, and he depicts the daily paper itself as both a shield protecting the individual's privacy, and a generator of new collective configurations. The narrator first perceives the newspaper as "something interesting" that his mother brings to him. This initial interest is immediately extinguished and replaced by an empty, unreceptive mood: "[I]t consisted only of newspapers. [. . .] I opened the *Figaro*. What a bore!"[62] Then in an abrupt tonal shift, mechanical reproduction is described in enchanted terms: the newspaper is a "spiritual bread"—"a miraculous, self-multiplying bread which is at the same time one and ten thousand, which remains the same for each person while penetrating innumerably into every house at once."[63] Expanding this populist tone, the narrator imagines his article being lifted up over the shoulders of an excited crowd. Although the *Figaro* is a historically elite newspaper, the narrator relishes its ordinariness, contending that because an article is only completed in the minds of its readers, its "final seal" retains a "trace of the commonplace."[64] A textual object that is simultaneously singular and multiple ("at the same time one and ten thousand"), the newspaper in Proust generates and dissolves distinctions at once.[65]

Most striking in this scene is the positive valence given the word "quelconque." Cultivating the point of view of an "impossible creature," the narrator strives to read simultaneously as an author and as a "lecteur quelconque"—a reader without qualities, any reader at all.[66] As noted in the introduction to this book, in its most basic sense, this gender-neutral adjective undoes distinctions, marking its object as neither specific nor generic, but as indeterminate or featureless. *Quelconque* acquired a pejorative meaning in the late nineteenth century, and came to qualify something not simply as lacking distinguishing attributes, but as dismissably ordinary or unremarkable. Proust activates this level of meaning in "Combray" when the narrator overhears his mother declaring some coffee and pistachio ice cream "bien quelconque" ("rather so-so").[67] Yet the Proustian *quelconque* can also signify in a third way: as the marker of superlative ordinariness, or remarkable insignificance. Hence when the narrator first sees Charlus at Balbec, *quelconque* ("whatever reason", "some reason") qualifies the Baron's mysterious, unspecifiable motives and desires.[68] *Quelconque* is also an adjective attached to Saint-Loup's lover, Rachel. An unqualifiable object in the narrative, Rachel is simultaneously common ("une poule" or "simple petite grue") and exceptional ("une femme d'un grand prix"). A prostitute and a remarkable artist, this "femme quelconque" is described in terms that liken her to the materiality of the novel itself: her face is compressed "like a piece of paper" between the narrator's and Saint-Loup's incongruous points of view.[69] The Proustian *quelconque* therefore designates its object as inestimable, or, as Ann Smock has put it, as simultaneously "beneath notice and beyond compare."[70]

The *Figaro* scene pivots on the *quelconque*—the adjective is repeated five times. In this passage, the *quelconque* marks the intersection of textual production and reception, authorial distinction and readerly anonymity. Relishing his indistinction, the narrator celebrates a disorienting mode of reading that is contradictory, even "impossible," requiring him to position himself at the intersection of "all contraries": "At the very moment in which I was endeavouring to be an ordinary reader ["un lecteur quelconque"], I was reading as author, but not only as author [. . .]. And when I became aware of too blatant a weakness, taking refuge in the spirit of the ordinary and astonished reader, I said to myself: 'Bah!'"[71]

We rarely hear the narrator's reported speech in this text—generally, he stands back and reports other peoples' speech—but in this scene, his voice takes on a surprisingly vernacular tone, his astonished "bah!" echoing his earlier "zuts" and chicken squawks, as well as Bergotte's stupefied stammer. Moreover, in this rare instance of autocitation, the narrator valorizes his own art not for its power to transcend time and abolish finitude, but simply for being a little prettier than the reader might expect: "Good heavens, they ought to be pleased! There are plenty of pretty things in it, more than they usually get."[72] Championing aesthetic categories that Kant banished from his theory of the beautiful (the pretty or merely pleasing), the Proustian narrator models a flagrantly unsophisticated mode of reading. In this scene, the novel opens a space of indistinction, in which boredom and fascination short-circuit into one another, an elite readership can be imagined as a "crowd," and a narrator who elsewhere carefully withholds his voice suddenly breaks into a triumphant "bah!"

"O sole mio"

In each of these episodes, a commonplace object (a spot of light, a patch of wall, three steeples, the daily newspaper) generates a punctive response, rather than a recuperative one. Instead of pulling back in order to instrumentalize the perception—"translate" it into theory—in each case the perceiver finds himself drawn into the scene. Startled by the perception of something at once exceptional and insignificant, he utters an undignified "zut" or "bah." At such moments, the ordinary or *quelconque* appears as an intensity that dissolves the language of judgment.

Proust's attention to the vicissitudes of distinction is nowhere more evident than in the Venice chapter of *The Fugitive*. In an episode that highlights the disorienting force of the ordinary in the *Recherche*, the narrator, hit hard by economic and romantic losses, undertakes a Venetian voyage with his mother in order to re-attune his sense of distinction.[73] The episode turns on the paradox of an everyday aesthetics, culminating in a reversal in which all the profits derived from the experience are annulled. Although he goes to Venice as an aesthetic critic, following in Ruskin's illustrious footsteps, the narrator departs in tongue-tied astonishment, witness to a radically inassimilable landscape. As Venice dissolves into a nameless "lieu quelconque" (a place without qualities, a featureless or indeterminate place), the would-be theorist, faced with this singularly ordinary scene, can only babble out a popular song.

In this episode, Proust explores the margins of distinction, venturing into the strange zone where the aesthetic meets the ordinary. In Venice, the line between art and everyday life is crucially blurred. A city in which *everything* is a work of art,[74] Venice appears in the *Recherche* as both the culmination and the cul-de-sac of a modernist fantasy of trans-aestheticization. This episode demonstrates the distinction-spoiling force of an everyday aesthetics: pushed to its limit, an aesthetics of the everyday implies a collapse of the border between art and non-art. Such a trans-aestheticized world would be utterly inestimable: precious to the point of worthlessness; distinctive to the point of indistinction. Object of the narrator's longing throughout the novel,[75] Venice turns out to be unknowable in the most unyielding way—simultaneously foreign and too familiar; strange and yet obvious; "singular" and yet insignificant, improper, "quelconque."

The association of Venice with decadence is a familiar literary topos: Chateaubriand, Byron, Balzac, and Ruskin (among others) have all written of the city's ruin.[76] In Proust's account, however, the trope of decay is given a modernist spin. What remains when the narrator loses his critical hold on Venice is not horrible, but unremarkable, or "whatever." In a reversal of the self-expanding dynamics of involuntary memory, Venice contracts the aesthetic subject upon himself ("me contractait sur moi-même") when it suddenly shrugs off his projections, appearing alien to all desire, simply *there*.[77] "I could no longer tell it anything about myself, I could leave nothing of myself imprinted on it," the narrator tells us.[78] This inassimilable space is embarrassingly banal, like Hamlet exposed as a mere actor with black costume and blond wig.[79] Abruptly dropped out of "the whole network of criss-crossing references woven around it," Venice now appears not terrifying but simply undressed, or poorly costumed: "So it was with the palaces, the canal, the Rialto, divested of the idea that constituted their reality and dissolved into their vulgar material elements."[80] And yet, broken into indistinguishable bits ("pareilles à toutes autres"), Venice nonetheless appears absolutely "singular."[81] As a "lieu quelconque," the city becomes the site of a tension between the inassimilable and the over-assimilated: between a particularity so particular that it cannot be named or objectified ("ça!") and a nameless, quality-less "mediocrity." *Quelconque* Venice marks the site where the invaluable and the valueless meet.

The scene in which Venice becomes a "lieu quelconque" might be read as an inverted, modernist sublime, in which the perceiver is astounded by insignificance, rather than by terror- and awe-generating totality.[82] The sublime, in Kant's *Critique of the Power of Judgment*, names a perception of such immeasurable and incomparable enormity that it threatens to expel the theorist from the realm of evaluation and discernment. Like *In Search of Lost Time*, Kant's third *Critique* is a text about the conditions of possibility for aesthetic judgment, and it bears witness to critique's ghost—a mood in which the distance necessary for criticism is abolished, and the critic finds himself gaping at the inassimilable. In Kant's narrative, however, the sublime can ultimately be contained on the condition that the subject's abstract, "incoercible" humanity be split from a more commonplace humanity: we realize our abstracting, theorizing potential, Kant suggests, by refuting "trivial" physical insignificance.[83] The marker of finitude and of the common business of living, the "trivial" emerges in this Enlightenment discourse as the remainder of an awe-generating aesthetic experience—the trivial is what must be sacrificed for the sake of theory.[84] Although Kant imagines the critic victoriously rising above nature by sacrificing all that is finite and commonplace in himself, the work of critique remains haunted by its limit, the point at which the judge, incapable of abstracting and assimilating the object of perception, finds his powers reduced to "an insignificant trifle."[85]

What shocks in the modernist "quelconque" is not the sheer enormity and incalculability of nature (as is the case in Kant) but rather, a strange "singularity of things."[86] Eroding Kant's tenuous distinction between the awesome and the trifling, Proust's Venice chapter dramatizes the disorienting potential of an everyday aesthetics. Quivering with contradictions, Venice is simultaneously too familiar and not familiar enough, over-assimilated and inassimilable, "mediocre" and "remote." Stripped of its proper name, Venice is at once close and distant, both/neither subject and object: "This unremarkable place was as strange as a place at which one has just arrived, which does not yet know one, or a place which one has left and which has forgotten one already."[87]

The recognition of Venice as a "lieu quelconque" destabilizes the entire edifice of aesthetic distinction. At the moment that the city is exposed as both exceptional and ordinary, the grounds for aesthetic judgment dissolve and the narrator finds himself aesthetically indisposed, filled with "disgust" ("dégoût").[88] If Venice first appears as an elevated version of Combray (Combray in a richer key), now the narrator can only compare it to the Deligny baths, a prestigious Parisian swimming pool floating in the Seine. A fashionable space in the middle of a river, surrounded by walls to keep out uninvited swimmers, the Deligny baths were simultaneously cordoned off and yet entirely permeable, suggesting a dubious distinction. In Proust's lifetime the baths were full of the unfiltered Seine.[89]

In the *Recherche*, aesthetic judgment is particularly vulnerable to stupid immobilization—the most astute critic always risks being struck dumb by the unwieldiness of the aesthetic object. The Venice chapter dramatizes precisely this intimacy between judgment and stupor, foregrounding the volatility of the object, its tendency to crumble and withdraw from the observer. The narrator does not speak while he is in the grips of the *quelconque*. Once again, the otherwise supremely articulate aesthete can only burst into song. This time he does not sing "à tue-tête," but silently, along with a musician serenading his hotel from a boat. As the aesthetic object swings between singularity and mediocrity, the narrator is transformed into "an attention strained to follow the development of *O sole mio*."[90] A song Adorno describes as a "Neopolitan semi-hit" and Julia Kristeva terms "a second-rate song of despair," already a commodified image of Italian-ness when Proust was revising *The Fugitive*, "O sole mio" is a cliché.[91] Noting that a series of prose rhymes play on "sole" in this passage, Malcolm Bowie declares that "the potency of cheap music [has never] been celebrated with such an expenditure of repeated syllables."[92] This "sentimental ditty" immobilizes the narrator in "religious" attention.[93] Recalling the interesting/uninteresting daily newspaper, the "insignificant" piece simultaneously fascinates and fatigues: "no doubt this trivial song which I had heard a hundred times did not interest me in the least."[94] The narrator silently sings along with the "vulgar" romance in a state of immobility, suspended between numbness and hypersensitivity, "motionless, my will dissolved."[95] If the catchy song does not exactly interest him, he is nonetheless struck, even stunned as he listens: "Each note that the singer's voice uttered with a force and ostentation that were almost muscular stabbed me to the heart."[96] Echoing the egg-laying tune he belts out after completing his first literary composition, the narrator's mental rendition of "O sole mio" inverts the image of Venice as the elusive object of an arduous quest. In Venice (or the "lieu quelconque" that was once Venice), the ideal aesthetic object proves to be indistinguishable from its cliché.

"The city that had ceased to be Venice" is one of a number of inassimilable objects in the *Recherche*, objects at once inestimable and theoretically profitless, from the "dappled pink reflection" and "little patch of yellow wall" to the "fugue" of shifting steeples and the singular/multiple *Figaro*. In the description of each of these objects, Proust's usual valorization of depths and essences gives way to an astonishing flatness, suggesting that these perceptual experiences—and the vocalizations they generate—could be anyone's. Instead of standing above phenomena in order to extract timeless truths from them, at such moments the perceiving subject is hardly different from the thing he looks at.

My objective in this chapter has been to highlight a minor, experimental side of Proust's aesthetic imagination. A canonical reading of European modernism asserts that modernist texts seek to counter the equivalences imposed by mass culture. According to this interpretation, texts such as *In Search of Lost Time* work to redeem commonplace modes of perception and to recuperate the banal by drawing it into a network of associations deemed aesthetically valuable. Proust's novel largely substantiates this view. Yet the *Recherche* also occasionally invites us to imagine a different kind of aesthetics. In instances of inarticulate, affirmation-provoking astonishment, the Proustian beholder enjoys the world in its common, undignified singularity, rather than as a mineable source of secret treasure. In Proust, the aesthetic subject is sometimes struck by an incomparable and yet unremarkable object which, indistinguishable from ordinary things, eludes critical judgment and evokes only a punctive stammer or a responsive call. At such moments, seemingly opposite modes of attention tend to shade into one another: the most rapt attention slides into boredom; the throes of rapture are indistinguishable from indigestion; the most distinguished artist is suddenly a child pointing toward a butterfly; and the most distinguished critic a bewildered traveler mouthing the words to a popular song.

Nuance

In *Phenomenology of Perception*, Merleau-Ponty describes a peculiar form of aphasia. Subjects stricken with this disorder are preoccupied with "nuance," or minor distinctions in tint, and fail to sort colors into general categories:

> [T]hey do it more slowly and painstakingly than a normal subject: they slowly place together the samples to be compared and fail to see at a glance which ones "go together." Moreover, having correctly assembled several blue ribbons, they make unaccountable mistakes: if for example the last blue ribbon was of a pale shade [d'une nuance pâle], they carry on by adding to the collection of "blues" a pale green or pale pink—as if it were beyond them to stick to the proposed principle of classification, and to consider the samples from the point of view of basic colour from start to finish of the operation.[1]

Here a classificatory impasse opens out onto other, more mutable and unpredictable ways of assembling phenomena. In his famous reading of this scene, Foucault allies aphasia with the "loss of all that is 'common' to place and name."[2] While Foucault insists on the isolating force of the aphasic's anxious and frenzied vision, which continuously disperses, splits, and fragments, this chapter takes color aphasia as an allegory for a more flexible and inclusive modality of aesthetic perception: one that highlights small, nearly imperceptible forms of difference. Unable to see the particular sensory data as representative of abstract essence or *eidos*, Merleau-Ponty's aphasics are hyper-aware of color gradations and intermediary shades. Their perception is oriented toward contiguity and contact: instead of reducing the samples to general categories at a glance, they are compelled to examine each one minutely. As if moved by the desire not only to look but also to touch the fabric of each ribbon, even when the patients manage to sort the samples "correctly" into color groups, they only do so after carefully comparing them by placing them next to one another.[3]

In an early fragmentary essay titled "A Child's View of Color," Walter Benjamin also allies heightened sensitivity to nuance with resistance to normative perceptual modes. Benjamin suggests that children, with their flexible, receptive sensory habits, are better attuned to nuance than adults are. Where adults are attentive to "things," "symptoms," and "intellectual cross-references," a child's view of color encompasses "an infinite range of nuances."[4] Benjamin associates nuance with childish practices of making and playing, and with a variety of everyday objects, from soap bubbles and "games with painted sticks" to decals, magic lanterns, and "pull-out picture books."[5] Viewed as a spectrum of nuances, Benjamin contends, color is not a mere symptom but a subtle, shimmering intensity: it ceases to be a "lifeless thing" and becomes "a winged creature that flits from one form to the next."[6]

What exactly is nuance, and what would a nuance-oriented reading practice look like? Which critical habits must we set aside in order to be attentive to the most minimal of variations, the weakest of distinctions? In this chapter, I place nuance in the orbit of the "prestige" of chapter 1 and the "quelconque" of chapter 2—as a concept that is closely bound to ordinary, unsophisticated practices of aesthetic perception. This might seem counterintuitive. The ordinary, after all, is precisely what falls beneath notice: a background noise or daily hum that we all perceive but pay little mind. Nuance, by contrast, would seem to name extremely fine-grained differences: a rare perceptual quality, not accessible to just anyone. Yet, as this chapter will show, modernism develops a new relation to nuance. At stake in modernist nuance is a paradoxically commonplace luxury of language, and a modality of attention that draws its energies from the everyday here and now.

If nuance appears to have little to do with the ordinary, this is because it is so closely linked to the concept of distinction. Indeed, despite Benjamin's insistence on the childishness of nuanced perception, nuance has historically been conceptualized as a highly-refined metric of social and semiotic discrimination. In its function as a marker of elite perception, nuance is related to the famed *je-ne-sais-quoi*: both concepts emerged in French during the seventeenth century, and both were key to the development of a complex social grammar of sophisticated taste.[7] As Eleanor Webster Bulatkin points out, "nuance" and "je-ne-sais-quoi" appear frequently in the same contexts in early modern texts; they share a quality of being "intangible" and "indefinable," yet "sufficiently perceptible for cognition."[8] In *Distinction*, Bourdieu also brings the two concepts into close contact, noting that the *je-ne-sais-quoi* is made up of "infinitesimal nuances" ("mille nuances infimes").[9] The late nineteenth century reaffirmed the bond between nuance and distinction: nuance, with its outdated aristocratic associations, emerged at the fin-de-siècle as the emblem of a new decadent subculture. Thus when sickly aesthete Des Esseintes, hero of Huysmans's 1884 novel, *Against Nature* (*À Rebours*), sets out to decorate his Fontenay mansion, he selects only those subtle and nuanced shades that "vulgar retinas" could not possibly appreciate. For Des Esseintes, "nuance" is the province of a "truly artistic individual" whose super-refined pupils are capable of perceiving color "in a more special and vibrant way" ("d'une façon plus spéciale et plus vive").[10] If today the word "nuance" still conjures the specter of ethereal fin-de-siècle perfumes, colors, and sounds, I would like to make a case for modernist nuance as something that is neither distinguished nor rare. Understood in the simplest sense, nuance is nothing more (or less) than everyday, minimal variation, such as one might see in the slowly changing textures of a cloud.

Although perfectly ordinary, nuance defined in this way is nonetheless precarious. Industrial modernity has little patience for the understated, unprofitable practices of seeing and feeling necessary to register such minor shifts in intensity and inflection. In *Minima Moralia*, Adorno contends that capitalism has damaged nuance beyond repair: nuances have been thoroughly commodified and "sold off as 'flavor.'"[11] Yet other thinkers identify something unreifiable in nuance. It offers what Roland Barthes terms an "apprenticeship in subtlety": a pedagogy oriented not toward mastering phenomena, but toward acquiring the lightest imaginable touch.[12] In this regard, we might understand hypersensitivity to nuance not as the hallmark of any one author's singular style, but as a twentieth-century aesthetic and critical attitude: one marked by a heightened attentiveness to material variability and vibrancy, to slight modulations of position, to distinctions so minute as to be nearly indiscernible. Perception oriented toward nuance is not subversive, but it is not necessarily the privileged feature of an elite and distinguished sensorium, either. Such attentiveness offers a quiet, evasive mode of resistance to routinized ways of viewing and ordering the world.[13]

To contemplate nuance is to consider questions of mood, atmosphere, and milieu. An ecological undertone is implicit throughout this chapter, which ultimately queries how literary texts might challenge our capacity to read the world in terms of extractable wealth—in terms, that is, of "natural resources" or "raw materials": mere consumable and profitable passive matter.[14] For Proust, the aesthetics of nuance implies a formalism of blurred contours and borders—a queer ecology that attunes us to the cloudy zone of contact between subject and object, and to the drift and transmutation of a subtly shifting lived environment.[15]

"Nuance" is the etymological cousin of "nuage" ("cloud"); it derives from the Old French "nue" and the Latin "nubes." If a *zut*-inducing pink reflection next to a strutting chicken, or a yellow patch of painting metonymically linked to some undercooked potatoes are paradigms for the ordinary/stunning "quelconque," a cloud (with its infinite gradations of color and shape) exemplifies the aesthetics of nuance. In Proust, cloudiness adheres to

objects seen from very far away or from extremely close by: cloudiness suggests a disturbance in the distance required to classify and delineate forms.[16]
As Hubert Damisch puts it, clouds are objects with "neither form nor consistency," in which any kind of figure may appear and vanish.[17] The vaporous
space of the cloud implies neither plenitude nor insufficiency. Blurry-edged,
indefinite, incalculable, clouds drift at the periphery of the perceptible world,
and at the edges of Proust's sublimation-centered aesthetic system. Because
clouds hover beneath the level of distinct shape, they can spread and share out
their properties, but cannot be replaced or redeemed into more essential
form. Without surface and without solidity, there is literally nothing to
peel back in a cloud, no secret content to be revealed. Clouds belong to an alternative economy, one in which objects continuously, slowly, gradually
metamorphose (vaporize, condense, solidify) without revealing hidden essence. As John Ruskin—Proust's favorite art critic—puts it in his homage to
Turner's clouds: "It is within the limits of possibility that a cloud may assume
any form."[18]

Indeed, a glance at the "cloud" section in the index of Ruskin's five-volume
Modern Painters reveals the form-exploding variety of clouds. The motley list
of entries includes: "brighter than the sky, or whitest paper," "unpaintable,"
"connected *with* the sky, not separate" (original emphasis), "cirrus: number of,
at sunrise, calculated," "curves in, all curves, rare," "edges often darker than
centres," "infinity and variety of," "mistaken for mountains," and "rain-
clouds: form of horseshoe."[19] Although Ruskin "conveniently" divides the atmosphere into three spaces, each characterized by a particular form of cloud,
he first warns that "in reality, there is no distinct limit fixed between them by
nature, clouds being formed at *every* altitude, and partaking according to
their altitude, more of less of the characters of the upper or lower regions. The
scenery of the sky is thus formed of an infinitely graduated series of systematic
forms of cloud."[20] Clouds are capable, in Ruskin's account, of generating endless streams of adjectives: his skies are alternately "mottled," "mackerel,"
"fleecy," "flakey," "fiery," "ragged," "ponderous," "checkered," "torn," "ribbed,"
"plumy," "honeycombed," "craggy," "silky," "opalescent," "inky," "sulphure-
ous," "elastic," and so on. So mutable as to escape final classification, the cloud
is not unqualifiable, but inexhaustibly qualifiable.

The dictionary of nineteenth- and twentieth-century French, the *Trésor de
la Langue Française*, assembles the following definitions of "nuance," each of
which shades subtly into the others:

> Intensity or degree of greater or lesser strength that a single color can take
> on–Tint distinguishable from others, within a single color, by the slightly
> different mixture of its components or by the subtle difference in intensity
> that these components present—Modification in intensity of a sound or of
> musical phrases—Variety or variant based on a difference of detail, often

subtle and difficult to discern, between two or several things or states otherwise the same, or between diverse states of the same thing—Very weak and almost indiscernible quantity of something —Intermediary state through which a thing can pass.

Intensité, degré plus ou moins fort que peut prendre une même couleur— Teinte qu'on peut distinguer d'autres, à l'intérieur d'une même couleur, par le mélange légèrement différent des composantes qui y entrent ou par la subtile différence d'intensité que présentent ces composantes—Modification de l'intensité d'un son ou des phrases de l'exécution musicale—Variété ou variante fondée sur une différence de détail, souvent subtile et difficilement discernable, entre deux ou plusieurs choses ou états par ailleurs semblables, ou entre les divers états d'une même chose—Quantité très faible et presque indiscernable de quelque chose—Etat intermédiaire par lequel peut passer une chose.

Presenting a modulation of degree so subtle that it escapes discernment, nuance (like a cloud) invites attunement to the very edges of form, the threshold of materiality. To perceive nuance—"small slopes on the surface of language," according to poet Pierre Alferi—we must hone our gaze on extremely minute gradations of difference.[21] Akin to what Naomi Schor terms the "insubordinate detail," nuance draws our gaze toward the periphery and the accessory—but unlike the detail, nuance is not a symptom or a clue.[22] An intermediary phenomenon, nuance can be understood as a variation *between* two states of the same thing (like a shade of red between two shades of red). Hence Lyotard defines nuance as an open-ended indeterminacy or "scarcely perceptible" harmonic wavering within determinate identity.[23] Lyotard allies nuance with timbre, and I will return to this concept in the last section of this chapter. For now, note that tuning into nuance orients us toward the horizontal (toward the axis of the *beside*) rather than the vertical (toward secret depths or transcendent heights). Lyotard suggests that nuance is perceived in terms of sensory texture, rather than (ocular) detachment: the mind cannot grasp, but can be "touched" by nuance.[24]

Leo Spitzer refers frequently to nuance in his 1928 essay on Proustian style. He notes that in his attempt to touch upon the "exact nuance" of a sound, a light, or a sensation, Proust often has recourse to a particular turn of phrase— one that brings out an intermediary register indirectly, by naming what lies closest to it.[25] Hence Proust often repeats the turn of phrase, "it was not *a* but *b*," or "if not *a* at least *b*," whereby *a* and *b* are offered to the reader simultaneously.[26] Proust's sentences tend to slow down, spill out, and multiply possibilities in order to render the nuances of the in-between. As we meander through the *Recherche*, we often find ourselves drifting this way and that through sentences that distend, puff out, engorge into one shape, then another. We float in the interstice of the hypothetical, suspended in the hiatus of an "if . . . then," an "unless," or an "either . . . or." Spitzer notes that the *Recherche* is full of the prefix "in-" and its variants: *immatériel, impalpable, inconnu, inaccessible, indéfini, ineffable, illisible, inexistant*, and so on.[27] This profusion of the "in-" suggests an escape from precision, a quality of being not-this (but not necessarily "that," either). Nuance is what cannot be directly grasped, but becomes perceptible in proximity. It offers itself to view not as an absolute negation of some other quality, but as what lies just *beside* the other.

One might expect nuance to signify in Proust as it does in Huysmans's decadent novel, *Against Nature*: as a rarified or delicate quality perceptible only to a privileged minority. After all, the kinship between nuance and distinction extends well into the twentieth century: in Bourdieu's analysis of the system of taste, the uninitiated masses are presumed to perceive only a "chaos of sounds and rhythms, colours and lines" in the very objects which, for the cultural elite, present a subtle web of references and counter-references.[28] And in Baudrillard's study of the bourgeois system of objects, the "dignity" of the bourgeois interior is characterized by its diffusion of discrete "nuances," such as beige and mauve, rather than bright colors.[29] Yet there is something peculiar about nuance that is left out of these accounts—a quality of minorness and non-systematicity that makes the hyper-nuanced object inappropriable to the distinction-seeking aesthete. Roland Barthes hints at this quality when he contrasts the opposition of primary colors (red vs. blue) to the "slight difference" that one glimpses in monochrome, or unmarked, "colorless" colors.[30] The very shades that Baudrillard interprets as signifiers of bourgeois propriety and good taste appear in Barthes's reading as ungraspable and unsettling. Orienting us toward a paradigm-thwarting, minute scale of distinction, organized around the "shimmer" ("moire"), such colorless or nuanced tonalities subtly shift depending on the angle of one's gaze.[31]

During the last years of his life, Barthes distanced himself from a semiotics grounded in the logic of castration and compensation. In works such as *Camera Lucida* and *A Lover's Discourse: Fragments*, as well as in his Collège de France lecture series, *The Preparation of the Novel* and—above all—*The Neutral*, Barthes abandons the project of semiological demystification, exploring instead a variety of different kinds of critical interest.[32] Inspired by Proust— whom he considers the central figure of his own "literary cosmogony"—he elaborates deliberately weak readings, skirting dualistic thinking in favor of nuance.[33] Attentive to minute gradation, amplification, and tonal distinctions, this minor theoretical mode abstains from classifying phenomena according to the binary pairs part/whole, manifest/latent. Instead, it plays with nuances, which Barthes also terms "differential intensities."[34] Barthes's reading plucks nuance out of the bourgeois interior and makes it the organizing figure of a posthumanist ethics. When he states (in the preliminary remarks to *The Neutral*) that he wants to read each figure so as to bring out its nuances, he adds that what he really wants is to *live* according to nuance. "Make no mistake," he warns, "this is not a call for intellectual sophistication" ("ceci n'est pas la requête d'une sophistication intellectuelle").[35] Barthes associates nuance with minor flaws or particularities, inassimilable details—"ce qui est raté"—as well as with the diffuse, lingering light one might see in a cloud.[36] This meteorological trope suggests that nuance is not the quality of an elite or inaccessible object. Rather, nuance emerges in Barthes's late work as a field of complexity or "continuous variation" that is also entirely commonplace, available (or equally unavailable) to all. Hence, in *The Neutral*, Barthes dreams of creating "nuance exercises" for children. These exercises would orient children away from dualistic, wide-ranging classifications and toward small differences and graduated distinctions. Instead of the traditional focus on definitions, synonyms, and antonyms, students might study an inventory of "micro-networks of words that are very similar but a tiny bit different," which, without denying difference, would illustrate the "price of the 'bit'" ("le prix du 'peu'").[37] We might understand Proust's famously complex syntax as pedagogical in precisely this way. Proust invites us to slow down and turn our attention away from hierarchical antinomies and toward nuance, with its microscopic atmospheric shifts and differential intensities.

In the *Recherche*, the scene in which the narrator meets the ambassador, Norpois, registers the difference between a socially profitable relation to nuance (as in Baudrillard's "nuanced" bourgeois interior) and a flagrantly useless, even childish attachment to it (such as Barthes imagines teaching with his "nuance exercises"). The novel's most explicit investor in cultural capital, Norpois is a virtuosic and detached classifier of artworks. Hoping to impress his sophisticated dinner guest and colleague, the narrator's father presents the diplomat with a piece of his son's writing—a "prose poem" that could well be an excerpt from the first volume of the *Recherche*, as it details the narrator's exaltation upon coming home from a walk in Combray. Rather than initiating the boy into the realm of social distinction, however, Norpois dismisses the narrator's hyper-nuanced style. For Norpois, the ideal writer is someone whose productivity leads him directly up the road to social recognition; the successful artist is "not the sort of man to stop along the way."[38] The narrator's heightened attention to sonorous detail is thus entirely pointless from the diplomat's point of view: "all those subtleties of a deliquescent mandarin seem to me to be quite futile."[39]

The distinguished ambassador is also unimpressed with the narrator's capacity as an aesthetic critic. Thanks to Norpois's recommendation, the narrator has finally been permitted to attend a performance by the celebrated actress, Berma. To his dismay, he finds himself utterly unable to judge what he sees. If Rachel, the former prostitute-turned-great-actress in the *Recherche*, represents an aesthetics of *quelconque* undecidability—she is simultaneously singular and nothing special—Berma's performance exemplifies the understated economy of nuance. What Proust shows us in this theater scene is that nuance orients us toward the cloudy, intermediary spaces at the limits of established critical schemas and hierarchies of taste.

The first time the narrator sees Berma perform, his critical faculties are stumped. Because he has not yet developed the capacity to subsume the nuances of the performance into a single formulation, he experiences a crisis of distinction, in both sense of the word. He is unable to read the performance in a way that will yield cultural capital. He struggles to distinguish foreground from background, star from secondary actors: although Berma is not supposed to appear until later in the play, "an actress entered from the back who had the face and voice which, I had been told, were those of Berma. The cast must therefore have been changed [. . .]. But a second actress now responded to the first [. . .]. [T]he second resembled her even more closely." A minute later, it seems to him that compared to Berma, both of these actresses' performances are comprehensible, marked by "noble gestures" that he can clearly distinguish and appreciate.[40] When Berma finally appears on stage, she speaks her lines in such a subtle, seemingly "monotonous" manner that the narrator is unable to differentiate her from the text of the play. Because she does not structure her monologues according to expected oppositions, but rather "mingle[s] together contrasts" that most actresses would emphasize, her delivery seems flat.[41] This understated delivery is perceived as an undifferentiated flood of words, and the actress seems to disappear into the language she recites: "I could not even, as I could with her companions, distinguish in her diction and in her playing intelligent modulations or beautiful gestures."[42] The problem is not simply that the actress's subtle delivery makes her indistinguishable from her role. Berma's performance is unjudgeable because the narrator cannot find the distance necessary to judge her. As he magnifies and unmagnifies the spectacle, picking up and putting down his glasses, he is disoriented by alternate, coexisting versions of the actress. These incompatible images overlap, neither more real than the other: "which of the two Bermas was the real one?"[43] Berma simultaneously vanishes into her role and multiplies on stage.

This disoriented perception—which does not subsume "close" into "distant" vision, detail into generality—exemplifies the mode of critical impasse that is in question throughout this chapter. When his father invites him to distinguish himself in front of Norpois later that evening by uttering the expected praise, the narrator misses the opportunity to confirm his (and his parents') good taste. Unable to derive any social profit from his experience at the theater, he can only stammer, lacking the words to describe the peculiarity of his disappointment: "I made no attempt to substitute ready-made phrases for the words that failed me but stood there stammering" ("je ne cherchais pas à remplacer les mots qui me manquaient par des expressions toutes faites, je balbutiai").[44] The narrator's embarrassing failure in front of

Norpois demonstrates that paying heightened attention to the formal qualities of the aesthetic object does not necessarily prove one's distinction. The
sense of distinction, after all, requires an acute capacity for discrimination.
As Bourdieu puts it, the operation of distinguished taste "demands that certain things be brought together and others kept apart, [and thus] excludes
all misalliances and all unnatural unions."[45] The narrator's extreme attention to the classification-thwarting intensities of nuance is therefore danger-
ously "over the top." Like the color aphasics who privilege minor resemblances
over generalizing comparisons and accretion over division—adding light
pink and green ribbons to a pile of blues—the social player who becomes too
interested in nuance (preferring to gaze at or stroke the cards in his hand
rather than play them) may find himself excluded from the game altogether.
Indeed, by the end of the evening, the narrator breaks the rules of the social
game to such an extent that he is definitely expelled from the diplomat's
esteem. Norpois will allude with disdain to this moment as one when it
seemed that the effusive adolescent would break down and kiss his hands.[46]

The remainder of this chapter is divided into two parts. The first section
examines the disorienting effect of Proust's descriptive practices, which pull
the reader up to the cloudy zone where delineated space gives way to what
Deleuze and Guattari call haptic space—an amorphous, infinitely variable aggregate of microscales, rather than a formal composition. In the second section, I turn to the relation between nuance and feeling. I argue that nuance
opens up an alternative economy of interest in Proust, organized around the
non-subject-centered drift of affect. Objects that appear particularly nuanced—
such as the vibrant hawthorn flowers, or the nebulous "petite bande"—are able
to spread their diffuse light through the novel, sharing out their qualities with
their surroundings, precisely *because* they resist classification. The peculiar
economy of Proustian nuance is best understood as an impersonal (meteorological) form of sublimation—an elemental, outward-spreading "dégradation," rather than a purifying substitution.

Too Close

Proust's earliest critics were bewildered by the extreme closeness of attention
that the *Recherche* requires of its readers. Bernard Grasset, who published
Swann's Way in 1913 at Proust's expense, flatly characterized the volume as
"unreadable" ("illisible").[47] Jacques Normand, who advised Fasquelle not to
publish *Swann's Way* in 1912, found his critical faculties stumped by the novel's
"unimaginable disproportion."[48] Normand suggests that the only possible way
to read Proust is to stick as close as possible to the text, following the author
step by step, "feeling one's way along" ("à tâtons").[49] Similarly, Henri Ghéon
(who reviewed *Swann's Way* in 1914) disparages the peculiar closeness of

Proust's vision, complaining that everything in the volume contains an inexhaustible "treasure of nuances."[50] Proust seems to suffer, in Ghéon's account,
from a sort of perceptual disorder. Instead of clearing vistas in the forest, he is
compelled to detail each individual leaf:

> The time that another would have spent clearing the forest, managing its
> spaces and opening up vistas, he spends counting diverse varieties of trees
> [. . .]. And he will describe each leaf as different from the others, vein by
> vein, both the front and the back.

> Le temps qu'un autre eût employé à faire du jour dans cette forêt, à y mé-
> nager des espaces, à y ouvrir des perspectives, il le donne à compter les
> arbres, les diverses sortes d'essences [. . .]. Et il décrira chaque feuille,
> comme différente des autres, nervure par nervure, et l'endroit, et l'envers.[51]

Rather than subordinating particular details to general, wide-ranging structures, Proust luxuriates in the textural minutia of what lies closest at hand.

We might conceptualize the theoretical impasse the narrator hits up against
at the theater—and which these early reviewers encounter in their readings of
Proust—as the disorienting effect of an extremely close reading. Proust's descriptions sometimes pull the reader right up to the edge of the perceptible—
the place where patterns become fuzzy and the border between inside and
outside, object and interpretation, becomes indistinct. If, historically, an intensified attention to detail has a disciplinary function—essential to the individu-
alization and classification of workers, patients, soldiers, students[52]—Proust's
intensification of detail functions to de-hierarchize, de-classify, de-individual-
ize. Inviting us to read so "closely" that we lose track of divisions and classifications, Proust diffuses and redirects the potentially paranoid, clue-seeking
energies of close reading. As art historian James Elkins points out, an extremely close reading magnifies the textural threshold where structure dissolves into perceptual substance, leading us up to the very limit of meaning,
where there are "no further signs to be read."[53] Because there is no limit to a
close reading, Elkins notes, it is inevitably "foggy," drawing the reader into the
uncertain sphere where lexeme blurs into morpheme, character into mark, and
the semiotic into the non-semiotic.[54] Proust is fascinated by what Elkins calls
the "point of unsurpassable closeness"—the zone where unaided vision hits its
limit, and clear lines dissolve into amorphous ones. Instead of assembling details into overarching laws, the Proustian aesthetics of nuance tempts us into a
reading so close that the reader, like a color aphasic amidst myriad multicolored ribbons, loses all sight of predetermined classifications. In two passages in
particular—the ekphrastic representations of the Hubert Robert fountain and
of a plate of asparagus—we are invited to linger at description's breaking point.

In eighteenth- and nineteenth-century realist novels, descriptions of
bourgeois interiors organize details so as to individuate and refine the

characters at their center: as Susan Stewart has suggested, the description of things in such texts serves as a backdrop to the description of the hero or heroine's development.[55] In Proust, description becomes so rarified, so hyper-attuned to nuance, that it swells out of bounds, flooding the line between background and foreground and even occasionally spilling onto the observer. In such hyper-refined description, the subject's centrality is eclipsed as the stable space holding the bourgeois hero at its center gives way to a more variable, blurred spatial assemblage. Helpful here is Deleuze and Guattari's distinction between two spatial modes: the metric, or striated; and the haptic, or smooth.[56] Suggestive of the strange insubstantiality of the cloud, haptic space is allied with close-range vision, while metric space relates to a more distant, optical spatial organization—it presumes an "immobile outside observer."[57] Deleuze and Guattari pile up descriptions of these two kinds of space, offering one analogy after another: the haptic is amorphous, the metric formal; the haptic involves nomadic movement and open spaces, the metric involves the sedentary, the interior space; the haptic implies an "aggregate" or "entanglement" ("enchevêtrement") of intricate microscales, perceptible in the "anti-fabric," felt, while the metric implies a delimited or closed woven fabric with top and bottom, vertical and horizontal elements; or again, the haptic is like patchwork, with its "infinite, successive additions of fabric," while the metric is like embroidery, "with its central theme or motif."[58] Haptic space is "irregular and undetermined," oriented toward "continuous variation," while metric space is "defined by a standard"; it "produces an order and succession of distinct forms."[59] In haptic space, points are subordinated to the intervals, lines, or trajectories between them; in metric space, lines are subordinated to points, or stops.[60] What is really important to note here is that the haptic and the metric, the close and the distant, are not really opposites: each is continuously being transversed by or reversed into the other.

We observe Proust's transition from metric to haptic space especially in extremely close descriptions. The nearer we get to the object, the more subtly and minutely its coordinates shift, until its properties appear to come unglued, both from one another and from the object itself. Optical classification gives way to a "zone of indiscernibility" that invites touch, rather than delineation.[61] Instead of a whole divisible into equal parts, the object appears as an amorphous, acentered assemblage or accretion of nuances. As we make our way through Proust's exorbitantly nuanced descriptions, we sometimes become aware of sliding out of ocular space into a nebulous realm so variable and replete with detail that it can no longer be easily seen or measured. The description of the Hubert Robert fountain in *Sodom and Gomorrah* is precisely such an instance of cloudification, or transfer from the optical to the haptic. The fountain appears classically composed and contained from a distance, but from close up, its impenetrable density and linearity gives way to an unpredictable proliferation of orientations, speeds, and trajectories:

> It could be seen from a distance, slender, motionless, rigid, set apart in a clearing surrounded by fine trees, some of which were as old as itself, only the lighter fall of its pale and quivering plume stirring in the breeze. The eighteenth century had refined the elegance of its lines [. . .]. But from a closer view one realized that [. . .] it was a constantly changing stream of water that, springing upwards and seeking to obey the architect's original orders, performed them to the letter only by seeming to infringe them, its thousand separate bursts succeeding only from afar in giving the impression of a single thrust [. . .]. From close to, exhausted drops could be seen falling back from the column of water, passing their sisters on the way up, and at times, torn and scattered, caught in an eddy of the night air, disturbed by this unremitting surge, floating awhile before being drowned in the basin. They teased with their hesitations, with their journey in the opposite direction, and blurred with their soft vapour the vertical tension of the shaft that bore aloft an oblong cloud composed of countless tiny drops but seemingly painted in an unchanging golden brown which rose, unbreakable, fixed, slender and swift, to mingle with the clouds in the sky.[62]

> Dans une clairière réservée entourée de beaux arbres dont plusieurs étaient aussi anciens que lui, planté à l'écart, on le voyait de loin, svelte, immobile, durci, ne laissant agiter par la brise que la retombée plus légère de son panache pâle et frémissant. Le XVIIIe siècle avait épuré l'élégance de ses lignes [. . .]. Mais de près on se rendait compte que [. . .] c'était des eaux toujours nouvelles qui, s'élançant et voulant obéir aux ordres anciens de l'architecte, ne les accomplissaient exactement qu'en paraissant les violer, leurs mille bonds épars pouvant seuls donner à distance l'impression d'un unique élan [. . .]. De près, des gouttes sans force retombaient de la colonne d'eau en croisant au passage leurs soeurs montantes, et, parfois déchirées, saisies dans un remous de l'air troublé par ce jaillissement sans trêve, flottaient avant d'être chavirées dans le bassin. Elles contrariaient de leurs hésitations, de leur trajet en sens inverse, et estompaient de leur molle vapeur la rectitude et la tension de cette tige, portant au-dessus de soi un nuage oblong fait de mille gouttelettes, mais en apparence peint en brun doré et immuable, qui montait, infrangible, immobile, élancé et rapide, s'ajouter aux nuages du ciel. [63]

What this meta-descriptive passage demonstrates is that the closer and more nuanced a reading gets, the more the seemingly refined object blurs and leaks: the fountain's continuity gives way to multiplicity, its immobility to movement, its rectitude and control to hesitation and contingency, and its smooth lines to "exhausted drops" and blurry "soft vapor." The description begins at

a distance from its object ("de loin") and then pulls us closer and closer in—
first "from a bit closer" ("d'un peu près") then "from close to" ("de près"). Just
when it seems as if we could not get any closer, the object splashes out of its
frame, saturating the threshold dividing foreground from background and
spectacle from spectators. The seemingly disciplined, classical cloud is about
to spray out and drench an unlucky passer-by: "a strong gust of warm air
deflected the jet of water and inundated the fair lady so completely that [. . .]
she was as thoroughly soaked as if she had been plunged into a bath" ("un fort
coup de chaude brise tordit le jet d'eau et inonda si complètement la belle
dame que [. . .] elle fut aussi trempée que si on l'avait plongée dans un bain").[64]
This odd final detail—described as "one of these little accidents"—indexes the
uncontainability of nuance. Proust pushes detail to such extremes that rather
than contextualizing the individual, it nearly submerges her.

What is most fascinating about this passage is the way it demonstrates the
disorienting effect of closeness. As the initially distant, stable point of observation is drawn closer and closer in, the contoured, centered, systematic
object metamorphoses into a non-totalizable assemblage. Similarly, in a
famous ekphrastic passage from "Combray," description becomes so minute
and rarified that the object seems to fall apart, unable to contain its own nuances. Here, the narrator has stopped to gaze at some asparagus on the table:

> What most enraptured me were the asparagus, tinged with ultramarine
> and pink which shaded off from their heads, finely stippled in mauve and
> azure, through a series of imperceptible gradations to their white feet—still
> stained a little by the soil of their garden-bed—with an iridescence that was
> not of the earth. I felt that these celestial nuances indicated the presence of
> exquisite creatures who had been pleased to assume vegetable form and
> who, through the disguise of their firm, comestible flesh, allowed me to
> discern in these incipient colors of dawn, these hinted rainbows, these blue
> evening shades, that precious quality which I should recognize again when,
> all night long after a dinner at which I had partaken of them, they played
> (lyrical and coarse in their jesting like a fairy play by Shakespeare) at trans-
> forming my chamber pot into a vase of aromatic perfume.[65]

> mon ravissement était devant les asperges, trempées d'outremer et de rose
> et dont l'épi, finement pignoché de mauve et d'azur, se dégrade insensible-
> ment jusqu'au pied—encore souillé pourtant du sol de leur plant—par des
> irisations qui ne sont pas de la terre. Il me semblait que ces nuances célestes
> trahissaient les délicieuses créatures qui s'étaient amusées à se métamor-
> phoser en légumes et qui, à travers le déguisement de leur chair comestible
> et ferme, laissaient apercevoir en ces couleurs naissantes d'aurore, en ces
> ébauches d'arc-en-ciel, en cette extinction de soirs bleus, cette essence
> précieuse que je reconnaissais encore quand, toute la nuit qui suivait un

dîner où j'en avais mangé, elles jouaient, dans leurs farces poétiques et
grossières comme une féerie de Shakespeare, à changer mon pot de chambre en un vase de parfum.[66]

Here again, metric space dissolves into an amorphous, haptic assemblage.
Like the fountain, which from a distance appears centered and "set apart" in
a clearing, the asparagus still-life is at first clearly framed on the table. As we
enter into the description, however, this frame falls away and the coordinates
of the object shift in relation to one another. Consider what happens to space
as our orientation shifts. We begin in front of ("devant") the object, and as we
are pulled in closer and closer in, our gaze is simultaneously redirected outward, as the colors of the vegetable zigzag from ground to sky and back again:
out (to "ultramarine"), down (to "rose" and "mauve"), up (to "azure"), down
(to "foot," "soil," and "earth"), up (to "dawn," "rainbow," and "blue evening
shades"), and finally, all the way down (to "chamber pot"). The sentence beginning with "these celestial nuances" bulges, piling clause on top of clause, as
though no quantity of adjectives could ever complete the portrait or exhaustively qualify the object. The last twist in the description—the metamorphosis
that transforms solid into liquid, food into waste, visual into olfactory
stimulus—pulls us in closer than we had bargained for, as the object of observation disappears from view only to splash out unexpectedly later on. Like the
description of the fountain, the asparagus still-life demonstrates that the
closer we get to the object, the more distinction clouds into indistinction, and
the more the object's properties detach, becoming free to merge with any
other object. This melting-down of the object such that its qualities loosen and
become transferable occurs even on the level of grammar: as Michel Riffaterre
points out, this passage implicitly twists the noun "asperges" until it morphs
into its verb form, "asperger"—to spray or splash.[67] Just as the Hubert Robert
fountain finally leaps out of its frame and onto a passerby, here the asparagus
still-life spills off of the table and into the narrator's chamber pot.

The asparagus are described as shading off imperceptibly—
"insensiblement"—from top to bottom, suggesting graduated differences in
tint so minute that they exceed visual discernment. The description of the
asparagus foregrounds the liminal qualities of the shimmering, nuanced
object by drawing our attention to the nebulous edges of distinct colors, the
zone where one tint first becomes perceptible or shades off subtly into another. Hence the vegetable's incipient colors ("couleurs naissantes") suggest
"hints" or "drafts" ("ébauches") of rainbows—the very first glint of color hovering free of definitive form.

Perceiving such hyper-rarified nuance, Proust suggests, is not the privilege
of a trained or sophisticated eye. As if acknowledging its own over-the-top,
paradoxically unsophisticated refinement, the passage describes the asparagus
tip as "finely stippled" ("finement pignoché"). In a familiar sense, "pignocher"

means to pick at one's food or nibble without appetite. As a painterly term, "pignocher" suggests an excessive finish or exaggerated workmanship; an attention to detail so extreme that distinctions become indistinguishable: "to paint meticulously, often returning with small brush strokes to the parts that are already done, finishing them to excess."[68] Proust is playing here on the possibilities inherent in the apparently "monotone," orienting us toward nuance as Barthes imagines it—not an index of sophisticated taste, but an almost imperceptible initial glimmer: "the idea [. . .] of the onset, of the effort toward difference" ("la notion [. . .] de début, d'effort de différence").[69]

This mobile still-life echoes the novel's famous *petite madeleine* episode, but in such a way as to subtly underscore the difference between an open-ended, object-oriented metamorphosis and a subject-centered one. In the initial scene of involuntary memory, the narrator declares that the sensations provoked by certain "inferior" objects are valuable insofar as they reveal to the subject his own "precious essence" ("essence précieuse"). The phrase "precious essence" reappears in the asparagus still-life, but here, by contrast, Proust insists on the materiality of this "essence," which manifests not as the fundamental core of selfhood, but as a transient substance that alternately takes the form of a tender stalk, a Shakespearean fairy-play, and a pot of perfumed urine. This is not the essence *of* the subject, but an essence that simply passes through the subject, metabolizing him just as he metabolizes it. In this occasion of close-up, everyday transfiguration, the ordinary world shines with nuance, appearing inexhaustibly variable in its multiplication of different modalities of intimacy and enjoyment.

Dégradation

In the *Recherche*, nuance is allied with heightened attentiveness to detail; it is what becomes perceptible at the closest range of a close reading, where metric order begins to dissolve. Closeness is not the only condition for perceiving nuance in Proust, however. Nuance also manifests as a nebulous quality that hovers around objects seen from afar. Rather than emerging as the effect of a too-close reading, this second sort of nuance appears as a cloudy patch blurring the contours of objects that have not yet been subjected to epistemological scrutiny. This cloudiness is not strictly visual: it is also represented as a faint, non-cognitive, sensory-affective buzz—an intermittent "hum" or "murmur" at the threshold of visual, olfactory, and acoustic perceptual pathways.

One of the remarkable features of Proust's novel is that it occasionally permits us a glimpse of a landscape that has not yet been colonized by desire's imperious possessiveness. This is not to say that at such moments we see the "thing in itself," but simply that certain scenes invite us to imagine an inexhaustibly *interested*—but not instrumentalizing—aesthetic engagement with the world. Interest, or in psychologist Silvan Tomkins's terminology, "interest-excitement," is the "general, impersonal affect" that serves as the basis for both human and animal attachments. In the most basic sense, interest is what commits us to the world, activating and amplifying our capacity to care for things.[70] As Tomkins points out, interest sustains not only perception but also the state of wakefulness.[71] It is an affect particularly allied with curiosity—with the development of perceptual skills necessary to explore one's environment, learn, and make memories.[72] Interest enables a multiplicity of ways of becoming acquainted with an object. It instigates not only the will to possess, but a flexible, non-dualistic engagement with phenomena that Tomkins describes as a *"changing* sampling of the object" (original emphasis).[73] This conception of interest is central to the minor aesthetic economy of nuance in the *Recherche*. A sophisticated, "strong" aesthetic disposition is dependent upon the capacity to symptomatize sensory experience and translate it into wide-ranging truths. This strong theoretical current sustains both the teleological rise-to-art plot and the regressive, unsatisfied jealousy plot for which Proust is so known. The impersonal, open-ended buzz of interest, on the other hand, enables a more modest theoretical trajectory—a flexible movement between sensory and conceptual horizons that makes nuance perceptible.[74]

When the narrator of "Combray" comes upon a flowering hawthorn hedge at Tansonville, the entire landscape seems to resonate with the sound and smell of awakening curiosity. We might imagine this as the first hint of impersonal interest—a perceptual-affective flutter without definitive origin, which never develops into a central theme. The hawthorns offer the perceiver not an object to penetrate, consume, or expose, but a multisensory rhythmic texture. "Buzzing" or "humming" with odor, these flowers engage the senses at the point of their conjunction. The first time the narrator perceives them, their "intermittent odor" strikes him as "the murmuring of their intense life" ("le murmure de leur vie intense").[75] This olfactory-auditory hum reemerges in the hawthorn hedge scene at Tansonville:

> I found the whole path throbbing with the fragrance of hawthorn-blossoms [. . .]. But it was in vain that I lingered beside the hawthorns—breathing in their invisible and unchanging odour, trying to fix it in my mind (which did not know what to do with it), losing it, recapturing it, absorbing myself in the rhythm which disposed the flowers here and there with a youthful light-heartedness and at intervals as unexpected as certain intervals in music—they went on offering me the same charm in inexhaustible profusion, but without letting me delve any more deeply, like those melodies which one can play a hundred times in succession without coming any nearer to their secret.[76]

Je [. . .] trouvai [le petit chemin] tout bourdonnant de l'odeur des aubépines [. . .]. Mais j'avais beau rester devant les aubépines à respirer, à porter devant ma pensée qui ne savait ce qu'elle devait en faire, à perdre, à retrouver leur invisible et fixe odeur, à m'unir au rythme qui jetait leurs fleurs, ici et là, avec une allégresse juvénile et à des intervalles musicaux, elles m'offraient indéfiniment le même charme avec une profusion inépuisable, mais sans me laisser approfondir davantage, comme ces mélodies qu'on rejoue cent fois sans descendre plus avant dans leur secret.[77]

Impenetrable and unknowable, the hawthorns offer an inexhaustible "rhythm" incomprehensible to thought, which one can only join—hence the narrator "mimes" it inside himself, "unites" himself with it. Like the asparagus still-life, the hawthorn passage repeats the *petite madeleine* scene—but again, with a crucial difference. In that founding scene of involuntary memory, the entire drama plays out within the closed sphere of the narrator's consciousness. He repeats the Cartesian gesture of blocking out as much of the world as he can: "I shut out every obstacle, every extraneous idea, I stop my ears and screen my attention from the sounds from the next room" ("[J]'écarte tout obstacle, toute idée étrangère, j'abrite mes oreilles et mon attention contre les bruits de la chambre voisine").[78] When the narrator does momentarily turn away from the olfactory stimulus, it is only in order to renew his mental powers: "feeling that my mind is tiring itself without succeeding, I compel it for a change to accept the distraction which I have just denied it, [. . .] to rest and refresh itself before making a final effort" ("sentant mon esprit qui se fatigue sans réussir, je le force au contraire à prendre cette distraction que je lui refusais, [. . .], à se refaire avant une tentative suprême").[79] Ultimately, his efforts are rewarded, and the memory rises up from "great depths" to be exposed on the "surface" of his consciousness. This experience of translating ungraspable formlessness into appropriable form is described as a "difficult task," an "important enterprise."[80] The scene in which the narrator is enraptured by the hawthorn hedge does not work in quite the same way. Instead of narrating the forceful interpretation of nebulous sensation, the hawthorn passage lingers on the mysteriously buzzing, humming threshold between the perceiving subject and the inassimilable object. Here, too, the narrator turns away from the object in order to return to it with fresh force: "je me détournais d'elles [les fleurs] un moment pour les aborder ensuite avec des forces plus fraîches."[81] Instead of turning *inward*, however, in this scene, the narrator turns his attention *outward*—up the embankment, where intermittent poppies and cornflowers lead into cloud-patched fields. In the instant of this perception, it is as if intentionality and cognition were suspended, eclipsed by the amplification of the senses. The perception, intense as it is, does not lead to epistemological riches. Even when the narrator returns to the object at hand, the feeling that the hawthorns provoke remains "obscure and vague." Although he makes a "screen" with his hands so that his gaze will not wander from the flowers, the narrator's feeling of pleasure never quite adheres to the hawthorns themselves, which do not help him to satisfy his epistemological craving:

> [I]n vain did I make a screen with my hands, the better to concentrate on the flowers, the feeling they aroused in me remained obscure and vague, struggling and failing to free itself, to float across and become one with them. They themselves offered me no enlightenment.[82]

> [J]'avais beau me faire un écran de mes mains pour n'avoir qu'elles sous les yeux, le sentiment qu'elles éveillaient en moi restait obscur et vague, cherchant en vain à se dégager, à venir adhérer à leurs fleurs. Elles ne m'aidaient pas à l'éclaircir.[83]

The hawthorns inspire the repeated expression of failure, "j'avais beau" ("in vain"). Yet the emphasis is as much on the enigmatic "beau" as on the discouragement implicit in the phrase. "Avoir beau" is to try and not succeed—but here, it suggests a non-success that opens onto other possibilities. Hence the narrator, unable to get to the bottom of the sensation or attach it definitively to the object before him, abandons the logic of depth or verticality in favor of the horizontal, or the "beside." Precisely because the hawthorns remain ungraspable, impenetrable, the perceiver becomes aware of another, even more festive variant of the flower, which in turn leads him to see Gilberte, Odette, and Charlus—each of whom will open up multiple variants of desirous possibility—on the other side of the hedge.[84]

As paradoxical as it may sound, one reason that the narrator is unable to classify or assimilate this experience is that the perception is so effortless. While involuntary memory sparks a laborious translation of matter into form, perceiving the hawthorns involves no work at all. As Elaine Scarry suggests, flowers—like clouds—are unusually easy to imagine. This is because, as she puts it, such objects partake of the imagination's "special expertise in producing two-dimensional gauzy images," as opposed to solid or thick phenomena.[85] With their diaphanous petals, flowers share with curtains or clouds the filmy quality that makes them easily imitated in the mind. They pass effortlessly into the zone of the imagination, eliciting no special labor of appropriation or translation. Indeed, the first time they appear in the novel, the hawthorns are distinguished by a certain cloudiness: "Higher up their corollas opened here and there with a careless grace, holding so unconcernedly, like a final, vaporous adornment, the bunch of stamens [. . .] which entirely beclouded them" ("[P]lus haut s'ouvraient leurs corolles çà et là avec une grâce insouciante, retenant si négligemment, comme un dernier et vaporeux atour, le bouquet d'étamines [. . .] qui les embrumait tout entières").[86] The vaporousness of the flowers is inseparable from their negligent or careless grace—by which we might understand a quality of given-ness, or even gratuitousness. Although the narrator discovers the hawthorns in church, they point the way out of a redemptive or compensatory economy. He can mime them easily, but he cannot penetrate beneath their odor in order to *make* anything of it: "my thought [. . .] did not know what to do with it" ("ma pensée [. . .] ne savait ce qu'elle devait en faire").[87] Instead, the flowers lend their qualities to other beings, spreading their vaporous attributes outward—horizontally, rather than vertically—first to Mademoiselle Vinteuil (with her creamy, freckled cheeks) and later to Gilberte and the "little band" of girls at Balbec.[88]

This instance of "vague," non-laborious flower-perception calls to mind Kant's conception of aesthetic beauty. Kant, after all, cites as examples of objects suitable for "disinterested," or "free" beauty ("pulchritudo vaga") "flowers, free designs, lines aimlessly intertwined in each other under the name of foliage."[89] The amorphous hum of interest that hovers around the nebulous, living hawthorns is not entirely equivalent to the aimless free play that grounds the Kantian perception of beauty, however, as that mode of calm contemplation is unconcerned with the actual existence of the object.[90] Nor is this sub-theoretical hum explicable in terms of the slippery circuits of psychoanalytic libido—always on the move to compensate for an original loss, its mobility indexing the insufficiency of all objects. Rather, the scene in which the narrator stands rapt in front of the hawthorn hedge suggests a mode of gentle attachment to the object's unknowable, inappropriable vitality—and to the inexhaustible murmur of a shared "intense life."

In Proustian involuntary memory, an everyday object seems to call out to the perceiver to be rescued or redeemed. As the narrator puts it, such "inferior" objects are interesting only insofar as their materiality—or the sensation it provokes—conceals the subject's own forgotten past.[91] The hawthorns do not lend themselves to this logic. They never shed their materiality and reveal the perceiver's essence to him. Instead, we might read their recurrent buzz as the pulse of an alternative, non-appropriative mode of aesthetic interest in the novel—one not rooted in the strict opposition between form and materiality, subject and object. A phenomenon that hovers just beneath definitive shape, belonging neither to the beholding subject nor to the object beheld, this murmur suggests the *near*-indifferentiation of nuance, or its sonic version, timbre. In a reading of Dickinson's "I heard a fly buzz—when I died," Paul Fry interprets the poem's "buzz" as the hum of existence, perceptible only after all signs and personal predicates have been willed away: the buzz marks a space in which clear distinctions blur and opposing poles become exchangeable. This slight vibration suggests not a complete collapse of difference, but its near disappearance, such that self and other, sound and silence, life and death, become "*almost* indistinguishable."[92] In Proust, the multisensory vibration that the narrator perceives (but cannot understand) is an unplaceable atmospheric effect: the first hum of impersonal interest, the first reverberation of desire's engine—if it were possible to imagine a type of desire that belongs as much to the landscape itself as to the perceiving human subject. Barthes has a word for this vibratory sensation of aliveness: coenesthesis (cénesthésie), the "shimmering state [état moiré] of the active and affected body."[93] The "bourdonnement" that the narrator perceives in the hawthorn passage is a sonic-olfactory shimmer, or "moire"—an atmospheric effect that encompasses both perceiver and perceived, but cannot be tethered to either.

In order to understand the peculiarity of this non-conceptual, coenesthetic event, we might consider more closely the sonic phenomenon of timbre, which Lyotard describes as philosophically synonymous with nuance. Timbre, like nuance, is difficult to define; one way to understand it is as the quality, character, or condition of sound, rather than what sound does—or, in other words, what remains of sound after pitch or loudness have been subtracted.[94] Like affect, timbre is associated with great flexibility of perceptual and cognitive response.[95] What is most interesting to note about timbre is that it is often perceived pre-attentively, or pre-reflexively—especially by Western listeners, who are biased toward the precisely arranged units of pitch.[96] The most subjective, or "perceptualized" element of sound, timbre is generally imputed to its "source" in order to maintain the illusion of a "seamless perceived world," but it is not measurably *in* any external object.[97] Because, unlike pitch (measurable in frequencies units, or Hz), the perception of timbre does not correspond to any determinate property of the acoustic signal, it is the "most malleable parameter of sound."[98] It is precisely this untethered timbral malleability that Proust foregrounds in his description of the hawthorn hedge. What Proust invites us to imagine in this passage is a multisensory timbral vibration that is not projected onto a particular source, but rather emerges at the threshold between perceiver and perceived. Creating new pathways between olfactory, acoustic, and visual perception, this amorphous hum enables numerous attachments, dismantling and diffusing the powerful Proustian sublimation machine in order to let its vibrations spread in other directions.

The hawthorn hedge presents itself, to borrow Merleau-Ponty's phrase, as a landscape "pregnant with many other visions besides [one's] own."[99] Allied with a buzzing, scent-exuding, textural proliferation of images, the hawthorns suggest a horizontal spread rather than a vertical or penetrative movement that would transform unknowingness into knowledge. The narrator's first encounter with the hawthorns in Combray reverberates through the novel: the flowers will reappear here and there through the text, without ever revealing a finalizable essence. When they appear for the last time along the twisting paths by Balbec, the narrator is content to "hear" their call without responding. A manuscript variant develops this moment at length, foregrounding the ungraspable quality of the flowers and the peculiar doubleness of the perceptual experience:

> I went nearer, but my eyes did not know at what adjustment to set their optical apparatus in order to see the flowers at the same time along the hedge and in myself. Belonging at one and the same time to many springtimes, the petals stood out against a sort of magical deep background [. . .]. And around the flower which opened up before me in the hedge and which seemed to be animated by the clumsy quivering of my blurred and double vision, the flower that rose from my memory revolved without being able to fit itself exactly on to the elusive living blossoms in the trembling hesitancy of their petals.[100]

> Je m'approchai, mais mes yeux ne savaient à quel cran mettre leur appareil optique pour voir les fleurs à la fois le long de la haie et en moi-même. Appartenant à la fois à beaucoup de printemps passés, les pétales se détachaient sur une sorte de profondeur merveilleuse [. . .]. Et autour de la fleur ouverte devant moi dans la haie, et que semblait animer le maladroit frémissement de ma vision incertaine et double, la fleur qui s'élevait de ma mémoire tournoyait sans pouvoir s'appliquer exactement, dans la tremblante hésitation de leurs pétales, aux aubépines vivantes et insaisissables.[101]

Here, past and present experiences overlap in a play of sensation irreducible to any definitive interpretation or representation of phenomena: the flowers quiver and tremble simultaneously in the world and in the perceiver's memory. The narrator states that he cannot identify the optical gauge or notch ("cran") that would permit him to assimilate the image before him to the image already inside him. Precisely because the outside image cannot be perfectly matched to the "quivering" and "awkward" interior one—there is no productive epiphany of involuntary memory to be had here—the flowers remain "alive" and "ungraspable." The passage itself, which Proust imagined including in the novel but ultimately left aside, doubles the gratuitous existence of the flowers, whose "call" from the side of the path need not be heeded.

The vaporous hawthorns cast a glow through the novel, but not by being sublimated in the traditional sense (elevated, compensated for, redeemed). Because their formless profusion inspires a layering of sensory responses, the flowers cannot be simply translated into or replaced by another (more valuable) form. Instead, the hawthorns will appear numerous times in the narrative, at Combray as well as at Balbec, slightly modified each time, without ever revealing the secret of their origination. In this sense, the hawthorns have more in common with the *petite phrase* in Vinteuil's sonata than with the *petite madeleine:* the nebulous flower will reappear throughout the novel, not as a lost or repressed object might reemerge in more acceptable or valuable form, but as a melody might reemerge, slightly altered, in a different key, with new ornamentation or dynamic markings, in a set of musical variations.

In *A Lover's Discourse: Fragments*, Barthes describes an impersonal, cloudy form of desire that sounds much like the sub-theoretical modality of aesthetic interest I have been elaborating here. Under a figure titled "clouds" ("nuages"), Barthes gathers descriptions of a content-less, non-declarative (and yet not repressed) temper. This nebulous mood or disposition ("humeur") hovers at the edges of jealousy, where jealousy cannot be declared. Neither a sign nor a state, this cloudy humor is a "derived, tempered, and incomplete effect" that emerges where the explicit expression of appropriative desire is displaced.[102] While jealousy symptomatizes its objects, turning the entire world into a decipherable collection of clues, this non-jealous, almost imperceptible drift of interest is imagined in meteorological terms, as if the subject were a landscape and moods simply passed through her from time to time: "all the tenuous shadows of swift and uncertain source which pass across the relationship change its light and its modeling; suddenly it is another landscape."[103]

Cloudiness in Proust, as in Barthes, is allied with love—not jealous desire, which reduces the sensory complexity of the object (and denies the loved one his or her own rich perceptual experience)—but a relation that acknowledges the object's vitality without consuming or destroying it. If asked to identify the most Proustian emotions, most readers would probably put jealousy at the top of the list. Jealousy strips the world of its perceptual and interpretive complexity, reducing the beloved to an epistemological object—a set of clues to be deciphered. It amplifies all stimuli correlating to its dualistic interpretive rubric, ignoring alternative interpretive possibilities. In jealousy, every detail is interpreted as a sign of the lover's potential infidelity. Hence in *The Captive* the narrator sustains his jealous attachment to Albertine by working to provoke her confessions. He longs to possess her to her very depths—to uncover the secrets concealed behind her enigmatic silences.[104] And yet the passages in which the narrator first encounters the girl—before she has become "Albertine"—set an entirely different tone. In these scenes of drifting perception, the narrator is attuned to the nuances that hover around the not-yet-appropriated other.

Proust describes the narrator's first contact with the still-anonymous Albertine in elemental, impersonal terms. This girl appears at first as just one incarnation of a series of cloudy objects in the novel, beginning with the hawthorn flowers. At first indistinguishable from her entourage, "la petite bande" ("the little band"), the not-yet-known Albertine is desirable because she materializes as the luminous reflection of a previously desired creature, Gilberte—who in turn first appeared on the other side of that vaporous hawthorn hedge in Combray. When the narrator first hears Gilberte's name, it passes by him like a cloud (casting a "petite bande" as its reflection):

> The name Gilberte passed close by me, [. . .] forming, on its celestial passage through the midst of the children and their nursemaids, a little cloud delicately coloured, [. . .] casting, finally, on that ragged grass [. . .] a marvellous *little band* of light, the colour of heliotrope, impalpable as a reflection and superimposed like a carpet on which I could not help but drag my lingering, nostalgic and desecrating feet.[105]

> Ce nom de Gilberte passa près de moi, [. . .] formant, passager céleste au milieu des enfants et des bonnes, un petit nuage d'une couleur précieuse, [. . .] jetant enfin, sur cette herbe pelée [. . .] une *petite bande* merveilleuse et couleur d'héliotrope impalpable comme un reflet et superposée comme un tapis sur lequel je ne pus me lasser de promener mes pas attardés, nostalgiques et profanateurs.[106]

Here the "little cloud" of Gilberte's name already radiates its cloudy luminosity onto other, to-be-loved girls: the "little band" the narrator will meet in Balbec. When the narrator first witnesses the little band's promenade at Balbec, before he begins the work of "imbibation" that will transform Albertine into a sign of his own jealous desire, he is similarly struck by a purely phenomenal, insignificant glimmer. The *petite bande* appears vaporous at first, "a singular stain," "a harmonious wavering," "an amorphous mass." As expansive and ungraspable as the hawthorn hedge, perceptible as a "vague, white constellation" or "indistinct and milky nebula," the *petite bande* is pure metamorphicity without fixed form.[107] Taking on one shape, then another—that of birds, flowers, a luminous comet—the *bande* is as forgettable and indistinct, as depthless and changing as a cloud.

The "reflection" first cast by Gilberte's name vanishes only to reappear, some time later, in the narrator's Balbec hotel room: "the darkness was not complete, and [the curtains] spilled over the carpet a sort of scarlet shower of anemone-petals, amongst which I could not resist placing my bare feet for a moment" ("l'obscurité n'était pas complète et [les rideaux] laissaient se répandre sur le tapis comme un écarlate effeuillement d'anémones parmi lesquelles je ne pouvais m'empêcher de venir un instant poser mes pieds nus").[108] Here, again, rather than seeking to capture and "translate" the phenomenon, the perceiver simply touches it with his feet. This urge to caress, to make contact (not with a dexterous hand, but with the flat, tender surface of a bare foot) is entirely unlike the laborious, appropriative engagement with phenomena necessary to "decipher" signs and transform materiality into spirit.

Cloudiness is a quality that hovers around an object that can be easily, effortlessly perceived, but not subjected to epistemological labor. So once, when the narrator is walking on the beach with Elstir, the *petite bande* emerges like a stain, a mirage, a marginal cluster or assemblage. "A few spots" or "a few spores," the *bande* is at once unmistakable and unidentifiable.[109] The narrator's desire to be introduced shrinks and swells with "an elastic force," and at precisely the instant that the introduction is definitively missed, he imagines that his gaze meets the gaze of one of the unknown girls as two clouds might pass one another in the sky. As the *petite bande* begins walking away, the narrator feels his gaze met by an unknown and unknowing look: "For a moment her eyes met mine, like those traveling skies on stormy days which approach a slower cloud, touch it, overtake it, pass it. But they do not know each other, and soon drift far apart" ("Un instant ses regards croisèrent les miens, comme ces ciels voyageurs des jours d'orage qui approchent d'une nuée moins rapide, la côtoient, la touchent, la dépassent. Mais ils ne se connaissent pas et s'en vont loin l'un de l'autre").[110] In the instant of their reciprocally unknowing, passing glance, the beholder is no different than the beheld. Here looking is made tactile, and rather than remaining untouched by his own metaphor, the observer is cloudified as well. In the preliminary time of this suspended non-acquaintance, it is as if the nebulous quality of the *bande* had transferred itself onto the narrator.

The notion that the given, phenomenological world is insufficient and must be repaired or redeemed by intellectual or aesthetic labor (assimilation, translation, deciphering) is often presented as a law in the *Recherche*. And yet occasionally in Proust the world appears not salvageable, but perfectly sufficient. Consider the following passage from *The Fugitive*, in which sublimation is imagined neither as a melancholic substitution nor as a purification, but as an ever-widening composition of nuances, concentric zones, and subtle harmonies:

> Andrée, and these other women, all of them in relation to Albertine—like Albertine herself in relation to Balbec—were to be numbered among those substitute pleasures, replacing one another in a gradual declension, which enable us to dispense with the pleasure which we can no longer attain, a trip to Balbec or the love of Albertine, pleasures which (just as going to the Louvre to look at a Titian consoles us for not being able to go to Venice where it originally was) separated one from another by indistinguishable nuances, convert one's life into a series of concentric, contiguous, harmonic and graduated zones, encircling an initial desire which has set the tone.[111]

> Andrée, ces autres femmes, tout cela par rapport à Albertine—comme Albertine avait été elle-même par rapport à Balbec—étaient de ces substituts de plaisir se remplaçant l'un l'autre en dégradation successive, qui nous

permettent de nous passer de celui que nous ne pouvons plus atteindre,
voyage à Balbec ou amour d'Albertine, de ces plaisirs (comme celui d'aller
voir au Louvre un Titien qui y fut jadis, console de ne pouvoir aller à Venise)
qui, séparés les uns des autres par des nuances indiscernables, font de notre
vie comme une suite de zones concentriques, contiguës, harmoniques et
dégradées, autour d'un désir premier qui a donné le ton.[112]

This passage perfectly describes the lateral mode of transfiguration that has
been at stake throughout this chapter. The key term here is "dégradation,"
which Montcrieff intriguingly translates as "declension," but which we might
render as "gradation" or "diminution." "Dégradation" in this context is not
pejorative—it does not imply a debasement or loss of value. Rather, it is a
painterly term suggesting a diminution of color or light, a gradation of tint, a
"gradual toning down or shading off."[113] We might also think of "dégradation" in geological terms: the disintegration or wearing down of rocks, strata,
and so forth, by atmosphere or water. In this sense, "dégradation" is an apt
term for Proust's easy, meteorological mode of sublimation. Proust is inviting
us to imagine a style of letting go or passing on that is neither a fall from some
original state of grace nor a preservation of the object ("which we can no
longer attain") in hope of a later recuperation. Instead, the object is neither
quite lost nor precisely retained.

In Proust, formerly loved objects persist in cloudy form, in tints or shades
that subtly set the tone for future loves. "Sublimated" in the most elemental
sense, the object undergoes a metamorphosis, not unlike the shape-shifting
that takes place when a body of water sublimates into a cloud. Just as the inas-
similability of the hawthorn hedge's timbral murmur leads the perceiver to
look away, up the embankment and across the hedge, Balbec disperses across
an imaginary canvas, shading into or shedding its light on Albertine—and
Albertine sheds hers on Andrée, and Venice on Titian. This horizontal spread
of interest occurs not despite, but precisely *because* the object is unattainable.
This is a remarkable description of sublimation because it accepts loss as its
central principle, but without the drama of psychoanalytic "lack," or castration. Sublimation is instead imagined as a "dégradation," a sharing out or
shading off of the loved object that makes the rest of the world lovable as well.
The "original" object cannot be grasped, but in wearing away, disintegrating,
dissolving (de-grading), it sets the tone for all subsequent desires, spreading
not an atmosphere of tragic absence, but a ripple effect of nuances.

Although the *Recherche* is in certain ways a distinction-producing machine, it also orients readers toward the extreme limit on either end of the
spectrum of taste. It draws us toward a marginal aesthetics of the unqualifiable, or *quelconque*, organized around objects too ordinary or commonplace
to be critically savored—and alternatively, toward a minor economy of nuance,
featuring hyper-distinguished, excessively qualifiable objects. Presenting a

modulation of degree so subtle that it escapes discernment, extremely nuanced objects invite attunement to the very edges of form, the threshold of
materiality. Opening onto the textural and the timbral, the affective and the
meteorological, the impersonal perceptual mode allied with an aesthetics of
nuance is neither quite "disinterested" in the Kantian sense, nor "interested"
in the Bourdieusian.

Nuance is form in its least systematic, most close-up or material—and
hence formless—manifestation. As such, it dissolves high-low, pure-impure
dualisms, orienting us instead toward gentler and weaker modalities of aesthetic interest. In Proust, nuance emerges at the threshold between extreme
attention and its release, between labor and ease, between the closest reading
imaginable and a non-appropriative perceptual mode that grants the object
its own unknowable vitality. The celebrated *petite madeleine* passage is the
primal scene for a dominant theoretical current in the *Recherche*: one that
celebrates the perfect correspondence of ephemeral material sensation and
lasting truth. The various manifestations of the nebulous hawthorn flowers,
on the other hand, are faint signposts marking the path of an alternative aesthetics. This winding pathway never leads to sublime vistas, but it allows us to
linger over nuanced objects and moods—haptic assemblages, timbral resonances, and cloudy *dégradations* imperceptible to the end-driven traveler.

PART 2

Mid-Century Experiments

{ 4 }

Profanation in Ponge

One morning, while bumping along on a public bus, prose poet Francis Ponge is wracked by an "aesthetic sob." What is it that moves him so? Nothing much: just a "contraction of the generally unremarkable [*quelconque*] landscape." Through the bus window, the world appears both gray and incandescent, the sky simultaneously shadowed and lustrous. "A beautiful day is also a meteor," the poet declares in a vain attempt to register the strangely ordinary intensity he felt that morning.[1] Yet as he labors to qualify this likeness—testing one method and then another, awkwardly offering and retracting analogies—we can scarcely see the beautiful thing to which he keeps directing our gaze. In this text and throughout his oeuvre, Ponge explores conjunctions of the singular and the common, inventing a new literary language in order to convey the formal variation and variability of the modernist ordinary.

Ponge is not usually thought of in relation to Proust. By placing Ponge's broken analogies in proximity to Proust's pastiches, exclamations, and hyper-nuanced descriptions, this chapter uncovers subtle lines of affiliation between the novelist and the poet. Both writers foreground unrefined modalities of aesthetic pleasure. Like Proust, Ponge valorizes a non-redemptive aesthetic perception—one that get as close as possible to ordinary objects without seeking to purify or elevate them into art. Yet while Proust's lyrical prose brings out the nuances of language, Ponge prefers a rougher grain. Attuned to small, non-transcendent objects and affects, he abjures the beautiful and the sublime in favor of the awkward—the *maladroit* and *malhabile*. He is drawn to landscapes that are slightly botched or spoiled: the platitudinous meadow, the pine forest cluttered with dead wood, the Provençal sky "glutted" with azure. Even Ponge's flowers have a tough and ragged quality. They are not humming assemblages of vitality, as in Proust, but something far less delicate: "badly washed cups" worked on by maintenance men butterflies with "shrunken rag" bodies.[2] Ultimately, Ponge molds the distinction-spoiling potential of Proustian aesthetic beholding into an overtly egalitarian theory of poetic construction: in his view, writing poetry is not a privilege of the elect few, but a mode of laborious play that is open to all.

Art for Ponge is thus anything but sacred and untouchable. Rather, it is *profane*, as Giorgio Agamben (drawing on Walter Benjamin) has theorized that concept: usable, to-be-played-with, not to be pocketed or held apart. Profanation, according to Agamben, is a kind of sacrifice in reverse. It indicates the act of returning to common use that which had been designated as property of the gods. Transforming display into free play, neutralizing or deactivating the partition between the ordinary and the extraordinary, profanation is another way of describing the de-instrumentalizing force of the aesthetic, which I have allied throughout this book with various alternatives to a purifying sublimation.[3] To profane, as Agamben puts it, is to "open the possibility of a special kind of negligence" that ignores the separation between spheres or registers.[4] Ponge cultivates such playful negligence, such disregard for hierarchies and lines of demarcation. For Ponge, the pleasures that matter are not reserved for poets and artists. There is no inherently aesthetic object or experience, no special class of aesthetic perceivers. As Vincent Kaufmann points out, by effacing the contractual expectations of conventional genres and allowing the rhetoric of each text to be shaped by the object it describes, Ponge strives to write in a manner that "puts everyone in the same place."[5]

This chapter investigates Pongean profanation from two points of view. The first section explores the poetics of awkwardness or exposed labor in Ponge, especially in his 1941 poem, *La Mounine, or Note Struck in After-thought on a Provence Sky* (*La Mounine ou note après coup sur un ciel de Provence*). Valorizing the sketch, rather than the finished masterpiece, and likening his own writing practice to the burrowing work of a small rodent, Ponge cultivates modesty and vulnerability as aesthetic strategies. In the second section, I examine the experiment with aesthetic value that Ponge undertakes in the critically ignored 1949 illustrated volume, *The Glass of Water* (*Le Verre d'eau*). In this text, Ponge challenges his reader to imagine a worth not dependent upon the logic of scarcity. He devises an alternative notion of "perfection": not completion or polish, but the quality of what is "potable" or simply good enough, sufficient as such, effecting little change and requiring nothing in return.

Awkward

Humility and modesty are keywords for Ponge, who consistently presents his own aesthetic labor in the humblest of terms. His is an art of refused inspiration. To call Ponge a "poet" is in fact something of a misnomer, as he resists this designation, and explicitly avoids stylistic virtuosity, or what he terms poetic "arrangement."[6] Instead, his writing centers on the object's utter particularity—"its raw quality, its *difference*."[7] How such enigmatically profane "difference" is felt and made perceptible but not sacralized and set apart: this is the difficulty at the heart of Ponge's work. While Proust and Sarraute investigate the everyday point of view of the aesthetic perceiver, Ponge draws our attention to the practice of writing, which he presents as a laborious and unsophisticated enterprise. Instead of polishing and perfecting ordinary language into poetry, Ponge chips away at elite forms, making poetry itself ordinary. Hence he frequently declares that the object he is describing "shouldn't amount to much," or that the thing in question "doesn't inspire [him] in the least."[8] Eschewing stylistic virtuosity in favor of hesitancy and incompletion, Ponge advocates writing "beneath one's powers."[9]

In keeping with the modesty and humility of his style, Ponge has a penchant for slight, inconsequential objects. He loves what Jacques Derrida terms the "throwaway" thing, the "nothing much," the "cheap whatever" ("le n'importe quoi de peu-de-prix").[10] Ponge began mapping the contours of such odds and ends in the shadow of surrealism's provocations. His first book, *Le Parti pris des choses* (*The Nature of Things*, written between 1924 and 1939 and published in 1942) is a catalogue of unremarkable little creatures and objects, from snails and shrimp to pebbles, cigarettes, and broken shipping crates. In the 1940s, Ponge refigured his approach to the ordinary. He developed a new genre—the notebook poem—and began the practice that he would continue for the rest of his career. He started publishing entire volumes of drafts, sketches, notes, and variants, all devoted to the attempt to circumscribe a certain everyday object or occasion: a pine forest; a table; a fig; a bus ride in Southern France; the metamorphosis of a bar of soap from austere stone to enthusiastic profusion of bubbles.[11]

Sartre claims that for Ponge, poetry constitutes "a general enterprise of scrubbing language clean" ("une entreprise générale du décrassage du langage").[12] Alternatively, one could say that Ponge wants to keep language dirty and close to the ground—open to play and transformation—rather than elevating it to some separate sphere. As this section of the chapter will demonstrate, this is a poetry that never leaves the messy workroom. We see Ponge's preference for rawness and incompletion both in the objects that he privileges and in his poetic method, which highlights the infelicitous not-quiteness of all analogy. In the early thing-poems and the later notebook poetry, Ponge brings the rough edges of things into relief. In his poems, things make and unmake themselves. They join and disjoin, form and unform. They get discountenanced, oxidized, mortified, and dispersed. Ponge loves to explore touchable, bendable, destructible envelopes and tissues, from the muscular elasticity of the orange peel to the lumpy, flaky ash of the cigarette. We witness this formal curiosity and restlessness, for example, in the early poem titled "Rain" ("Pluie"), which explores the many material forms that rain can take: it falls like a curtain, like peas, like grains, like marbles, like hard candy, like a sheet, like a cord. These varied formal manifestations engage the environment differently, at different tempos ("allures"). Rain streams, drops, scuds, sluices, shatters, and springs again, producing a concert of ringing, gurgling, and gonging. The poem thus becomes a miniature storm of activity, a "complicated mechanism" that the poet-mechanic sets in motion for us.[13]

Although of the same generation as André Breton, Ponge's disdain for aesthetic heroism and his view of aesthetic creation as everyday labor set him apart from his avant-garde contemporaries. In contrast to surrealism, with its "objets trouvés" and spontaneous, seemingly magical automatic writing, Ponge resists all forms of glamour. He, too, fills his poetry with found objects, but his "ready-mades" are never done. He is no magician, Ponge insists, but a simple clockmaker, a repairman of language. Inviting us to watch him work, Ponge foregrounds the smallness and powerlessness of object, poem, and poet alike. This insistently ordinary, unsophisticated practice of aesthetic making is not to everyone's taste. Jean Paulhan, for example, disparaged Ponge's new method of unpolished composition in 1942, writing in a letter to the poet: "the more you advance, the more you are penetrated by what you don't know."[14] Samuel Beckett was similarly unimpressed by Ponge's willingness to expose his own weakness, noting dismissively in 1949, in reference to a preface by Ponge that he had just translated, that the poet comes off as "oddly vulnerable" ("drôlement vulnérable").[15]

Beckett goes on to disparage Ponge's style, with its "muffled verbs and parentheses."[16] Indeed, Ponge skirts eloquence at every turn, privileging instead a modernist aesthetics of awkwardness. Awkward derives from "awk," meaning upside down or backward, turned the wrong way around. An awkward object is ill adapted for use, clumsy in operation; an awkward person is bungling and ungainly, lacking in dexterity or skill. In French, to be "adroit" is to be able to easily attain a result, thanks to innate or learned dispositions. To be "maladroit" or "gauche," then, is to lack facility, to show how hard you are trying, and thus to spoil the impression of ease. Being *gauche*, Roland Barthes notes, is a matter of "press[ing] too hard," like a child with a pencil.[17] In his play with awkwardness, Ponge valorizes the seemingly deficient, setting aside fantasies of closed or finished form.

With its implication of vulnerability and exposure, awkwardness registers a failure of sophistication. At the same time, there is something resistant, or even defiant, about the awkward, which thwarts familiar means-ends rationality. As Mary Capello suggests, the awkward—like dashes in a Dickinson poem—is "what neither yields nor seeks to fit."[18] Hence Baudelaire imagines the poet in modernity as an ungainly albatross, almost comically "awkward" ("maladroit," "gauche") with its oar-like wings dragging at its sides. If the awkward implies laboriousness, it also suggests uselessness, impracticality: a clumsy version of aesthetic non-instrumentality, awkward is the tool held in the wrong hand, or turned upside down. Ponge helps us to see that there is something productively awkward about the very notion of the aesthetic, which frees objects from both exchange and from end-oriented use (it profanes them, in Agamben's terms). For what could be more unplaceable, more difficult to categorize or describe, less yielding to the grasping hand, than a thing without purpose?

Awkwardness is thus the tone of aesthetic autonomy in Ponge: the awkward names a thwarted relation to purposiveness. As such, it transforms work into aesthetic play. By presenting the suspension of instrumentality in terms of the *maladroit*, rather than as an index of aesthetic sophistication, the poet desacralizes the practice of writing. To write in order to expose the awkwardness of things is an act of profanation: an act that makes common the construction of poetry, placing it within the (fumbling) reach of anyone at all.

As an aesthetic paradigm, the awkward is less seductive than the commoditized, dominated mode of "cuteness" that Sianne Ngai has recently allied with Ponge's interest in tender, defenseless objects of domestic consumption, like oranges and potatoes.[19] According to Ngai, cuteness is perfectly aligned with the logic of commodification: the cutest object is the most hyperobjectivated, the most utterly reified. Hence the more a thing signifies its dominated status, the cuter it becomes. If it is difficult to resist the wide-eyed malleability of the adorable plush toy or baby doll, the awkward bears the traces of its construction in a way that invites us to become aesthetic makers, not consumers. Naming an "off" or askew relation to instrumentality, the awkward registers a stubbornly anachronistic residue of craft, out of place amidst the sleek products of late capitalism.[20]

Ponge is especially drawn to those things that resist consumption—the prickly blackberry with its slightly fecal associations, the abandoned hermit shell crab, or the broken container, useless once emptied of its precious cargo. His quintessentially awkward object is an abandoned shipping crate, "still brand new" ("tout neuf encore") but used up and cast aside. Muffling the pathos of abandonment, the poet playfully describes this busted crate as "somewhat aghast" ("légèrement ahuri") to be in such an "awkward situation" ("pose maladroite"):

The Crate

Midway between cage and cachot, or cell, the French language has cageot, a simple little open-slatted crate devoted to the transport of fruit that is sure to sicken at the slightest hint of suffocation.

Devised in such a way that after use it can easily be broken down, it never serves twice. Thus its life-span is shorter even than that of the perishables it encloses.

So, at the corners of every street leading to market, it gleams with the unassuming lustre of slivered pine. Still brand new and somewhat aghast at the awkward situation, dumped irretrievably on the public thoroughfare, this object is most appealing, on the whole—yet one whose fate does not warrant our overlong attention.[21]

Le Cageot

A mi-chemin de la cage au cachot la langue française a cageot, simple caissette à claire-voie vouée au transport de ces fruits qui de la moindre suffocation font à coup sûr une maladie.

Agencé de façon qu'au terme de son usage il puisse être brisé sans effort, il ne sert pas deux fois. Ainsi dure-t-il moins encore que les denrées fondantes ou nuageuses qu'il enferme.

A tous les coins de rues qui aboutissent aux halles, il luit alors de l'éclat sans vanité du bois blanc. Tout neuf encore, et légèrement ahuri d'être dans une pose maladroite à la voirie jeté sans retour, cet objet est en somme des plus sympathiques,—sur le sort duquel il convient toutefois de ne pas s'appesantir longuement.[22]

This text, sandwiched between descriptions of blackberries and candles in *The Nature of Things*, highlights the awkward before and after of value-production. Ponge asks us to sympathize here not just with the commodity, but also with the commodity's demise, its afterlife as trash. He depicts the crate's exit from the realm of the useful and entrance into the realm of rubbish, which Michael Thomson has theorized as an "in-between category": neither transient nor durable, rubbish occupies a "region of flexibility" between these crucial poles in the production of value.[23] Inviting us to see the way things hover in and out of their relation to preestablished ends, Ponge underscores the object's liminal position, describing the word itself ("cageot") as "midway between *cage* and *cachot*." The "appealing" and forgettable object also hovers between singularity and generality: although it is one particular instance, it is reduplicated innumerably, shining modestly "at the corners of every street leading to the market." While surrealism valorizes the hunt for the marvelous object hidden amidst flea market trash, Ponge demonstrates that there is nothing extraordinary about his ubiquitous, perishable container. Like the lowly, surplus stalk in Manet's *L'Asperge*, Ponge's crate is less "found" than forgotten: its recuperation only serves to highlight its leftover status. The crate is built to be broken without effort, and the text mimics this ease and light-handedness throughout. Ultimately, the poem ends with a gesture of abandonment, gently tossing "le cageot" to the curb. Unlike Baudelaire's tragically awkward poet-albatross, Ponge's crate is not meant to be redeemed: it is simply glimpsed at the moment of its transition from the transitive to the intransitive, or from the purposive to the purposeless.

Ponge does not let us forget that this crate—like all of his chosen objects—
is made of language, which for him is the ultimate source of missed connections and suspended ends. He often draws our attention to his own sense of
verbal awkwardness, insisting that he is "not eloquent."[24] Early in his life,
Ponge tended to become tongue-tied at the very moment that eloquence was
most called for. At nineteen, despite being a brilliant student, he failed the
oral entrance exam for a philosophy degree: "inability to express himself"
("incapacité à s'exprimer") was the examiner's note. He would not open his
mouth, "despite the jury's friendly insistence."[25] The following year he was
again held back by ineloquence in his entrance exam for the prestigious École
Normale Supérieure.[26]

It is no wonder, then, that inarticulacy became a central feature of his poetics. Ponge's prose turns on occasions of tongue-tiedness. He describes his
writing process as a zigzag between identifying the perfect phrase and plung-
ing back into blunder, or what he calls the "thick forest of awkward expressions" ("la forêt épaisse des expressions maladroites").[27] If the Proustian "zut"
belongs to a minor constellation of inarticulate aesthetic moments in the *Recherche*, in Ponge such babble takes center stage, becoming the very substance
of poetry. Returning repeatedly to expressions of missed adequation, Ponge
composes what he terms "description-definitions" that call attention to their
own hesitant construction. As he puts it in a lyrical prose fragment titled "The
Carnation" ("L'Oeillet") his labor can yield only modest results: "I won't rest
till I have drawn together a few words that will compel anyone reading or
hearing them to say: this has to do with something like a carnation" ("Je
n'aurai de cesse avant d'avoir assemblé quelques mots à la lecture ou l'audition
desquels l'on doive s'écrier nécessairement: c'est de quelque chose comme un
oeillet qu'il s'agit").[28] Resolutely unpolished, unfinished, and imprecise,
Ponge's style is calibrated to undermine any conclusive statement.

In a 1947 conference talk titled "Tentative orale" ("Verbal Attempt"), Ponge
lays claim to awkwardness as the structuring—and destructuring—force of
his poetics. He explains in this piece that the things he loves most are defined
by his incapacity to speak about them.[29] To be "this awkward" ("maladroit à
ce point"), Ponge notes, is to suffer from a sort of linguistic vertigo: as he puts
it, a gaping hole is perpetually opening beside him, and all he can do to keep
his balance is to focus his attention on the nearest material object. Here Ponge
gives us a glimpse of the ungainliness that conditions his relation to language
and determines the small, proximate objects of his poetry. As if flaunting the
disorientation that keeps him reaching for the closest thing, Ponge ends this
lecture by leaning down to kiss the table goodbye.

The argument I have been making is that for Ponge, awkwardness is both
the very condition of the speaking being and a specific mode of resistance
against the sacralization of art. As he fumbles his words, Ponge stages an
"effort against poetry."[30] "I believe my vision to be quite commonplace" ("Je

crois ma vision fort commune"), he insists.[31] Underscoring this "commonplace" quality, Ponge habitually exposes not only his drafts, but also the lexical research that poem-construction requires: his prose poems contain long
lists of definitions and etymologies. Tellingly, before settling on the title *La
Rage de l'expression*—which Lee Fahnestock translates as *Mute Objects of
Expression*—he had considered the titles "Endless Dictionary" and "The De-
lights of the Dictionary" for his second collection of work.[32] Ponge likes to
include even lexical dead-ends in his poetry, citing definitions that he has
looked up that are not particularly revealing or appropriate for the context.
As he puts it, he gnaws his way through authoritative forms, piling up waste
as he goes: "I work *in* or *through* the dictionary a bit in the manner of a mole,
pushing words and expressions to the right and left, burrowing my way
through them."[33] This is why he thinks of his own writing not as a monumental edifice or statue, but as something thrown away or caste aside, like rubble
or debris.[34] For Ponge, poetic contemplation requires the willingness to get
dirty: he compares writing to the act of digging up particles, flakes, roots,
worms, and other little creatures with a plough or shovel. Derrida highlights
this side of the poet's work when he writes that Ponge "does not run away
from dirt, he writes with dirt, against dirt, on dirt, about dirt."[35] This is a
poetry that stays close to the ground, exploring its undistinguished depths.

   Resistant as it is to polished completion, the notebook poem is a genre especially calibrated for awkwardness.[36] In his intentionally unfinished variations, Ponge lays bare the scaffolding of his texts, exposing the difficulty of
speaking of (or for) what he calls the "mute" world. Although each poem
strives to circumscribe something commonplace, this orientation toward
simplicity yields voluminous results. In these texts, Ponge labors to convey a
singular indeterminacy that cannot be pinned down. This attempt to describe
the unspecifiable quality of things draws him close to Proust. In a 1979 interview, Ponge likens Proust to Cézanne and Van Gogh, noting that these three
artists are linked by a shared preoccupation with what it means to be moved
by the particular—not by "the sky," but by "that blue there!" ("ce bleu là-
bas!").[37] In his own work, Ponge stutters around this differential quality, this
certain something that language, oriented toward general category, can only
evoke by ostensive gesture ("that blue!"; "zut!") or by an accumulation of imperfect descriptors.

   We see Ponge working to approximate such unspecifiable particularity especially in *La Mounine, or Note Struck in Afterthought on a Provence Sky* (*La
Mounine ou note après coup sur un ciel de Provence*), a notebook poem I evoked
in the introduction to this chapter. *La Mounine* comprises nothing but a series
of incomplete attempts to convey the look of a landscape—and particularly, a
patch of sky—glimpsed through a bus window early one April morning.
No final or finished composition can or should result from this aesthetic
perception: the only alternative to complete silence, Ponge determines, is to

publish accounts of the failure of description ("des descriptions ou relations *d'échecs de description*").[38] Although he details the scene over and over again, Ponge does not want to get it right. Instead, he strives to put this meteoric apparition in its place—to make it ordinary, to integrate it into the texture of things. The beautiful thing is profaned, brought down to size, opened to playful use and reuse.

Ponge's description of a stunning and ordinary apparition seen from a moving bus echoes Proust's description of the Martinville steeples in "Combray." Both are pieces of lyrical prose—the Proustian narrator explicitly calls his childish composition a "prose poem"—and both highlight the beautiful object's capacity to stupefy the observer, compelling him to mimic it in language. Both scenes explore a singular whateverness that thwarts established categories. (Ponge's list of working titles for the volume in which *La Mounine* was published includes various versions of "whatever": "quoi que ce soit," "quelconque," and "sujets quelconques.")[39] In Ponge as in Proust, the aesthetic subject catches sight of the object (steeples, a patch of sky) while merely passing through. In both cases, the reader is presented with multiple versions of the event—two in Proust, and many in Ponge's recursive notebook poem—such that the objects described seem to waver and blur before our eyes. Finally, just as Proust's narrator ends his act of composition with a joyful squawk, Ponge highlights the poetic potential of babble in *La Mounine*. Babble for Ponge takes the form of analogies that continuously miss their mark. Yet we might understand such broken or disarticulated poetic language in Michel de Certeau's terms, as joyfully "multipl[ying] the possibilities of speech" rather than shutting them down.[40]

La Mounine is the account of a non-happening. Ponge works hard to depict almost nothing at all: just a minor rearrangement of the given, a barely perceptible opening in the sky. In a slight tensing or diminution of space, statues suddenly appear beneath a sky strangely transparent, like a window into the night. This apparition has no consequence, no effect, except to return things (temporarily) to a zero-degree of being. The poet recounts the non-events again and again in the attempt to isolate the cause of the puzzling "aesthetic sob" that overwhelmed him that morning on the bus between Marseille and Aix-en-Provence.

The entire text circles around the paradox of illuminated shadow, or shadowed illumination. In some versions of the event, Ponge indicates that the sky has blanched. At other moments he perceives not a clearing, but a darkening of the sky, a shadowing or congestion or inky saturation, as if an octopus has released its ink, or a blotter has been filled with water. Sometimes the sky appears shadowed and incandescent at once, resembling "a pane of clear glass in a frosted skylight."[41] The prose mirrors this perplexity by moving in two directions at once—toward bifurcation (the direction of the conjunction "or," as in the title, *La Mounine, or Note Struck in Afterthought on a Provence Sky*), and also toward a succession of analogies (the sky is like a meteor, like an inky octopus, like poison, like the explosion of blue petals, like a blotter or rag). Sydney Lévy writes of this "paradoxical" sky that it is as if each of its directions—toward dark and night, toward light and day—is so excessive that it shades into its opposite.[42] Indeed, we lose all sense, reading *La Mounine*, of where darkness ends and light begins. And yet Ponge returns again and again to the perplexing ordinariness of this scene, and to his inappropriate, misplaced sob. How can a landscape so "generally unremarkable" move him to tears?

In this piece, Ponge turns himself into a sculptor of language, but as he works, he roughs up the text, foregrounding incongruity and non-adequation. In the following passage, for example, he labors to relay the analogical relation linking this beautiful sky to night:

> There's nothing more closely resembling night. . . . That's going too far. Let's simply say: there's something of night in this sky, it evokes night, it's not all that different from night, it has an undertone of night, it has undertones of night, it has the same tones as night, it amounts to night. This daylight amounts to night, this ashen-blue daylight.[43]

> Rien ne ressemble plus à la nuit. . . . C'est trop dire. Disons seulement: il a quelque chose de la nuit, il évoque la nuit, il n'est pas si différent de la nuit, il a une valeur de nuit, il a les valeurs de la nuit, il a la même valeur, les mêmes valeurs que la nuit, il vaut la nuit. Ce jour vaut la nuit, ce jour bleu cendres-là.[44]

The similitude initially posited is canceled, and then hesitantly reconstructed. In place of a simple declaration of likeness, the text draws our attention to that indeterminate, indefinite "something" that binds one term of the analogy to the other. Working as it does by way of exemplarity, analogy tends to concretize its object. Yet in Ponge, the principle of analogic connectivity—its "as" or "like" function—runs wild. The effect is to underscore not resemblance, but very slight distinctions between terms. Likeness is only rendered in a broken, imprecise language of near-equivalence and not-quite-resemblance: each successive proposition wears away at and destabilizes the precedent, and verbs of comparison (to resemble, to evoke, to amount to) pile up. Does this day have "undertones" of night or simply "an undertone"? Does it "amount to" night, or merely "evoke" night? In this text, Ponge comes close to expressing something like metaphysical anguish—and yet the serious intensity of the occasion is perpetually undone: rather than a masterpiece, we get a sketch—modest, imprecise, and inconclusive.

In *La Mounine*, Ponge works to register a radiant *thisness* that remains ungraspable, as if the apparition were just outside the poem's frame. Part of the text's challenge to visibility resides in the way it stages the convergence of precision and imprecision. As Ponge narrows in on the particularities of the perception, his heap of lexical scraps and leftovers grows bigger. Although he claims that his objective is to "preserve" that Provence sky from time, *La Mounine* is ultimately more concerned with ruining or undoing a spectacular impression than with memorializing it. We might even describe the poem as a catalogue of such methods of ruination.

Ponge spoils the beauty he describes in a variety of ways. Throughout the text, for example, he negates his own propositions. He calls this a method of "successive eliminations," and it takes the form of frequent interjections, such as, "that's not the right word," "that's going too far," and "why no!" He also destabilizes the impression in more subtle ways. The poem opens with a simple declaration ("True daylight didn't appear until Martigues"), but this tone of certainty is soon undermined as Ponge modulates and reformulates the terms of his description. Unable to settle on a single analogy, he stammers around the object of perception, describing it in anaphoric near-repetitions— as, for example, "a veiled effulgence, a veiled splendor, a veiled glimmer, a veiled radiance."[45] In a parallel to this stuttering reformulation, the precise time of the event shifts subtly from the beginning to the end of the poem: first it was "around nine," and then "between eight-thirty and nine," and finally "around eight."[46] The oddest and most deflating effect of the text, though, is the way Ponge incorporates his research, letting us see the lists, questions, notes, and dictionary definitions that would normally get relegated to the trash. The poet simply refuses to distinguish between preparatory and fin-ished work: there is no final version of the poem.

The feeling that Ponge attempts to describe in *La Mounine* is qualified only by its "intensity." Recalling Barthes's definition of "nuance" as a "differ-ential intensity," Ponge is referring here to an affective quality that escapes conceptualization. "Intensity" suggests the strain of an experience that is un-usual in an unmarked and unmeasurable way.[47] Whatever it is that the early morning bus passenger feels, that feeling is suddenly amplified tenfold ("déc-uplé"). And yet the scene is not majestic—this is not Beethoven's storm, Ponge tells us, but Leonardo da Vinci's. As Ponge puts it: "A thunderstorm like a shower, the ensuing sun as a dryer; really, my dear Beethoven, was it worth making such a grandiose production of this?"[48] Instead of Beethoven's sublime spectacle of sound, we are invited to picture one of Leonardo's sketches, in which, according to Ponge, "the importance of such a meteor is put in its rightful place."[49]

What does Ponge's identification with Leonardo da Vinci tell us about *La Mounine* and the Pongean aesthetics of awkward beauty? Leonardo's work is marked by its unfinished quality, and by its valorization of sfumato and anamorphosis—techniques that blur distinctions and distort classical form. According to Monique David-Ménard, Leonardo "searched everywhere to bring to light the moment when the distinction between beings and things is not established, the moment [. . .] when the separation of types of beings is made without being assured."[50] Leonardo's passion, as David-Ménard puts it, was to "draw forth this moment of the indecisive."[51] This is an apt description of Ponge's project as well. Like Leonardo, Ponge establishes contrasts only to slowly rub away at them: he strives to capture moments of imprecision, when things give way to their other: *this* into *that*, day into night, "glimmer" into "radience," shadow into luster.

The poet initially seeks to "pocket" this aesthetic experience. As he writes in an August 1941 letter to his cousin, he sought to put the impression in his wallet—"je cherchai aussitôt quelque expression pour l'empocher, la mettre en portefeuille"—but could not.[52] In an echo of the hawthorn hedge scene in Proust's "Combray," Ponge presents his own aesthetic response as a failure. The words would not present themselves "no matter how I lifted my eyes to the sky" ("J'avais beau relever les yeux au ciel, [. . .] le mot, ou les mots, ne se présentaient pas").[53] And yet, like Proust, Ponge invites us to find satisfaction in the irrecuperable ordinariness of the encounter. Its worth lies precisely in the way it eludes the perceiver's grasp—not in its beauty, but in this "j'avais beau," which can be translated, roughly, as "however hard I tried."

Throughout *La Mounine*, Ponge plays with the clunky machinery of analogy, exploring various forms of likeness. The apparition in question—"this beautiful day"—shares qualities with many things, from a landscape sketch by Leonardo da Vinci to a splotch of ink or an explosion of petals. Ultimately, though, it is equivalent to nothing else. As he inscribes an experience that he does and does not call "beautiful," Ponge resists lyricism. Although he is describing the sky, he will not let the poem get off the ground. Instead, he mutes his own "aesthetic sob" by surrounding it with heaps of prose, covering it over with one abandoned analogy after another.

In an October 1941 letter to his friend Gabriel Audisio—composed shortly after a summer spent writing *La Mounine*—Ponge figures himself as an awkward apprentice alchemist, alone in a dark laboratory:

> I worked all summer and I'm working still each day until 2 or 3 in the morning. [. . .] I feel something like an apprentice alchemist (or chemist), feverishly carrying on with his precision experiments in a lab in which the electricity has just gone off (and will never come back on). It takes him ages to identify his vials, he touches fifty of them before finding the right one, and when he's found it, the crucible has gotten cold and he has to reheat it, etc., etc.

> J'ai travaillé tout l'été et je travaille encore jusqu'à 2 ou 3 heures du matin chaque jour. [. . .] Je me fais un peu l'effet d'être un apprenti alchimiste (ou

chimiste) qui continuerait fiévreusement ses expériences de précision dans un laboratoire où l'électricité vient de s'éteindre (et ne se rallumera jamais). Il lui faut un temps fou pour identifier ses fioles, il en tâte cinquante avant d'atteindre la bonne, et quand il a trouvé la bonne, le creuset a refroidi, il faut qu'il s'occupe de le réchauffer, etc., etc.[54]

Here the scientific impulse (toward rigor, perfection, and rightness) is detached from instrumental ends. This image of the poet as blundering technician is a variation on Ponge's notion of the poet as a mole burrowing through dictionaries. It is a distinctly undignified conception of poetic labor. Ponge calls upon science here, but does not present it as a form of unquestionable authority: the point, rather, is that all of this "precision" leads nowhere, yields no final answers. The artist gropes toward exactitude, but the awkward precision he seeks is not "for" anything. This is precision in the dark, a precision that one can only feverishly feel for.

At the end of twenty pages or so of notebook scratchings, representing about three months of work, Ponge concludes *La Mounine* by retracting a conclusion. He ends with an "opening" (a "début"): "It's along the lines [c'est dans le sens] of what just precedes that there should be a continuation and completion of the poem whose *opening* would be fairly close to what follows" ("à peu près comme ci-après").[55] Here Ponge inscribes five stanzas of free verse, each line of which has already been tested out (considered, debated, turned over and over) in the preceding pages. The last word is "Etc."—a pseudo-technical Latin abbreviation that opens the text rather than closing it, exemplifying the poem's laborious, interminable attempt to capture that obscure yet luminous apparition.

In other draft compilations, Ponge concludes with a sort of final offering—a contained and detachable poem, the fruit of all this labor, so to speak. By contrast, in *La Mounine* he first adds up comparisons, piling one analogy upon another, only to ultimately dismiss them all. None is quite right. Publication here therefore takes the form of abandonment: echoing "The Crate," Ponge gives up, letting the text go. Making no attempt to close *La Mounine*, the poet simply withdraws, acknowledging that he has succeeded only in composing "awkward, labored pages" ("des pages malhabiles et efforcées").[56] In this notebook poem, we see Ponge's attraction to the infelicities of language itself—his interest in the way, as he puts it, "nothing coincides," and nothing is quite equivalent to anything else. The poem will never be complete. The poet can never arrive at the final truth of the thing because it will always say to him "no, I'm something else" ("non, je suis encore autre chose").[57] Yet *La Mounine* is not a failure in all senses. In the poem's frayed analogies, its incompletion, and in the effort it puts on display, Ponge lets his reader feel that his precarious vision is ours as well, and that we, too, could build something as beautifully awkward as this.

"As such, nothing more"

O world of insipidity and insignificance, here you attain perfection!
—PONGE, "LE RESTAURANT LEMEUNIER"

The first part of this chapter explored Ponge's penchant for the awkward, a concept that names a fumbling, laborious relation to aesthetic non-instrumentality. The following section examines Ponge's experiments with the quality of effortless inconsequentiality he calls "perfection." Like the awkward, Pongean perfection is a desacralizing, profanatory force: it undoes distinctions, placing poetry within the grasp of anyone at all.

"Perfection" is a word that crops up frequently in Ponge, but in unfamiliar guises. Uninterested in ideal or finished forms, Ponge links perfection with incompletion and variation. His is a "paradoxical," "unsellable," and "deal-breaking" ("rédhibitoire") perfection, and it appears in diverse manifestations.[58] Soap offers the very paradigm of "aesthetic perfection."[59] But the shape of a pebble is also an example of perfection. So is the thorny inkiness of the ripe wild blackberry, haughty and unappetizing as it may be. Ponge claims that plants are perfect in their rooted immobility. The snail is a model for poetry in the way it "perfectly" secretes its slime. Proverbs are perfect in their stupidity. Ponge discovers that even "platitude" is perfect in its way—"la platitude est une perfection," he dreams one night.[60] Ponge's egalitarian conception of perfection thus has little to do with polish or refinement. Instead, it is closely allied with its supposed opposite, the imperfect.[61]

How to qualify the inconsequential perfection of a glass of water: this is the challenge Ponge takes on in the notebook poem, *The Glass of Water* (*Le Verre d'eau*), first published in 1949 as a collaboration with the artist Eugène de Kermadec. As we have seen, *La Mounine* explores the poet's struggle to describe an everyday perception that is not quite commensurate with the available categories. *The Glass of Water* highlights another side of Ponge's preoccupation with the conjunction of singularity and commonness. This text, still untranslated into English and largely ignored by critics, foregrounds the difficulty of conceptualizing that which is superlatively precious and yet widely available. Getting one's mind around the glass of water is surprisingly difficult, Ponge says, because this object is so perfectly translucid, limpid, even "pure"—and so commonplace. As he puts it, "how to qualify this perfection that dispenses itself without reckoning," this perfection that "everyone can grasp?"[62]

To declare a clean, drinkable glass of water the most commonplace object imaginable would seem to require an act of willful ignorance. Who today could ignore the fact that water is an increasingly rare commodity? But for Ponge, writing in postwar France, it appeared as the very prototype of the highly valuable yet entirely accessible thing—as ubiquitous as a pebble, he says. As an object, the glass of water could not be more ordinary: "ça court les rues" is the expression Ponge invokes. Literally, it "runs the streets," meaning that it is everywhere, it is nothing special, nothing rare. In France, tap water runs from every faucet, collects in every sink.[63] Indeed, Ponge insists on the utter lack of effort necessary to attain this object: enjoying a glass of water requires no special training or expertise; this pleasure can be yours "without the slightest fatigue or expense."[64] Ponge loves the image of lifting a glass to one's eyes and looking at it from all sides, without any expenditure of effort. He works hard to render the ease of this gesture, returning to the image again and again, as in the following embedded lines of verse:

> If diamonds are said to be of beautiful water
> Of what water is the water in my glass?
> How does one qualify pure perfection?
> Pure perfection cannot be qualified
> Pure perfection remains unqualified . . .
> Which runs through the streets, scales every floor
> Dispenses itself at all the faucets
> Where each according to his thirst can gather his dose
> Lift it level with his eyes
> Then down it in one gulp

> Si les diamants sont dits d'une belle eau
> De quelle eau donc dire l'eau de mon verre?
> La pure perfection comment qualifier?
> Perfection toute pure ne peux qualifier
> Pure perfection reste inqualifiée . . .
> Qui court les rues, grimpe à tous les étages
> Se dispense sur tous éviers
> Où chacun à sa soif peut en cueillir sa dose
> L'élever à hauteur de ses yeux
> Puis la boire d'un trait[65]

Like the specter of Lemoine's precious yet mundane synthetic diamond that so fascinated Proust, Ponge's diamantine glass of water exemplifies the paradox of commonplace perfection. Ponge is drawn to the *verre d'eau* precisely because it is so unremarkable: "it's the symbol of nothing, or at least, of not much." Without taste, without odor, without color, and almost without form, the glass of water signifies above all "an extraordinary lack of qualities." And yet, despite its unqualifiability, it is sometimes—to the throat parched by hard work or fever or strong sentiment—"the most precious thing."[66]

   Playing on the transparency common to both objects, Ponge declares the glass of water to be as precious as a diamond. The poet is invoking Adam Smith's famous "water-diamond paradox" here: how is it that useless objects are highly valued, while the most useful objects are worth almost nothing? As Smith puts it:

> The things which have the greatest value in use have frequently little or no value in exchange; and, on the contrary, those which have the greatest value in exchange have frequently little or no value in use. Nothing is more useful than water; but it will purchase scarce any thing; scarce any thing can be had in exchange for it. A diamond, on the contrary, has scarce any value in use; but a very great quantity of other goods may frequently be had in exchange for it.[67]

Ponge reevaluates the logic that would subordinate "use" to "exchange." Ordinary as it is, the glass of water is nonetheless incomparable: immeasurable and perfect, it is a flower without equal, "fleur sans pareille." It is nothing more or less than itself. "How to qualify this perfection that bestows itself without counting?" the poet asks. "Comment qualifier perfection pareille?"[68]

"Transparent" as it may be, the glass of water is also problematic. It is easy enough to praise its beauty, Ponge explains. What is remarkable about this object is the way that its "charms," its "preciousness," and its "beauties" are at every moment shot through by insipidity and worthlessness. In a formulation that recalls the magic tricks of involuntary memory and the performative ventriloquism of Proustian pastiche, Ponge declares that platitude works away at the object's value, annulling it, smoothing it out, dissolving it, and making it disappear "like a three-card trick":

> Of course the glass is a delightful object, a most precious thing [. . .]. But the most difficult task lies ahead of us, for now we must—and how?—give an idea of its true particularity, which is more or less the following: namely, that the greatest simplicity, one-ness, uniformity, even platitude, an incredible worthlessness and valuelessness, a character that is unrefined, crude, tasteless, insipid (insipid and tasteless can now be spoken one right after the other without pleonasm: it's no longer quite the same thing), odorless, colorless, cheap . . . at each moment TRAVERSES its charms, its preciousness, its beauties, annulling them, smoothing them out, dissolving, leveling, hiding, bleaching, rubbing away, erasing, digesting, rendering passable, sterilizing, cleansing, making them disappear (like a three-card trick), compensating for them.

> Bien sûr le verre est un objet de ravissement, une chose des plus précieuses [. . .]. Mais le plus difficile reste à faire, car maintenant il faut—et comment faire—, il faut donner idée de sa particularité véritable, qui est à peu près la suivante: à savoir que la plus grande simplicité, unicité, égalité, platitude même, une invraisemblable nullité, non-valeur, un caractère rustique, fruste, sans goût, insipide (insipide et sans goût peuvent être maintenant

dits l'un à la suite de l'autre sans pléonasme: ce n'est plus tout à fait la même chose), inodore, incolore, bon marché . . . TRAVERSE à chaque instant ses charmes, ses préciosités, ses beautés, les annule, aplanit, dissout, nivelle, cache, décolore gomme, efface, digère, rend potables, stérilise, assainit, escamote (comme au bonnetau), rembourse.[69]

The glass of water contains the most crackling contradictions. What distinguishes this object is the way its worthlessness and its preciousness meet, each traversing, working through, making and unmaking the other. Like Proust, Ponge incites in his reader a mixture of enchantment and disbelief. He flaunts the magic trick: mere words can conjure a glass of water! And yet he spoils the trick, too, by letting a flood of verbs overwhelm the description, unsettling it with a litany of likenesses.

Fascinated by the proximity between the superlative worth of the glass of water and its insignificance, Ponge declares that this object is literally the vital minimum. The most humble of offerings, it is the very least that one can give ("la moindre des choses que l'on puisse offrir").[70] In this sense, the quenching effect of the glass of water is comparable only to other, similarly minor pleasures:

> [O]pening the window, putting on a clean shirt, washing your hands, lighting a fire, lighting a lamp, receiving a letter or a handshake, or a simple salute, or a smile, stopping walking or stopping working, or stopping to think for a minute, your child getting a good grade, the sea making a pebble shine, or the sun a piece of straw.

> [O]uvrir la fenêtre, passer une chemise propre, se laver les mains, allumer un feu, allumer une lampe, recevoir une lettre ou une poignée de mains, ou un simple salut, ou un sourire, s'arrêter de marcher, ou de travailler ou de réfléchir une minute, que votre enfant ait une bonne note, que la mer fasse luire un caillou, ou le soleil un brin de paille.[71]

If the glass of water is a gift almost too humble to be recognized as such, Ponge wants nothing more than to offer us something just as ordinary—a text that would be equal parts limpid and insipid, without any consequence other than one of fleeting refreshment. And he puts it: "for you, whoever you may be, in whatever state you may find yourself, here is a glass of water. This book is a glass of water."[72] Hence his attempt to describe this object will prove once and for all that he is not a poet: "This time, I won't be bothered with poetry," he declares.[73] For, like the object itself, the poet's textual rendering of the colorless, tasteless glass of water must "go down in one gulp," leaving scarcely a trace.[74]

One of the concepts Ponge works away at in this text is the notion of satisfaction or refreshment. He returns repeatedly to the verb "désaltérer," which means to "quench one's thirst," but also indicates an inversion or cancellation of the verb "altérer," which in turn means to make other, to change or modify; or (more pejoratively), to deteriorate, degrade, falsify.[75] What kind of alteration does "désaltérer" imply, exactly? It cancels the spoilage of "altérer," but does not thereby ameliorate—instead, it simply satisfies, restoring one to oneself, to one's zero degree. It therefore indicates a mode of profanation, albeit the effortless inverse of the laborious "awkward." Without qualities, Ponge imagines, water cannot really modify the body of its drinker.[76] Unlike rum or milk, it does not "work" in the body that consumes it: it adds nothing.[77] Merely washing superfluous matter away, water makes no difference, incites no alteration. This addition that adds precisely nothing implies a subtle shift in atmospheric conditions nonetheless: Ponge wants to offer us his book "as one places a glass of water on the table, and the entire atmosphere of relations is changed."[78] He insists that this gift adds up to nothing, demands no recompense, and yet "refreshes everything, changes everything."[79]

It is not quite right to call the glass of water "beautiful," Ponge explains, since this is too obvious; as with the atmospheric intensity felt one morning at La Mounine, "beautiful" goes without saying ("belle va trop sans dire").[80] The glass of water is at once more and less than beautiful. If its simplicity is hard to qualify, part of the problem, according to Ponge, is that the word "potable" in French means not just "safe to drink" but "mediocre," merely "passable." Something is rotten in the French language, he exclaims, if you cannot express the idea of a simple sufficiency without also signifying a lack of distinction, a deficiency in refinement.[81] Ponge's aim in *The Glass of Water* is thus that of all his work: to open a non-pejorative space in language to signify *what we all can have*—what is precious but not uncommon, what is undistinguished, unsophisticated, and perfectly good enough. As he puts it, the glass of water "lacks nothing." It "affirms itself as such [comme tel], nothing more."[82]

While *La Mounine* explores the slight distinction between near-synonyms and the almost imperceptible mismatch between likenesses, *Le Verre d'eau* highlights Ponge's fascination with tautology—with the way the object is sufficient to itself, satisfactory in itself. Ponge claims, for example, that just as a glass is "most itself" when it is full of water, water remains "most itself" in a glass.[83] As we have seen, it is important for Ponge that water does not intoxicate, but merely "dis-alters" you ("vous désaltère"), quenching your thirst and returning you to your own most neutral state.[84] He even suggests that there is a homology between the look and sound of the phrase "glass of water" ("verre d'eau") and the thing itself. It is superficial and a bit precious to say this, Ponge admits, but note how the phrase itself is framed on either end by a container, a little vase ("V" and "U"); note the crystalline symmetry of er-re in "verre"; note the transparency and muteness of those reflected "E"s; and note the heaviness of that "eau," which fills the empty *verre*, weighing it down.[85]

Tautological simplicity, or transparency, is thus key to this text. Ponge's friend and collaborator, Kermadec, explores the pictorial possibilities of such transparency in the series of prints he created for the book.[86] Kermadec, like Ponge, belonged to no established aesthetic movement or group, choosing instead to go his own way. Never commercially successful and rarely discussed by critics, Kermadec preferred the less prestigious and grand media of watercolor and pencil to oil, and his penchant for open, exposed lines is evident in his *Glass of Water* lithographs (Figure 4.1). Dwarfing Ponge's text with its comparatively massive dimensions, Kermadec's glass of water flaunts its spontaneity and all-at-onceness, in contrast to the poem's slow, iterative versions and revisions.[87] Yet both the image and the text draw our eye to the play of line and page, and to the confusion of inside and outside, content and container. Both Ponge and Kermadec emphasize the object's transparency and lightness, inviting us to rest our gaze in blank spaces.

Ponge also underscores the analogy between transparency in writing and transparency in musical composition, comparing *The Glass of Water* to the clean, spare lines of Bach's *Well Tempered Clavier*.[88] Like Bach's composition,

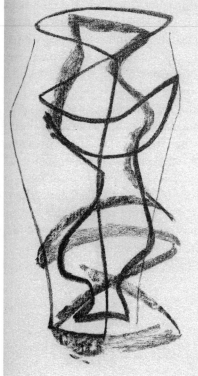

22 Mars.

Si des diamants sont dits d'une belle eau
de quelle eau donc dire l'eau de mon verre?
Comment qualifier cette fleur sans pareille?
— Potable.

Si les diamants sont dits d'une belle eau
De quelle eau donc dire l'eau de mon verre?
Si de belle eau sont dits certains diamants...
Que de belle eau soient dits certains diamants...

Moins précieuse non je ne puis trop le dire
Ni plus simple non plus mais plus courante oui
Mais d'usage plus libre et potable à mon goût

Plus ou moins précieuse on ne saurait le dire
Mais plus courante oui et potable à mon goût

Moins chère en quelque sens mais plus chère
en quelqu'autre

Moins chère à acquérir Plus facile à avoir
Plus facile à cueillir à quelque robinet
Plus chère d'être libre à tous les robinets

La pureté court les rues, grimpe à tous les
étages et se dispense sur tous les éviers. En
vente libre à tous les robinets.

O pureté tu n'es donc pas si rare
Tu cours les rues
Grimpes à tous étages
Te dispenses sur tous éviers...
Et l'on te cueille à tous les robinets

FIGURE 4.1 Francis Ponge and Eugène de Kermadec, *Le Verre d'eau*.

Source: Special Collections and University Archives, Rutgers University Libraries.

Permission to reproduce this page was granted by Quentin Laurens of the Galérie Louise Leiris, Paris.

the poem is a set of exercises or contrapuntal variations that alternate between relatively unbound (prelude-esque) and relatively strict (fugal) compositional forms.[89] To read the recursive drafts of *The Glass of Water* is to "practice" the text, to participate in its construction. This poetic exercise is intended to prove to each of us that we too can become poets. As Ponge puts it, his objective in writing about the glass of water is to "open to all the ways and means, the difficulties and pleasures of poetry."[90]

In this regard, *The Glass of Water* exemplifies Ponge's conception of his own poetry as a gratuitous offering or gift. In this text, as in *La Mounine*, a luminous but perfectly banal occasion is made perceptible to us. At stake in these essay-poems is a non-sublime opening in the fabric of things, a very slight redistribution of the given. Exploring what is incomparable in the most ordinary objects and in the least sophisticated modes of enjoyment, Ponge invites us to pay attention to occasions of profanation, when the distinctions between the valuable and the worthless, the rare and the common cease to hold. His poetry therefore troubles the economic and aesthetic logic that grants the greatest worth to the rarest and least usable things. The Pongean aesthetic object—a rain shower, an abandoned crate, a sky seen from a bus window, or a glass of water—is anything but distanced and untouchable. Whether they appear awkwardly incomplete or perfectly sufficient, such apparitions are nothing special—and yet unlike anything else. Ponge refuses to make poetry look easy, but even as he exposes the quotidian hard work of poem-building, he lets us see that we too are part of this sketched and drafted world, and equally imbricated in its forms.

While Ponge explores aesthetic experience from the perspective of the poet-laborer, his contemporary, Nathalie Sarraute, ruins the scene of sophistication in a different way. The following chapter argues that Sarraute, too, explores the awkward labor of aesthetic enjoyment. But if Ponge mobilizes a Proustian poetics of babble, spoiling fantasies of perfection by displaying the residue of poem-construction, Sarraute's fiction draws on a more sociological side of Proust. Exposing the institutional norms and practiced habits of speech, perception, and sociability that the performance of distinction demands, she shows us how hard it can be to put on a display of good taste.

{ 5 }

Sarraute's Bad Taste

In matters of taste, more than anywhere else, all determination is
negation; and tastes are perhaps first and foremost distastes, disgust
provoked by horror or visceral intolerance ("c'est-à-vomir") for the
tastes of others.

—BOURDIEU, *DISTINCTION*

Nathalie Sarraute inherits Proust's experiment with distinction and pushes it
to new extremes. Like Proust and Ponge, Sarraute foregrounds the unsophisticated side of aesthetic experience, calling into question the division between
the category of "art" and merely "ordinary" objects. Yet Sarraute stages more
explicitly sociological—and much more dysphoric—scenes of aesthetic encounter. Exploring the problem of aesthetic taste from the perspective of the
mid-century striving bourgeois perceiver, she invites her reader to look
closely at the rituals of speech, gesture, and feeling that practices of refinement require.

In many ways, and more precisely than the work of either Proust or Ponge,
Sarraute's fiction exemplifies Bourdieu's sociology of culture. According to
Bourdieu, judgments of taste are always judgments of class. Such assessments
function pragmatically, marking the social status of the subjects who make
them while also reinforcing the legitimacy of the objects socially designated
as works of art. Like Bourdieu, Sarraute dismantles mechanisms of power.
Exposing the struggle for control over symbolic codes and classifications that
subtends the enjoyment of art, she demonstrates that there is nothing un-
learned, ahistorical, or "disinterested" about aesthetic taste. As Bourdieu puts
it, taste not only classifies its object (as beautiful or ugly, distinguished or
vulgar); it also "classifies the classifier."[1] In novels such as *The Planetarium* (*Le
Planétarium*, 1959), *The Golden Fruits* (*Les Fruits d'or*, 1962), *Do You Hear
Them?* (*Vous les entendez?*, 1972), and in the radio play, *It's Beautiful (C'est

beau, 1972), Sarraute represents mid-twentieth-century bourgeois society as organized around competition for cultural capital. Sarraute's characters strive to maintain or elevate their positions in the hierarchy of social space by proving their capacity to appropriate cultural treasures not only materially, but symbolically as well.

Sarraute's depiction of the aesthetic sphere is ultimately moodier and less schematized than Bourdieu's, however. Like Bourdieu, Sarraute demonstrates that aesthetic judgments both symptomatize and reinforce principles of class inequality and social exclusion. But she also exposes the uncertainty inherent in such verdicts, foregrounding the impure, subtle mixtures of feeling that bind us to those objects socially designated as works of art. While Bourdieu's *Distinction* (1979) investigates how the cultural fantasy of "pure" aesthetic taste successfully reproduces and naturalizes class distinctions, in Sarraute's fiction, the social players supposedly best-equipped to manipulate works of art are perpetually *embarrassed* by their attempts to derive cultural capital from acts of aesthetic evaluation.

Drawing on Proust's micro-phenomenological style, Sarraute invites us to concentrate on minutely graduated sensations and unfamiliar, uncategorizable mixtures of feelings. Against those who chide Proust for his "excessive minutia," Sarraute writes that she wishes Proust had been even more extreme in his close-ups instead of drawing back to analyze and classify observations from a distance. Using a cartographic metaphor, Sarraute suggests that she is still working with Proust's map, but that rather than directing readers to overarching "grand immobile lines," her texts plunge us into a disorienting sensory-perceptual contact with things.[2] By foregrounding ambiguous moods rather than oppositional classifications and by drawing attention to nearly imperceptible distinctions and to happenings too minuscule to be qualified as events, Sarraute, like Proust, undertakes a recalibration of aesthetic interest. But while Proust is attuned to gorgeous ordinary things—dazzling yet commonplace patches of light and nebulous, hyper-nuanced assemblages—Sarraute orients us toward the uglier side of taste. She tests out the shelf life of distinction, representing aesthetic pleasure as always in the process of "turning," spoiling, or going bad. The sticky and unsettling tone that Sarraute cultivates with her clichés, her piles of quasi-synonyms, and her minor paradoxes functions as a gauntlet thrown down to the critic, who cannot easily "digest" the text and translate it into her own terms.

Another way to understand the stakes of Sarraute's project is to say that she is interested in the dysphoric side of nuance—not the Barthesian glimmer or the Proustian cloud, but the *-âtre* (or *-ish*)—a suffix that blurs the precision of qualifiers, drawing them into the orbit of the not-quite, the tending-toward, the quasi, or almost (*presque*). If Proust's novel presents a constellation of luminous points and cloudy, multi-sensory apparitions, Sarraute privileges weak figures of a limper variety—from the "limp paw" ("molle menotte") to the heap of stuff, like the "mushy" and "grayish" ("grisâtre") "something" that spills out of a German sofa after the child narrator lacerates it in Sarraute's fictional autobiography, *Childhood* (*Enfance*, 1983). Sarraute's texts are also suffused with visual/olfactory images of a sweet-acrid gas—suggesting an amorphous tone or ambiance that is not emitted by any identifiable source. The narrator of her early novel, *Portrait of a Man Unknown* (*Portrait d'un inconnu*, 1948), describes a vague, ambiguous, mixed feeling that subjects seem to inhale, rather than express: "one had, at times, the sensation of absorbing involuntarily, of deeply inhaling something thick and sugary that left you all buzzing and numb" ("on avait, par moments, la sensation d'absorber malgré soi, d'aspirer à pleins poumons quelque chose d'épais, de sucré, qui vous rendait tout gourd et bourdonnant").[3] As we shall see, this sugary, slightly repugnant atmosphere is the feeling-tone that Sarraute cultivates throughout her work.[4]

The recent "affective turn" in literary and cultural criticism enables us to appreciate Sarraute's interest in the sociality of emotion—a preoccupation that baffled her contemporaries.[5] Sarraute teaches us to understand the conventions of aesthetic enjoyment both sociologically and phenomenologically. She approaches taste from a dual vantage point, representing it both as a force of social classification, and as a historically contingent mixture of feelings that is never entirely classifiable. Sarraute has a word for the mixed or muddled feelings and sensations that exist at the limits of typology: *tropisms*. "Tropism" is a term borrowed from biology, where it signifies the turning of an organism as a response to given stimuli, such as light or gravity. Sarraute's theory of the tropism—which she defines as "incessant and rapid fluctuations of states in perpetual transformation"—can be read as a theory of publicly mediated affect: feeling as it is materially registered in, refracted through, and productive of particular social contexts.[6] In *The Age of Suspicion* (*L'Ère du soupçon*, 1956), Sarraute describes tropisms as intersubjective, shifting assemblages of feelings at the limit of cognition:

> They are indefinable movements that slip very rapidly at the limits of our consciousness; they are at the origin of our gestures, of our words, of the feelings that we manifest, that we believe we feel and that it is possible to define.

> Ce sont des mouvements indéfinissables, qui glissent très rapidement aux limites de notre conscience; ils sont à l'origine de nos gestes, de nos paroles, des sentiments que nous manifestons, que nous croyons éprouver et qu'il est possible de définir.[7]

Elsewhere, Sarraute qualifies these "feelings in nascent state" as unnamed, incomplete, "minuscule dramas."[8] Because these "movements" develop and disappear with extreme rapidity, the only way to allow the reader to perceive them is by slowing down and closing in on images that might provoke analogous sensations in her. Sarraute therefore works to "decompose" these movements and "make them play out in the consciousness of the reader like a slow-motion film."[9] Although Sarraute is often associated with the *nouveau roman* movement of the 1950s and '60s, her theory of "tropistic" affect distinguishes her from the anti-phenomenological structuralist ideology of her contemporaries.[10]

As a fuzzy concept at the limit of categories, the tropism is similar to Raymond Williams's "structure of feeling": a formation "at the very edge of semantic availability."[11] Williams employs the term "structure of feeling" to denote "practical consciousness" rather than "official consciousness": a social (never simply "personal"), present-tense, flexible, uncertain, active modality of experience, not yet assimilated or converted into a fixed form or finished product. Structures of feeling are social in an extremely *micro* way: not simply effects of institutional or class relations, but "emergent or pre-emergent" qualitative shifts that "do not have to await definition, classification or rationalization before they exert palpable pressures and set effective limits on experience and on action."[12] As Jonathan Flatley notes, this term enables us to talk about the sociality of affect, and to investigate how the social is linked to the personal in ways "that are more ephemeral and transitory than set ideologies or institutions."[13] Structures of feeling, like tropisms, are nascent and fleeting, and they thwart mind-body, cognition-feeling dichotomies, as well as the facile opposition of ideology versus "lived experience." Thinking in such terms requires attending to modes of perception and cognition that are neither unmediated, or "direct," nor quite ideational. As Williams suggests, this is not about "feeling against thought, but thought as felt and feeling as thought: practical consciousness of a present kind in a living and interrelating continuity."[14] Like Williams, when Sarraute distinguishes between the present-tense microrhythms of the tropism and the more stagnant temporality of social conventions and institutions, she is not drawing an absolute ontological division between (pre-social) feeling and (social) action or speech. Rather, she is stating her interest in the difficult task of representing how struggles for social distinction *feel* in the uncertainty of the present.

This chapter is divided into three sections. The first part investigates Sarraute's penchant for infelicitous performative statements. If the performative declaration, "this is beautiful," works to divide and classify, distinguishing both the speaker and the object, aesthetic judgments in Sarraute's fictions never sound so authoritative. Instead, Sarraute amplifies the static surrounding speech acts of aesthetic judgment, foregrounding not the felicity of the declaration, but the embarrassingly infelicitous (or quasi-felicitous) "periperformative" noise around it. In the second section, I examine Sarraute's representation of the aesthetic object in the age of André Malraux's Ministry of Culture, which established a grandiose, pseudo-religious role for art. In Sarraute, the objects designated as artworks appear inappropriate to such grand ends. Instead, they are strangely unwieldy, like the potato-esque "petit pan de mur jaune" that so dazzles (and nauseates) Proust's Bergotte. The paradigmatic ungraspable art object in Sarraute is the gray stone statuette in *Do You Hear Them?*. Out of place everywhere, the statuette appears alternately precious and unremarkable. As such, it confers only dubious prestige on its distinction-seeking collector. Finally, in the third section of the chapter, I investigate Sarraute's cultivation of an aesthetics of bad taste. Focusing on her fondness for overripe, sticky-sweet, or *douceâtre* images, from creepy dolls and sinister babies to mercurious-chloride-laced spoonfuls of strawberry jam, I argue that Sarraute establishes her own minor aesthetic category: a moody mixture of sweetness and disgust. While Proust works to dissolve the border between natural objects (clouds, chickens, patches of light) and art, Sarraute explores the fragile distinction between the work of art and the mass-produced commodity in the mid-twentieth century. The *douceâtre* suggests a non-dramatic, non-cathartic modality of disgust—a disgust so slight that unlike the dysphoric formlessness of the sublime, it cannot be heroically cast off.

"It's beautiful, don't you think?"

It is difficult to say where conventions begin and end.
–J. L. AUSTIN, *HOW TO DO THINGS WITH WORDS*

One way in which Sarraute implicitly revises Bourdieu's theory of distinction is by foregrounding infelicitous or unsuccessful acts of evaluation. Like Bourdieu, Sarraute demonstrates that the art object has no proper content or inherent value, because it owes its existence to institutional frameworks and to the ingrained perceptual habits of the "initiated." She frequently draws our attention to the performative quality of aesthetic judgments, which is to say that statements of aesthetic worth in her novels are not simply descriptions, but actions—speech acts which classify both the speaker (as distinguished enough to make such distinctions) and the object (as worthy or unworthy of such attention). Aesthetic judgments are performative because they function as demands for social recognition, and as symbolic investments that legitimize the object in question, granting it a certain kind of life.[15]

But while Bourdieu emphasizes the bourgeoisie's mastery of symbolic forms,[16] Sarraute's fictions foreground instances of thwarted critical language—moments when an observer, reader, or critic can only point, multiply adjectives, or repeat conventional formulations. If Bourdieu investigates the conditions and consequences of felicitous or productive judgments—what Austin might call the "total speech act in the total speech situation"[17]— Sarraute is attuned to infelicity, or quasi-felicity, and her novels intensify the semiotic and affective noise that accompanies evaluative acts. In Kant's "Analytic of the Beautiful," the pronouncement "this is beautiful" is endowed with a special performative force. In speaking of beauty as if it were a property of things, the speaker "judges not merely for himself, but for everyone": he does not simply count on the agreement of others, but "demands" it from them.[18] By contrast, Sarraute's fictions return repeatedly to scenes in which the declarative, "c'est beau" sticks in the speaker's throat or comes out as babble. And instead of confidently speaking for everyone, Sarraute's aesthetic judges tend to implore others to agree with them.[19] This is precisely the subject of her 1972 radio play, *It's Beautiful*, which opens with a man prompting his wife to state that some unnamed object is beautiful:

> HE: It's beautiful, don't you think?
> SHE, *hesitating*: Yes . . .
> HE: You don't think it's beautiful?
> SHE: *as if against her will*: Yes . . . yes . . .
>
> LUI: C'est beau, tu ne trouves pas?
> ELLE, *hésitante*: Oui . . .
> LUI: Tu ne trouves pas que c'est beau?
> ELLE, *comme à contre-coeur*: Si . . . si . . .[20]

In Sarraute, characters cannot call something beautiful without adding, "don't you think?" Here, the ellipses that punctuate the woman's lines, along with the italicized stage directions ("hésitante," "comme à contre-coeur"), infuse a seemingly simple verbal exchange with ambiguity. What interests Sarraute is not simply conflict or disagreement over aesthetic value, but the affective static that attends all acts of aesthetic judgment. She returns again and again not to outright performative misfires, but to slight infelicities, when a conventional or ritualized utterance just barely fails to "come off," or when it is impossible to determine whether the speech act has succeeded or not.

Although Sarraute shares Bourdieu's interest in the relation between habits of perception and structures of privilege, if she had written *Distinction*, it would read more like the work of sociologist Erving Goffman. Both Goffman and Sarraute focus on the dramaturgy of face-to-face interactions and foreground flusterings and faux pas—instances when situations break down, rather than when they go smoothly. Like Goffman, Sarraute is attuned to minor, barely perceptible, but shared configurations of experience: she suggests, for example, that certain words *irritate* us, inducing "a sensation of disagreeable tickling or light burning" as if they had lodged just beneath the skin.[21] And like Goffman, Sarraute highlights the "intense" or "barely apparent flusterings" of embarrassment, a particularly contagious affect that functions as an index of a broken or threatened social bond.[22] Embarrassment, Goffman argues, might *feel* personal, but because it "disrupt[s] the smooth transmission and reception by which encounters are sustained," it pertains to the "encounter as a whole."[23] Sarraute's description of the tropism as provoking a ripple effect of social feeling likens her theory to Goffman's, who writes that "embarrassment seems to be contagious, spreading, once started, in ever widening circles of discomfiture."[24]

Sarraute's 1962 novel, *The Golden Fruits*, which dramatizes the reception of a novel titled *The Golden Fruits*, is explicitly about the perils of asserting cultural domination through the appreciation of a work of art. This novel explores the fractures and warpings, woofs and warbles that attend speech acts of aesthetic judgment. It consists entirely of verbal squirming and fidgeting around statements such as "it's the best book of the last fifteen years," and "there were those that came before *The Golden Fruits* and there are those that come after." In this text, aesthetic judgments are performatives that only partially "come off," because they tend to index the speaker's desire to be recognized rather than her effortless sophistication. For example, the following passage turns up the affective interference around an evaluative speech act, figuring an everyday verbal exchange as a desperate (and only vaguely requited) demand for legitimation:

> Listen. I'm calling out—answer me. Just so that I know that you're still there. I'm calling to you with all of my strength. *The Golden Fruits* . . . do you hear me? What did you think of it? It's good, isn't it? And the gloomy voice responds . . . "*The Golden Fruits* . . . it's good. . . ."

> Ecoutez. J'appelle, répondez-moi. Juste pour que je sache que vous êtes toujours là. Je crie vers vous de toutes mes forces. Les Fruits d'Or . . . vous m'entendez? Qu'en avez-vous pensé? C'est bien, n'est-ce pas? Et la voix morne répond . . . "Les Fruits d'or . . . c'est bien. . . ."[25]

If this "call" is answered, however half-heartedly, the elliptical gaps in the passage orient our attention toward the vulnerability of such symbolic exchanges. Later, when admirers of *The Golden Fruits* attempt to prove their good taste by specifying why the book is so extraordinary, Sarraute presents their evaluation without ellipses, but as babble, a heap of contradictory adjectives: "Macabre. Macabre and candid. A sort of innocence. Bright. Somber. Piercing. Confident. Cheerful. Human. Relentless. Dry. Damp. Chilly. Scorching."[26] Here, the performative declaration of aesthetic worth gives way to sheer semiotic noise. Judgments of aesthetic appreciation do not "stick" to the work, which resists definitive classification. Sarraute's objective here is not simply to demystify the scene of aesthetic judgment by exposing the interest and acquisitiveness hidden behind displays of "disinterested" pleasure, but to highlight the inevitable failure of such appropriative schemes. After all, the aesthetic sign is inherently ambivalent: it indexes an immense and heterogeneous network of references and yet appears by definition autonomous and self-contained, pointing only back toward itself. Art is "legitimate" to the

extent that it seems both original *and* hyper-referential; it must simultaneously cite convention and flaunt its rupture of convention. This ironic relation
to originality makes the work of judgment increasingly difficult for the
distinction-seeking spectator or critic.

In Kant, the speech act, "it's beautiful," conjures the fantasy of an instan-
taneous bond between perceivers. In Sarraute, however, this statement is
often offered up in desperation, when there is nothing else to say, as an anxious attempt to save face when one's reputation is on the line. In *The Golden
Fruits*, a well-respected critic is called upon in public to explain why the novel
is as good as he claims (he has failed to cite the book a single time in his laud-
atory article). Under the suspicious gaze of his peers, the critic becomes increasingly flustered, unable to hold the situation together. "You know you're
putting me in an awkward position," he admits, but insists that "everything is
beautiful in *The Golden Fruits* . . . anything at all . . ." ("n'importe quoi").[27] As
he turns the pages, however, the text appears graceless and emaciated:
"gauche, thin, fragile, fleshless." He searches in vain for the "splendid" and
"admirable" passages, but the words merely "flutter for an instant" and fall
flat.[28] Finally, in a gesture of pity and respect for social etiquette, someone
holds out the familiar ready-made phrase:

> Eyes emptied of all expression turn slightly in their sockets: the poor guy is
> waiting for someone to lend him a hand . . . everyone hesitates, a bit con-
> fused, everyone digs around, but she . . . here it is, I have what he needs, here
> you go, old boy, take it: "It's very beautiful."

> Des yeux vidés de toute expression tournent légèrement dans leurs orbites:
> le pauvre bougre attend qu'on lui donne quelque chose . . . chacun hésite, un
> peu confus, chacun fouille, mais elle . . . voilà, j'ai ce qu'il faut, tenez, mon
> brave, prenez: 'C'est très beau.'[29]

Spoken with some degree of deference, this proffered statement almost mends
the situation. But then a tone-deaf speaker echoes the phrase, amplified with
excessive enthusiasm: "it's verry beautiful" ("c'est trrès beau"). These words
"explode," spraying the embarrassed critic with shrapnel ("il est criblé
d'éclats"). The garishly rolled *r*—a noisy index of the speaker's "outrance," his
misreading of social cues—marks the end of *The Golden Fruits*' prestige for
the critic, who now can only save face by casting off the novel ("perhaps I was
wrong . . ."). Aesthetic judgments, Sarraute demonstrates, are not simply effective or ineffective, but fluctuate in intensity and effects. Spoken inappropriately, by the wrong speaker, in the wrong context, and they are not simply
"unhappy," but positively toxic. As *The Golden Fruits*' cachet expires, and it
morphs into a "poor thing," it does not merely lose its capacity to confer investor profit. It becomes a sort of social poison, ruining the distinction of
anyone who attempts to lay claim to it. Hence when the novel has hit a point

of particularly low prestige, an untimely admirer exclaims, "Personally, I like *The Golden Fruits*," and it is as if he has touched an electrified object: "A current runs through the *Golden Fruits* which my twitching hand cannot drop, I'm electrocuted, frozen in place."[30]

Aesthetic judgments in Sarraute never work with the punctual crispness that Austin attributes to the illocutionary act. (Indeed, even in Austin's own account, performatives rarely fulfill all of the conditions for felicity.[31]) Sarraute is especially interested in exploring the conditions and consequences of dissonance between statement and feeling, such as stating that something is beautiful in a half-hearted or excessively enthusiastic tone. Austin argues that feeling the "appropriate" affect is a condition of any felicitous performative, but he acknowledges that a mismatch between feeling and statement does not necessarily result in explicit misfire. Instead, the "insincere" performative, or "abuse," does not quite "come off," but nor is it "void" and "without effect." As he puts it, "when I say 'I promise' and have no intention of keeping it, I have promised but. . . ."[32] Interestingly, in attempting to qualify the effect of a minor conflict between feeling and convention, Austin has recourse to Sarraute's favorite punctuation mark, the ellipsis. Sarraute's texts are riddled with suspension points. Trails of little black dots spread through her oeuvre like stains, introducing an ambiguous warble or slight dissonance into all verbal exchanges. Frequent references in Sarraute to involuntary corporeal movement (laughter, nail-biting, scratching) function similarly, indexing the uncontrolled and uncontrollable presence of the body in judgments of taste, and unsettling the smooth transmission of meaning without halting it entirely.

Sarraute's idiosyncratic syntax adds to this noisy effect. While the performative works by attaching the indexical first person pronoun to certain verbs (in the present, indicative, active), Sarraute dismantles such statements, as if to test out the charge and force of deixis once it is separated from its anchoring pronoun. Sarraute also multiplies indexicals like "here" and "now" within the impersonal space of third-person narration. Such indexical markers seem to float free, not indicating any particular conjunction of space and time. Sarraute likes to squish and twist adjectives, too, allowing their connotations to seep onto neighboring words by piling them in lists of near-synonyms, or by repeating the softening suffixes "-aud" and "-âtre" (which we might translate with the English suffix "-ish"). So objects in Sarraute are not "short" but "shortish" ("courtaud"); not "gray" or "white" but "grayish" or "whitish" ("grisâtre," "blancheâtre"); and not "sweet" but "sweet-ish" ("douceâtre"). As one of Sarraute's characters puts it, words must be held down, their sharp points dulled, stippled, and swaddled, until they are nothing but "big flabby knobs" ("des grosses boules un peu molles").[33] Finally, Sarraute heaps up adjectives so that our attention is drawn to non-oppositional differences—the barely discernible distinctions or gaps between near-synonyms.[34]

Although Austin initially establishes strict conditions for the felicity of performative language, he eventually acknowledges that the line between the "explicit performative," the impure, "quasi-performative" ("half descriptive"), and the descriptive statement is fuzzy and may involve a number of "transitional stages."[35] He therefore invents a term for performatives whose effect does not quite coincide with the instant of their utterance: perlocutionary acts. The distinction between the illocutionary and the perlocutionary inheres in the mere difference of a preposition: "in" versus "by." While the illocutionary utterance can be defined as the "performance of an act *in* saying something," the perlocutionary more ambiguously achieves certain effects "*by* saying something."[36] Hence if a paradigmatic illocutionary act is *to warn*, a perlocutionary act is *to convince*. Other perlocutionary verbs include *to persuade, to deter, to tempt* (although Austin suggests that this one can be illocutionary, too), *to seduce*, and *to pacify*. The illocutionary demands; the perlocutionary cajoles. As Austin points out, "'trying to' seems always a possible addition with a perlocutionary verb."[37] The perlocutionary act is less punctual than the illocutionary, more improvisatory and less conventional, more vulnerable to the uncontrollable participation of others. It is therefore more difficult to determine exactly when it has achieved its effects (and precisely what these effects might be).[38] Sarraute is fascinated by the vague and unpredictable perlocutionary atmosphere pervading all aesthetic judgments.

Austin's category of the *quasi*-illocutionary, or perlocutionary act is intriguing, but one suspects that he introduces this term mainly as a place to stash the impurities that he wants to disassociate from the illocutionary act. Eve Kosofsky Sedgwick explicitly valorizes the aesthetic and political potential of the perlocutionary, inventing a general term that encompasses a wide range of quasi- or not-quite performatives: the "periperformative." Sedgwick suggests that if the statement "we (hereby) consecrate this ground" is an explicit (illocutionary) performative, then statements such as "we cannot consecrate it" or even "we get a kick out of consecrating this ground" or "we wish we had consecrated it" are *peri*-performative. Periperformatives hover between description and performance; they are *about* performatives, they "allude to" or "cluster *around*" performatives.[39] The periperformative, Sedgwick suggests, effects a sort of unwinding or loosening or wearing at the compact event of the performative. It "has the property of sketching in a differential and multidirectional surround that may change and dramatize [the performative's] meanings and effects."[40]

Sedgwick's discussion of the periperformative helps us to understand what is at stake in Sarraute's repetition of noisy, incomplete, or seemingly unsuccessful statements of aesthetic judgment. Sarraute, after all, is interested less in explicit occasions of felicity or infelicity, social triumph or humiliation, than in utterances that just barely "succeed" (such as "oui c'est beau") or that ambiguously

fail (such as "c'est trrès beau"). She draws our attention to the minute gradua-
tions and fluctuations of low-grade discomfort and irritation that subtend acts
of aesthetic judgment. In theorizing the periperformative, Sedgwick is not discussing dramatic, punctual instances of performative misfire, but rather a generalized atmosphere of subtle and ambiguous infelicity. Hence, she argues that
Henry James's novels constitute "an exploration of the possible grounds and
performative potential of periperformative refusals, fractures, warpings of the
mobile proscenium of marital witness."[41] Following Sedgwick, we might say
that Sarraute's novels constitute an exploration of the fractures and warpings
that attend class-affirming scenes of aesthetic judgment.

Sarraute presents aesthetic experience as irreducibly social—both dependent on and productive of social meanings and classifications. Like Sedgwick,
she emphasizes the importance of witness as a condition of performative felicity. The performative, as Sedgwick points out, does its work by relying on
"the tacit demarcation of the space of a third-person plural, a 'they' of
witness—whether or not literally present." The performative utterance, of,
say, a dare, therefore "invokes the presumption, but only the presumption, of
a consensus between speaker and witnesses, and to some extent between all
of them and the addressee."[42] While Austin argues that a performative's felicity is dependent on conventional speech being spoken "correctly" and "appropriately" in the correct and appropriate context, Sedgwick is interested in
what would happen to the performative scene should consensus break down
and the witnesses abstain from complying. She invites us to imagine the scene
of a dare, warped by the witnesses' periperformative chorus: "Don't accept
the dare on our account," which would alter the "interlocutory (I-you-they)
space of our encounter."[43] Such periperformative non-compliance is one way
that a person might "disinterpellate from a performative scene."[44] The imagined witnesses' "count me out" functions similarly to the wife's half-hearted
response, in It's Beautiful, to her husband's demand for aesthetic agreement
("yes . . . yes . . ."). Such plays around a more binding statement demonstrate,
as Sedgwick puts it, that the performative's rhetorical force "rarifies or concentrates in unpredictable clusters, outcrops, geological amalgams."[45] In other
words, the periperformative ("it's beautiful, isn't it?"; "it's verry beautiful")
foregrounds the fragile and shifting parameters of the convention to which it
alludes—the bourgeois tradition of aesthetic appreciation in this case, instan-
tiated by the conventional declaration of beauty. Instead of explicitly disinter-
pellating from the scene of aesthetic appreciation (as Sedgwick's hypothetical
dare-resisters do with their courageous "count me out"), Sarraute's characters
tend to squirm around the act of legitimation they are obliged to perform.
The result is sometimes a statement so ambiguous ("yes . . . yes . . .") that it is
impossible to determine whether it is "felicitous" or not.

The category of the "periperformative" is useful because it includes not
only speech acts, but also broken or suspended speech. Sarraute expands the

range of periperformative disturbance to include the atmospheric effects of minor bodily movements and tics. Her novels rarely provide descriptions of bodies, but frequently evoke habitual, aggravating corporeal movements— such as fidgeting, nail-biting, and sweaty-hand-holding. In the 1972 novel, *Do You Hear Them?*, laughter is presented as a noisy, periperformative disso- nance infiltrating and disturbing two men's appreciation of a little piece of gray stone sculpture. In this highly theatrical novel, a man sits at his coffee table with his neighbor, admiring an inherited pre-Colombian statuette, while his children's uninterpretable laughter floats down from upstairs, peri- odically punctuating the men's conversation. This laughter does not quite function as an explicit "count me out," but it nonetheless troubles the statu- ette owner's attempt to make a clear and definitive value judgment. Conta- gious (like embarrassment), laughter functions in this text like suspension points between clauses, upsetting—ever so slightly—the order of things. The semiotic vagueness of this laughter—a corporeal/affective agitation that the novel references and describes but cannot cite—unsettles the bourgeois ritual of aesthetic appreciation taking place between the father and the neighbor. The novel registers the shifting effect of the laughter on the interlocutors, who struggle to codify it as a non-threatening sign of the innocence and freshness of childhood. They find, however, that the laughter does not stay put in this category. Soon it sounds frivolous, slightly malicious, and strangely fake: "Happy. Young. Carefree. A trifle sets them off. It's just that little tremolo . . . it seems a bit forced . . . as if fabricated. . . ."[46] The men will never succeed in definitively codifying the noise.

By juxtaposing the juvenile laughter to the men's assessment of the statue, Sarraute foregrounds the sociological function of both expressions of pleasure—while also indicating that an element of each mode of exchange es- capes cognition. Taking pleasure in gazing at a carved piece of stone, Sarraute suggests, is a sociologically pragmatic act as well as a (partially) opaque corpo- real phenomenon. In this regard, enjoying a work of art is not unlike "getting" and laughing at a joke. Both (adolescent) laughter and (adult) aesthetic appre- ciation function to bind members of a particular group while alienating out- siders. Although the men imagine their ritual to be serious and sophisticated, they are incapable of defending it from the noise that floats through the walls: "it pierces through the closed door, it insinuates itself. . . ."[47]

Do You Hear Them?, like *It's Beautiful* and *The Golden Fruits*, is explicitly about the peril of making declarations of aesthetic appreciation. As in *It's Beautiful*, such declarations do not quite work as they should. Here is the man's (implicitly unspoken) response to his neighbor's statement, "It's beauti- ful, don't you think?" ("C'est bien beau, ça, vous ne trouvez pas?"):

Don't push me, this is a provocation, I'm only doing it, as you know, be- cause I'm forced to, coerced, my voice, you hear it, is flat, feeble, my lips open with difficulty to repeat after you, because you insist: Yes, it's beautiful. . . .

Ne me poussez pas, c'est de la provocation, je ne le fais, vous le savez, que forcé par vous, contraint, ma voix, vous l'entendez, est atone, toute molle, mes lèvres s'entrouvent avec difficulté pour répéter après vous, puisque vous l'exigez: Oui, c'est beau. . . .[48]

As in the radio play, points of ellipsis, little visual and auditory stains in the text, index the noisiness of the performative, drawing our attention to an embarrassed and embarrassing gap in the verbal exchange. The speech act that should function as a symbolic investment, legitimizing or distinguishing both the statuette and the speaker, comes out atonal, flabby, and feeble. The speaker describes himself as an actor who continues acting after all the spectators have left the theatre,[49] and we might interpret the awkward infelicity of such acts of aesthetic judgment as moments in which Sarraute is indexing the inappropriateness of residual bourgeois standards of evaluation in the context of the late twentieth century. On the one hand, what's at stake in this novel is a post-1968 generational conflict, in which the performative power of the evaluative statement is continuously interrupted and undermined by that irrepressible, youthful laughter from upstairs. On the other hand, it may be that artwork in modernity—defined against any hierarchy of genre conjoining particular representational techniques and subject matter with a given audience—*always* embarrasses the judgments intended to hold it in place. As the artwork increasingly flaunts its subversion of pre-established criteria, the difficulty of responding "appropriately" becomes more acute. Sarraute takes as her subject matter precisely this mismatch between the reader or spectator's perceptual and behavioral habits, and the kind of attention that the modern artwork demands: an intensified attention to nothing special. Embarrassment in Sarraute's novels is not so much a punctual event (as it is, for example, in Balzac's *Lost Illusions* when Lucien fails to observe established rules of conduct and wears the wrong outfit to the opera), but a condition—a sort of low-grade, constant buzz or hum of discomfiture that suffuses the entire texture of the novel, fluctuating in intensity.

If an "enchanted" experience of culture is one that forgets the acquisition of the code, Sarraute withholds the privilege of such forgetfulness from her characters and readers alike. In reading her, we are constantly made aware of the time and affective labor implicit in seemingly effortless acts of aesthetic appreciation. "Distinction," after all, is essentially a performance of legitimacy that convinces "like a successful bluff"; as in gambling, the more practiced one is at playing the game, the more natural it looks. Profiting maximally from the field of cultural goods requires a "sense of the right moment to invest or disinvest."[50] In Sarraute, characters fumble their hands, bet too soon or too late, and reveal how hard they are trying instead of impressing others with the attitude of indifferent detachment that is the ultimate sign of good taste.

Inestimable Objects

Sarraute is alert to the instability of aesthetic signs: objects designated as distinctive, rare, or original are always vulnerable in her novels to wild highs and lows of estimation. *The Planetarium* opens with an interior-decorating fantasy turned nightmare: a woman returns home in anticipation of the "exquisite harmony" that awaits her in her newly redecorated kitchen. She expects to find "an ensemble of perfect taste, sober, elegant."[51] But instead, she is horrified to discover that the half-finished décor suggests a "poor, facile harmony, already seen everywhere." The colors are crude, the cathedral-inspired round door looks fake and vulgar—"a real bathroom door"—and the workmen have tracked dirt onto the floors and left stains on the walls. "They haven't finished, it's all in disarray, sawdust on the ground, the toolbox is open, tools scattered across the floor. . ." ("ils n'ont pas fini, il y a du désordre partout, de la sciure de bois par terre, la boîte à outils est ouverte, des outils sont épars sur le parquet. . .").[52] Inverting an image of rare, effortless taste into its messy negative, Sarraute reveals the affective and material labor required to construct the fantasy of authentic distinction.

This half-finished, work-stained kitchen illustrates Sarraute's relation to distinction in general: she relentlessly exposes the scaffolding (or pragmatic foundations) subtending the ideal of impeccable taste. Nonetheless, Sarraute is not primarily concerned with ideological demystification. Her objective is not simply to strip the aura from objects socially designated as art, but to explore the multiple (and often dissonant) tones that surround such objects during moments of cultural crisis, as historically specific practices of appreciation cease to function as they once did. Works of art in modernity, Sarraute suggests, do not exist outside of these circuits of captivation and degradation, esteem and oblivion. Her novels examine the peculiarly indeterminate status of art at mid-century, inviting us to take stock of what distinction-producing objects look (and feel) like from different angles and over time, as their symbolic value rises, plummets, rebounds, wavers. At the end of *The Planetarium*, the oval door appears to float "in limbo," suspended between opposing categories of taste. Is it ancient and original, or tacky and touristic? ("Vieille porte massive de couvent ou porte de pavillon tocard?")[53] Like Ponge's laborious, insistently incomplete prose poetry, Sarraute's fictional space appears half-built, a messy work station in which no one can fully invest belief.

In *In Search of Lost Time*, Proust also investigates circuits of symbolic value and foregrounds the dissonance between material and symbolic appropriation. Hence the Duc and Duchesse de Guermantes hang Elstir's paintings in their home, but disparage them as ordinary and unrefined, while the narrator is so awed by the works that he holds up a dinner party for nearly an hour admiring them. Sarraute explores scenarios of distinction-seeking that are much less clearly demarcated: she cuts out any meta-fictional discourse that would establish the definitive value of the artwork in question, and drops us into a discordant echo chamber of talk. Alternately precious and commonplace, the artwork itself vacillates between appearing semiotically blank and excessively codified. In Proust, the reader is led to side with the narrator's appreciation of Elstir's originality, while dismissing the Duc's vulgar appraisal.[54] In Sarraute, works of art are symbolically inappropriable, impossible to appraise with confidence. They are interesting precisely because they are only partially capturable within any given institutional frame, and are never severed from the world of ordinary appetites and everyday perceptions.

Bourdieu argues that when social agents appropriate symbolic capital through acts of aesthetic evaluation, they are (unconsciously) activating an incorporated "network of oppositions": coarse versus refined, light versus heavy, spiritual versus material, free versus forced, and so on.[55] What's odd in Sarraute is that art objects don't stay put in any category of value. Instead, they tend to oscillate from one end of the spectrum to the other, appearing incomparable one moment and unremarkable the next. Sarraute exploits this ambivalence inherent to the aesthetic sign. In her novels, art objects are strangely volatile, inappropriate everywhere and always slipping out of the categories that make them culturally legible and profitable.

Do You Hear Them? offers the most striking example of this volatility. The entire novel is built around an unqualifiable object, an inherited pre-Columbian statuette of uncertain value. The object's owner attempts simultaneously to convince himself of his property's worth, and to ensure its (and hence his own) future legitimacy by shaming his children into adopting the pose of proper respect. This drama of bourgeois collection allegorizes the vicissitudes of aesthetic distinction more generally. After all, the practice of establishing, maintaining, and passing on a private museum is a means of signaling one's capacity to accumulate the signs and symbols of power.[56] In Sarraute's novel, the statuette may have originally been brought back from a trip by the owner's father.[57] As such, it suggests the fantasy of a "found" treasure, and hence, potentially signifies an even greater capacity for sublimation on the part of its owner than if it had been plucked from a circuit of pre-approved aesthetic objects (as the Guermantes pick up Elstir's *Bunch of Asparagus*, following Swann's advice). Yet, looted from a culture about which its owner knows nothing, silently bearing a history of which its French keepers are ignorant, the statuette proves to be unwieldy as a signifier of bourgeois cultural capital.

Moreover, the pre-Columbian artifact is an important object in the history of the French avant-garde: its cachet is indissociable from its prior appropriation by ethnographic surrealism.[58] For Bataille, such an object is valuable precisely by virtue of its association with his conception of sacred violence and the "low." In his ethnographic journal, *Documents*, Bataille incorporates photographs of pre-Columbian artifacts along with images of slaughterhouses and big toes. The appeal of the pre-Columbian artifact in 1930 was that it appeared so foreign to bourgeois practices of aesthetic appreciation. Hence, the problem that Sarraute's collector faces (circa 1970) is not simply how to derive cultural capital from an object that was not originally made to sit on a coffee table and reflect its proprietor's good taste, but how to turn a symbol of anti-bourgeois contestation into the centerpiece of a private family collection. *Do You Hear Them?* is not only about the difficulty of aestheticizing a looted sculpture; it is about the perils of bourgeoisifying an object already appropriated by the avant-garde. Throughout the novel, the statuette generates more embarrassment than self-congratulatory pleasure. Suspended between the neighbor's pious esteem ("truly, you have a superb piece here") and the children's mocking laughter, sometimes the statuette appears as a precious object to which words cannot adhere: "it resembles nothing."[59] At other times, however, the piece looks strikingly unsophisticated: a "dirty beast" ("sale bête") made out of lumpy, dirty gray, badly cut stone ("pierre grumeleuse, d'un gris sale, grossièrement taillée").[60]

The statuette hovers between aesthetic and semiotic possibilities. It is appropriable materially, and (sometimes) symbolically, but never both at once. This poses a problem for its owner, as the bourgeois cultivation of personal distinction requires not simply possessing objects of "quality," but fully mastering the discourse surrounding them—a mastery which, according to Bourdieu, "cannot be acquired in haste or by proxy."[61] It is not enough simply to display a rarity in one's house; the bourgeois collector or connoisseur must be able to demonstrate his symbolic appropriation of the object as well. This means mastering the "technical, archaic, and esoteric" discourse that separates "informed" from "mere passive consumption."[62] As Bourdieu puts it, "the objects endowed with the greatest distinctive power are those which most clearly attest the quality of the appropriation, and therefore the quality of their owner."[63] Made for unknown purposes, acquired by someone else, indexing a history of colonial appropriation as well as one of avant-garde contestation, placed on the table by a neighbor, the statuette is not an object of "quality," but a thing of unqualifiable value, and a dubious signifier of bourgeois luxury and charisma.

Do You Hear Them? is a novel that explores the sociology of taste in late modernity. It also dramatizes a crisis in the concept of "culture" in 1960s–1970s France. The instability of aesthetic value in this text is not simply a private problem for the bourgeois collector. Rather, the collector's anxious attempt to compel his children to share in his aesthetic pleasure can be read as an allegory of the French state's promotion of art in the name of the *patrimoine.* Indeed, the statuette's owner sometimes imagines official state agents (a school director, a social worker) entering the family home in order to arbitrate the disagreement between him and his children.

Sarraute wrote *Do You Hear Them?* following a decade of intense state appropriation of culture in France. From 1959 to 1969, André Malraux presided over the first Ministry of Cultural Affairs (*Ministère des Affaires culturelles*). The Ministry used art as a tool of diplomacy, sending France's museum treasures out on loan so that the French cultural heritage could be admired by all.[64] It also sought to instrumentalize art as a medium of cultural cohesion during an era of unprecedented capitalist modernization, as a corrective to the lure of mass media and entertainment largely imported from the United States. A July 1959 decree stated that the Ministry would strive to "render the works of humanity, and especially of France, accessible to the greatest possible number of French citizens, ensure the widest audience for our cultural patrimony, and promote the creation of both the works of art and the spirit that enrich that heritage" ("rendre accessibles les oeuvres capitales de l'humanité, et d'abord de la France, au plus grand nombre possible de Français, assurer la plus vaste audience à notre patrimoine culturel, et favoriser la création des oeuvres de l'art et de l'esprit qui l'enrichissent").[65] As Herman Lebovics puts it, Malraux wanted to make art into a "new magical bond"—one that could "replace the lost community and the dissipated aura of religious rites" at a time when American words and images were rapidly circulating through France.[66] Saddling "Art" with the sacred task of preserving French national unity and international prestige during a moment of perceived "cultural drift," the Ministry fundamentally transformed the relation of the French state to the aesthetic sphere.[67]

Between 1961 and 1968, Malraux oversaw the creation of eight "Houses of Culture" ("Maisons de la culture") in major provincial towns. These institutions were imagined as "cathedrals to culture" in which, in the words of Malraux's *directeur de cabinet*, Antoine Bernard, the greatest possible number would be able to experience high art in conditions favorable to "communion" with the works.[68] According to the official dogma, "cultural needs" are universal, and the Ministry could democratize high-level aesthetic experience simply through geographical redistribution of consecrated works.[69] The idea was that the uninitiated would be transformed by such proximity to art. As Malraux put it: "any sixteen year-old child, no matter how poor, should be able to have true contact with his national patrimony and with the glory of the spirit of humanity" ("il faut que [. . .] n'importe quel enfant de seize ans, si pauvre soit-il, puisse avoir un véritable contact avec son patrimoine national et avec la gloire de l'esprit de l'humanité").[70] According to Michel Beaujour, the democratization of high-level aesthetic experience via the *Maisons de la culture* was intended to "raise ordinary people above their ordinary consciousness."[71]

Art is no laughing matter for Malraux, and the father in *Do You Hear Them?* approaches his collector's piece with a similar attitude of religious gravity. His children, however, dismiss such "moribund" cultural expressions, preferring mass cultural entertainment—jukeboxes, magazine covers, foosball—and they view their father's reverence for the statuette with hilarity. When given the opportunity to engage with the object, they work to squash its status as signifier of aesthetic value. First they try to make it indistinguishable from any other consumable commodity (they decorate it with cookie box paper), and later reduce it to sheer use value (they use it as an ashtray stand). I will return to both of these examples below.

The father's ambivalent attachment to the object occasionally gives way to unadulterated pleasure, but only when he can envision the statuette framed within the safe, neutral haven of the national museum. In the following passage, he briefly enjoys the statuette as a "pure" aesthetic object:

> Free . . . all cords . . . all moorings cut . . . alone . . . pure . . . through great empty rooms, over old shining floors . . . toward that, just that, in the corner over there, near the window . . . placed there, offered . . . no, not offered, it doesn't offer itself up, it solicits nothing. That's precisely its force. Nothing. From anyone. It's sufficient in itself. It's there. Having come from who knows where. Torn from who knows what. Calmly declining everything that comes to stick to it: all images, all words.

> Libre . . . tout cordon . . . toutes amarres coupées . . . seul . . . pur . . . à travers les grandes salles vides, sur les vieux parquets luisants . . . vers cela, juste cela, dans le coin là-bas, près d'une fenêtre . . . posé là, offert . . . non, pas offert, cela ne s'offre pas, cela ne sollicite rien. C'est là sa force. Rien. De personne. Cela se suffit à soi-même. C'est là. Venu on ne sait d'où. Arraché on ne sait à quoi. Repoussant calmement tout ce qui vient se coller à cela: toutes les images, tous les mots.[72]

The perceiver jubilates in the feeling of freedom from circumstance that the experience of pure taste affords. Liberated from all function and seemingly without history or even qualifiable identity, the statuette conforms to Kant's criteria for disinterested aesthetic beauty. It is unqualifiable, without content, beyond compare. And yet even this rare occasion of euphoria in Sarraute is marred by a slight dissonance. The snag in the description—"no, not offered"—reminds us that the "yes" of aesthetic appreciation requires a crucial negation: a "no" to all traces of time, labor, and desire.

Sarraute also makes it clear that this fantasy of disinterested pleasure requires a particular institutional frame in order to work: only when the statuette's owner imagines abdicating his status as personal collector is he able to fully aestheticize his property. The art object can be enjoyed when it is decontextualized (in imagination), severed from the bourgeois home, and deposited in the national museum. Only once it is authenticated and bureaucratized in the state-sanctioned space of the Louvre, subjected to the rational classification of experts, does the statuette appear to gleam "freely."

In *In Search of Lost Time*, Proust disrupts privileged hierarchies of value by presenting Bergotte's museum epiphany as surprisingly ordinary, at once overwhelming and underwhelming, bound up in the everyday exigencies of digestion and consumption. Sarraute takes a step beyond Proust's vulgarization of museum space by presenting her character's "disinterested" aesthetic experience as laboriously constructed. Actively projecting the decontextualizing concept of the museum around the statuette, the father struggles to keep adjectives from sticking to the object:

> There, from out of the stone creature it spills, it spreads . . . a movement? No. A movement disturbs, frightens. It's there. It's always been there. A radiance? A halo? An aura? The hideous words touch it for an instant and are immediately cast off. And he who is there . . . no, not he, he is this infinite . . . which that fills . . . no, not "infinite," not "fills," not "that." Even "that" is wrong . . . it's already too much. Nothing. Not a word.

> Là, de la bête de pierre cela se dégage, cela s'épand . . . Un mouvement? Non. Un mouvement ça dérange. Ça fait peur. C'est là. C'était là depuis toujours. Un rayonnement? Un halo? Une aura? Les mots hideux touchent cela un instant et sont rejetés aussitôt. Et lui qui est là . . . non, pas lui, il est cet infini . . . que cela emplit . . . non, pas "infini," pas "emplit," pas "cela." Même "cela," il ne faut pas . . . c'est déjà trop. Rien. Aucun mot.[73]

As this passage demonstrates, enjoying an object "without interest" is hard work for Sarraute's characters. In her fictional world, this sort of laborious interior monologue is the only form that aesthetic pleasure can take.

It is not long before the precious statuette is subject to a market crash in value, and it appears unworthy of display, deserving of being thrown in the basement with all the other junk:

> What's that rough stone statuette doing here, it's dirty gray, a squat, clumsy beast, with a crushed muzzle, with ears like wheels, like tires . . . it doesn't belong on this coffee table. . . . Nor over there, on the chimney where it replaced . . . we had to put something there . . . the marble grandfather clock with its broken pendulum. . . . It should have stayed in the basement among the broken armchairs, the old trunks, the old tubs, the basins and pitchers of chipped enamel. . . .

> Que fait ici cette statuette en pierre rugueuse, d'un gris sale, celle d'une bête pataude, courtaude, au mufle écrasé, aux oreilles pareilles à des roues, à des pneus . . . elle n'est pas à sa place sur cette table basse. . . . Ni là-bas, sur

la cheminée ou elle a remplacé . . . il fallait bien y mettre quelque chose . . .
la pendule de marbre au balancier cassé. . . . . Elle aurait dû rester à la cave
parmi les fauteuils crevés, les vieilles malles, les vieux pots, les cuvettes et
brocs d'émail ébréché. . . .[74]

As the precious object shifts from "there" ("là-bas") to "here" ("ici"), it becomes ordinary, its crushed muzzle suggesting all sorts of broken-down,
time-worn things: ripped chairs, old trunks, chipped enamel basins. And yet
when Sarraute topples the statuette from its sanctified museum corner to the
dank, junk-filled cellar, she is simply shifting our perspective on the strange
volatility of the object culturally designated as "art." If the first passage presents the little statue as timeless, the second description plays with this fantasy,
noting that the statue was placed on the mantle in order to replace a broken
clock. If the first passage presents the statuette as perfectly, self-sufficiently
functionless, the second passage also depicts it as functionless—but in the
manner of a useless, busted chair or broken container. And while the first description insists on the object's lack of proper or designatable identity, noting
that no adjective could possibly adhere to it, the second description foregrounds a different sort of unqualifiability, describing the object as a con-
glomeration of borrowed and imprecise attributes, which make it comparable
to anything at all.

Later in the novel, the father bequests (or imagines bequesting) the statuette to his children. When he visits (or imagines visiting) their room, he discovers that they have—intentionally or absent-mindedly, we cannot know
which—turned their precious inheritance into an ashtray. Flanked on one
side by a pile of letters and postcards, the statuette now bears an odd protu-
berance on its back: "it's a giant oyster shell . . . full probably to the brim with
cigarette butts, with ashes, and the creature now serves as its support . . ."
("c'est une coquille d'huître géante . . . pleine probablement jusqu'aux bords
de mégots, de cendre, et la bête lui sert maintenant de support . . .").[75] Precisely by forgetting about the object and abandoning it to its minor role as the
support for a container of worthless residue, the children succeed in liberat-
ing it from the obligation to signify its owner's good taste.

This is not the end of the story, though: severed from the economy of distinction and reduced to sheer use value, the statuette will reenter the circuit of
symbolic exchange once again. At the end of the novel, we are again invited to
imagine it wrenched from the sphere of bourgeois domestic propriety. This
time, however, it is inculcated into an economy of ascetic aristocratism—
authenticated and labeled at the Louvre. When one of the children, now grown
up, passes by the statuette on the way toward the museum exit with out-of-
town friends, "they approach and stand still before it in reverent silence." The
friends then "lean over and respectfully read the inscription."[76] Instead of
shining freely in its singularity as it does in the first museum fantasy, now the
object is simply another piece in the national collection. The museum is

likened to the Panthéon or the Père Lachaise cemetery—a graveyard for art, a neutral resting place for officially sanctioned emblems of the state.

Yet because all of these displacements are presented as possibly paranoid projections, rather than diegetically "real" events, we are not sure at the end if the statuette has been appropriated definitively into a museum collection, or if the squat little beast has been sitting on the coffee table all along. Like the round door in *The Planetarium*, it seems to hover between categories and classifications. Ancient convent door or tacky villa? "Superb piece" or decorative ashtray? We will never be able to tell. In the universe of Bourdieu's *Distinction*, objects are essentially legible signs: their legitimacy is recognizable even for those social players ill-disposed to invest in them. Sarraute, by contrast, organizes her fictions around dubiously legitimate objects, things impossible to evaluate because they appear alternately distinguished and unrefined. Her novels invite us to linger at the interstice between classifiable type, and to explore the messy process by which singular things are typified, assimilated into circuits of exchange.

Thus far, I have discussed ways in which Sarraute represents the spoiling of distinction. In the final section of this chapter, I want to consider Sarraute's own cultivation of an aesthetics of bad taste. My wager is that throughout her oeuvre, Sarraute invites us to pay special attention to a particularly diminutive or docile brand of disgust. This is not the intense abjection found in Sartre or Bataille, but a barely tolerable modality of aversion. If Sartrean "nausea" is a response to the sheer contingency of things, Sarraute's saccharine tonality is the atmosphere surrounding the semi-commodified, quasi-consumable aesthetic object in late modernity.

Too Sweet

> It's comforting to use these partitions in order to put everything back
> in place, to separate and stow it all away in compartments, properly-
> labeled drawers. . . . You only have to open them, it's there, known,
> classified. One can amuse oneself by taking a bit from here and a bit
> from there, making subtle mixtures for those with delicate tastes:
> adding tenderness to rancor, vindictiveness to generosity . . . exquisite
> compositions. . . .
> —SARRAUTE, *FOOLS SAY*

> *Douceâtre*: that which verges on sweetness, which is of a bland, insipid
> sweetness.
> —*TLFI*

In many ways, as this chapter has demonstrated, Sarraute's mid-century novels explore the same social universe that Bourdieu's *Distinction* so dramatically charts out. In Bourdieu's mapping, the market in cultural goods can be clearly divided up, with sugary, easily palatable products on one side and more bitter or refined fare on the other: impressionism versus abstraction; the *Blue Danube* versus Ravel's *Concerto for Left Hand*. While Bourdieu highlights the symbolic mastery of the dominant class, which is adept at manipulating this market, Sarraute foregrounds instances of failed appropriation, when artworks cannot be appraised and transformed into symbolic assets. Sarraute's characters approach artworks with words like "original," "authentic," and "masterpiece." But the works themselves, made up of platitudes and used-up forms, cannot sustain this type of attention. In an era in which practically anything proves to be museum-worthy—from a bicycle wheel to a Brillo box or a can of (fake) "artist's shit"—and in which an increasingly sophisticated advertising industry aestheticizes every last household product and device, art objects become blanker than ever—both more and less accessible as durable goods or distinctive signs. Sarraute shows us that as art itself veers toward pastiche, growing more ambiguously intimate with ordinary, consumable things, it becomes increasingly unwieldy as a source of social profit.

Sarraute's novels demonstrate that those who seek distinction by flaunting their mastery of symbolic forms are haunted by the commodity-character of the artwork in modernity. This platitudinous, already-digested quality is a problem for her characters: they cannot quite figure out how to handle the artwork's ambiguous forms or unravel its dubious ironies. *The Golden Fruits* is instructional in this regard because it is about the problem of deriving cultural capital from a pastiche. Characters in this novel argue about whether another novel titled *The Golden Fruits* is an intentional or accidental copy: does it offer "concentrate of platitude" ("du concentré de platitude"), or mere "platitude in the raw" ("platitude à l'état naturel")?[77] The novel is at first described as a supreme work of art: "a jewel," a "perfect little thing," a "pure masterpiece." Nothing breaks its smooth, shiny surface—no crack or fissure through which a "foreign body" might enter. This is "Beauty" incarnate.[78] Later, however, the same text is dismissed as "weak and flabby," like mush for toothless people, and it is disparaged as a bad copy, like a twig or stone masquerading as real food at a child's tea-party, and which adults, out of pity and embarrassment, must smack their lips around and exclaim "oh isn't that good" ("oh que c'est donc bon").[79] As this work of art falls from a position of supreme value to one of valuelessness, it also slips out of a rhetorical register of opticality into a register of orality, suggesting something that you are compelled to put in your mouth—but that you can't quite swallow. One speaker notes that the author must have intended to produce an object that would be impossible to consume: "he wanted the reader to starve to death in front of it" ("il voulai[t] que le lecteur crève de faim devant ça").[80]

In the postscript to *Distinction*, Bourdieu contends that the entire language of aesthetics is "contained in a fundamental refusal of the *facile*." "Pure taste" is purely negative in its essence, because it is based on "disgust" for all that seems "vulgar," "shallow," "cloying" ("tape-à-l'oeil"), "rose-water," "syrupy," or "sugary" ("douceâtre").[81] For Bourdieu, excessive sweetness works as a purely aversive force: it is disgusting, and disgust is constituted, as theorists from Kant to Kristeva have argued, by "the vehement rejection or exclusion of its object."[82] Sarraute, on the other hand, insists on the sticky, unclassifiable, slight grossness of the *douceâtre*, an adjective she frequently allies with objects or feelings that can neither be incorporated nor rejected, or that are just barely tolerable. By highlighting the perilous sweetness of art objects—including her own texts— Sarraute works to annul the cultural profits that we might derive from them. Unlike postmodern pastiches, such as Warhol's soup cans and coke bottles, which, according to Jameson, are offered up for our effortless consumption as depthless, emotionless, and ahistorical commodities, Sarraute's pastiches present a distinctly unpalatable flavor.[83] Sarraute might not want us to "starve to death" while we read her, but she does want to leave a bad taste in our mouths.

The poet André du Bouchet writes in a 1949 letter to Sarraute that he is struck by her "ad nauseum" repetition of the word "douceâtre."[84] Indeed, look up "douceâtre" in the dictionary, and you find a quotation by Sarraute.[85] "Douceâtre" implies not a strong modality of disgust, but a weak one, and is associated with the feminine, the diminutive, the infantile. Hence the *Trésor de la langue française* cites Sainte-Beuve's declaration that after the age of creation and fecund invention, men turn to the "tasteless" and the "douceâtre," and Barrès's lament that "France is moving imperceptibly toward a *douceâtre*, exhausted, feminine civilization, which is distancing it progressively from warrior virility." There is something small, minor, and underwhelming about the *douceâtre*. We see this in the Goncourt brothers' description of an orator holding a "*douceâtre* word" in his mouth for a moment, as if it were a "delicious candy." This minor quality is also evident in a passage from Sartre's *Nausea*: in a miniature version of the intense existential nausea he will later experience, Roquintin experiences "a sort of *douceâtre* disgust" upon holding a pebble at the beach. Finally, "douceâtre" suggests a murky *quasi* quality: it qualifies what is neither *this* nor *that*. "Douceâtre" is listed as a synonym of "doucereux" (syrupy, sugary, sweetish), which in turn is listed as a "(quasi-) antonym" of "authoritarian, brutal, caustic." This term is difficult to define because it signifies a not-quite-sweet quality, a quality of touching on or edging toward sweetness ("qui tire sur le doux"). Throughout Sarraute's work, the *douceâtre* is closely linked to the concept of "fadeur"—not any particular taste, but a monotonous insipidity, a strangely nauseating lack of identifiable taste or character.

As it explicitly lacks a precise, delineated object, we might understand the *douceâtre* as a feeling-tone or mood, rather than a specifiable feeling. "Mood" is essentially an affect without "explicit occasion or object" or a feeling that seems to be searching for its appropriate object.[86] Annette Baier notes that if emotions generally have an object—they are about *something*—moods, "if they are about anything," are about "nearly everything."[87] Suggesting a minor, non-cathartic form of disgust, allied with the infantile, the feminine, the cutesy, the sticky, the diminutive, and the commercial, the *douceâtre* is the dominant mood of Sarraute's fiction, which often has recourse to nursery rhyme rhythms and creepily sweet fairy tale tropes.

An air of indigestible sweetness leaves its trace throughout Sarraute's first published text, *Tropisms*, which opens with a scene in which sticky clusters of shoppers stand transfixed in front of a shop-window doll whose eyes and teeth turn on and off at regular intervals. *Tropisms*, first published in 1939, is the only one of Sarraute's texts exclusively devoted to the reproduction of *atmosphere:* the volume presents neither plot nor character. Instead, it is full of images suggesting a "menacing sweetness": lunching ladies chirp and chitter, bodies squirm and fidget in domestic spaces, sticky little hands are available to be squeezed and adorable little cheeks are offered to be kissed or "devoured." The text returns again and again to figures of threatening docility or childishness. Objects and bodies are eerily docile, excessively obedient: hands are grabbed, fondled, kneaded; children are held, "absorbed," or even gobbled up "to the last crumb."

Indeed, the book presents itself as at once hyper-consumable and unconsumable: a slim, diminutive object, just over one hundred pages, comprised of prose fragments, some only a single page long. Above all, these textual bits are meditations on triviality. In a letter rejecting the volume for publication, Jean Paulhan notes the work's "curious subtlety."[88] Subtlety—suggesting at once tenuity, delicacy, abstruseness, dexterity, and cunning—is an apt descriptor for this peculiar text, comprising two dozen pieces that turn around states and spaces of the minute, marginal, and disempowered: childhood, old age, shopping, domesticity, gossip.

Tropisms immediately presents the conjunction of shopping and aesthetic absorption. The opening fragment's crowd of window-shoppers is described as an oozing mass, an immobilized swelling or congestion (an "engorgement"). These spellbound consumers remain glued to the window-front doll before them, "offered up," as Sarraute puts it. While Sarraute's surrealist contemporaries liked to represent mannequins as violently reified and fragmented bodies, here the storefront mechanical doll is not horrifying but just vaguely disquieting, its semi-animated face anticipating the various fidgeting, squirming bodies that populate the volume.

In another passage, Sarraute describes a group of characters who live "the life of women": shopping, gossiping about marriages, worrying about whether a certain gray goes with a certain blue. Sarraute depicts the women as at once "voracious" and "delicate," and cites them repeating: "what he needs is a housewife . . . housewife . . . housewife. . . ."[89] This echoed cliché emblematizes

Sarraute's particularly domestic avant-garde poetics. Interested, precisely, in the language of a ladies' tea, Sarraute stretches, pulls, and twists the platitudes of an everyday scene of shopping. Just as the women themselves "roll" the impoverished matter of their own lives into a "little gray pellet" ("une petite boulette grise"), Sarraute kneads her material into something less than a recognizable drama. There is no catharsis here, no transgression; only these little "bits," "figurines," and "pebbles" ("boulettes," "fèves," "galets").

In a tropism that reflects especially on the project of the volume as a whole, an anonymous "she" would like to thrust commonplace, personality-less clichés away from her, but they stick around so aimiably: "they hung around her calmly, they smiled at her, pleasant, but dignified, very proper, they had worked all week long." These dated repetitions of Balzac and Flaubert are so worn down from use that they have become ungraspable: "they had so often been observed, depicted, described, been so sucked on, that they had become all smooth like pebbles, all polished, without a nick, without a hold" ("ils avaient été tant regardés, dépeints, décrits, tant sucés qu'ils en étaient devenus tout lisses comme des galets, tout polis, sans une entaille, sans une prise"). Sarraute cultivates not a subversive, but a sweet aesthetics—a sort of cookies-and-milk avant-garde, one that presents itself as "very good" ("bien sage").[90]

A little too well-behaved, perhaps—too diminutive, too affirmative. The very first tropism that Sarraute wrote (which appears in the 1957 Minuit edition as the ninth) presents a portrait of domestic anxiety, of sweetness and docility so excessive that it becomes menacing:

> She was crouched on a corner of the armchair, squirming, neck strained, eyes bulging: "Yes, yes, yes, yes," she was saying, and she approved each part of the phrase with a shake of her head. She was frightening, sweet and flat, all smooth, and only her eyes stuck out. There was something eerie and disquieting about her and her tenderness was menacing.

> Elle était accroupie sur un coin du fauteuil, se tortillait, le cou tendu, les yeux protubérant: "Oui, oui, oui, oui," disait-elle, et elle approuvait chaque membre de phrase d'un branlement de la tête. Elle était effrayante, douce et plate, toute lisse, et seuls ses yeux étaient protubérants. Elle avait quelque chose d'angoissant, d'inquiétant et sa douceur était menaçante.[91]

Throughout *Tropisms* bodies fold, twist, and squirm, as if trying to take up less space. Sarraute's language, too, twists and squirms; the text is largely made of accumulative, anaphoric syntax that moves like the body in fragment 2: "shuffling, shuffling, always in the same place, turning around and around."[92] Sarraute is interested here in creating a literary language that could approximate the restrained force and repetition of skin peeling, scratching, or turning in insomnia. Phrases backtrack and repeat, generating a nursery rhyme rhythm for Sarraute's characteristically sweet, homey brand of anxiety. *Tropisms* tends to pile up near-synonyms, amassing lists of only slightly differentiated words or phrases. Repetition of muted, gentle oxymorons exposes the pliancy of words: "desperate satisfaction"; "strange tranquility"; "menacing sweetness"; "slight worry full of joy."[93] Language envelops us as it does the child dragged on a walk by his parents in fragment 17. Dense, gluey air sticks to his skin and eyes: "agglutinated," he is compelled to "absorb" his parents' words. Feeling moves through space in Sarraute's textual world: material, viscous, it filters from one room to another, clinging to people and things like "sticky drool."[94]

Like her 1930s surrealist contemporaries, Sarraute is fascinated by the figure of the doll, and her works are replete with wax statues, blinking storefront mannequins, stiff new gift dolls, and characters who resemble "big dolls that have just been assembled."[95] Sarraute's play with docility suggests an alternative to the surrealist obsession with the figure of the *femme-enfant*, however. Denis Hollier notes that the surrealists idolized "woman," but only insofar as they could simultaneously objectify her and imagine her as deadly: "they wanted her to arouse in them a fear and trembling that would amplify and sanctify the emotions of which she was both source and object."[96] If the surrealists were drawn to monstrously violent and violated feminine figures—from Caillois's praying mantis to Hans Bellmer's erotic dismembered dolls—Sarraute invites us to explore a more diminutive and subtle modality of sweetness.[97]

Sarraute particularly exploits this tone of sweet revulsion in *Childhood*. Throughout the text she mixes appealing images with repugnant ones, as when the child narrator, Natasha, submits to her mother's command to chew her food until it is "as liquid as a soup."[98] Anticipating a pleasant visit from her grandparents, the child is instead forced to inhale nasty gas and have her tonsils removed; a kindly maid wards off her own nausea by coating her hair with vinegar, thereby nauseating Natasha; small children are violently destructive, ripping apart upholstery and stuffed animals. In a particularly *douceâtre* scene, Natasha is compelled to accept a spoonful of strawberry jam with medicine (calomel) mixed into it. The jam, with its "unsavory whitish streaks" appears both delicious and revolting. (Calomel, or mercurous chloride, was commonly given to children at the turn of the century to treat constipation and for teething, before the dangerous effects of its toxicity were made known.) Here, the child is suspiciously examining the jam, which does not seem quite right:

A spoon filled with strawberry jam approaches my lips . . . I turn my head, I don't want any more . . . it has a hideous taste, I don't recognize it . . . what has happened to it? Something has been slipped into its usual good flavor . . . something repugnant is hiding there . . . it makes me sick, "I don't like it, it isn't real strawberry jam." "Yes it is, look, you see very well that it is." . . . I examine with interest the thin layer of jam spread in the saucer, the straw-berries are like the ones I know, they're only a little paler, less red or dark pink, but on them, or between them, there are unsavory whitish streaks. . . .

Une cuiller emplie de confiture de fraises s'approche de mes lèvres . . . je détourne la tête, je n'en veux plus . . . elle a un goût affreux, je ne la recon-nais pas . . . que lui est-il arrivé ? dans sa bonne saveur de toujours quelque chose s'est glissé . . . quelque chose de répugnant s'y dissimule . . . elle me fait mal au coeur, "Je ne l'aime pas, ce n'est pas de la vraie confiture de fraises. —Mais si, voyons, tu vois bien que c'en est." . . . J'examine avec beaucoup d'attention la mince couche de confiture étalée sur la soucoupe . . . les fraises sont bien comme celles que je connais, elles sont seulement un peu plus pâles, moins rouges ou rose foncé, mais il y a sur elles, entre elles, comme de louches traînées blanchâtres. . . .[99]

The narrator will henceforth associate strawberry jam with "something repug-nant, slyly introduced, hidden beneath the appearance of the delectable."[100]

Consider the difference between Sarraute's *douceâtre*—a cloying form of distaste—and the hero-ifying drama of formlessness that Kant discusses in the *Critique of the Power of Judgment*. Disgust is an important concept in Kant's third *Critique* because it is the absolute limit-point of aesthetic pleas-ure. Disgust is the only affect that threatens aesthetic representation with collapse:

There is only one kind of ugliness which cannot be represented in accord-ance with nature without destroying all aesthetical satisfaction, and conse-quently artificial beauty, viz. that which excites *disgust*. For in this singular sensation, which rests on mere imagination, the object is represented as it were obtruding itself for our enjoyment [gleichsam, als ob er sich zum Ge-nusse aufdränge] while we strive against it with all our might. And the ar-tistic representation of the object is no longer distinguished from the nature of the object itself in our sensation, and thus it is impossible that it can be regarded as beautiful.[101]

A feeling perilous to taste, disgust collapses the distinction between the arti-ficial representation of the object and its nature in our perception. Disgust's forcefulness, for Kant, undermines the necessary distance between object and imagination. Like the Kantian beautiful, the disgusting is singular and non-subsumable. But unlike the beautiful, the disgusting does not stay in place so that the subject can enjoy it disinterestedly. Rather, disgusting (non) objects "insist, obtrude, thrust themselves" upon the subject; by forcing en-joyment, disgust "can be neither beautiful, nor ugly, nor sublime, give rise neither to positive nor negative, neither to interested nor disinterested plea-sure."[102] Sarraute recasts the intensities of Kantian disgust. She is interested in a disconcertingly mild modality of distaste—"a very slight repulsion"—which leaves the subject with nothing definitive to turn *from*, nothing precise to defend against.[103]

While Kant imagines disgust as a overwhelming feeling that thrusts itself forcefully and violently upon the subject, Sarraute tones it down and mixes it up, experimenting with a weaker—just barely tolerable—form of the affect. We might think of the *douceâtre* as the quality of an object that is indigestible or unconsumable because it has already been chewed on too long. Sticky, moist, lacking flavor, the *douceâtre* has neither the existentialist pathos of Sartrean "nausea" nor the transgressive appeal of Bataille's "informe." It is too weak for that. If, according to Kant, the "disgusting" ruins aesthetic pleasure, collapsing the distance necessary for the circulation of mimesis by "insisting on our enjoyment," Sarraute's *douceâtre* does not quite insist, but rather, sticks around like a guest you can't get rid of, or a hand you must keep holding.

Just as deixis and rarified description are particularly associated with Proustian aesthetic disorientation, and analogy-heaps correspond to Ponge's "awkward," *cliché* is the form of language most closely allied with the Sarrautian *douceâtre*. Throughout her oeuvre, Sarraute explores the phenomenology of cliché. Cliché—originally a typesetter's term dating to the early nineteenth century—suggests the particularly modern notion of words worn down by overuse. Given Sarraute's interest in extra-linguistic, affective rhythms, it is not surprising that she is also preoccupied by a type of language that halts thought ("invites you not to think") or "prevents the genesis of an image" but provokes *feeling*.[104] Signifier of "unseeing blandness," cliché has no inherent content; all that separates cliché from idiom is the feeling of aggravation cliché provokes in those who identify it as such.[105] Sarraute associates cliché with gentle annoyance; a smile; a weak, moist bond; docile participation in a childish circle game; or an object held so long in one's mouth that it becomes "all smooth" ("tout lisse").

What sort of aesthetics doses itself out to the reader like an (indigestible) sweet morsel or a (slightly toxic) bite of jam? Sarraute makes us aware that reading is an act of consumption: in reading her, we are constantly compelled to accept that luscious and sickening spoonful. If, as Du Bouchet puts it, Sarraute's prose has the effect of making the reader docile, it also makes us hyper-aware of our own submission.[106]

Bourdieu shows us that aesthetic taste is inseparable from taste for food or clothes or interior design. Sarraute goes one step further, demonstrating that the sweet, doll-like passivity and malleability of the commodity taints the things that are supposed to transcend such ordinary circuits of exchange. In *Childhood*, for example, the narrator's mother is first described as an ideal aesthetic object. The mother shines as unqualifiable and incomparable:

"far from all possible comparison."[107] But when she is considered in relation to a hairdresser's mannequin, the value of her beauty comes into question. The word "beautiful," it turns out, adheres perfectly to the mannequin. Brought into proximity with this storefront commodity, "maman" falls from her pedestal, transformed into a pseudo- or sort-of mother: a "marâtre" (stepmother). This transformation of the ideal mother into a not-quite mother echoes the murky category-shifts undergone by other ideal objects in Sarraute, such as when the indescribable statuette in *Do You Hear Them?* becomes a "dirty beast," or the cathedral-inspired door imagined to signify "exquisite harmony" in *The Planetarium* suddenly resembles "a real bathroom door."

Sarraute tropes her own *douceâtre* aesthetics in a passage from *Do You Hear Them?*, in which the anonymous patriarch finds that his children have adorned his statuette with a sweet little ruff made from the type of embossed paper found in cookie boxes. Here, the statue's owner is describing his children's perverse action:

> What have they done? Like the good-for-nothings that they are, like kids that tie a saucepan to a cat's tail . . . they have made a necklace, a ruff out of waffle-paper like the kind that you find, with all due respect, at the bottom of a box of cookies, or chocolate . . . and they have put it around the neck of that statue.

> Qu'est-ce qu'ils ont fait? –Ils ont, comme les vauriens qu'ils sont, comme des gamins qui attachent une casserole à la queue d'un chat . . . ils ont fabriqué avec du papier gaufré comme celui qu'on trouve, sauf votre respect, au fond des boîtes de biscuits, de chocolat . . . un collier, une fraise qu'ils ont passé au cou de cette statue.[108]

When their father demands an explanation, the children insist that the ruff suits the statue perfectly: "it gives it a *je ne sais quoi*."[109] Although they are mocking the codes that make artwork symbolically appropriable and profitable for bourgeois collectors like their father, the children are also drawing attention to the precariously thin line between sophistication and vulgarity. In a gesture that mirrors Sarraute's own cultivation of a *douceâtre* aesthetics, by "sweetening" the statuette, the children make it less consumable within an economy of distinction. By making the *douceâtre* the feeling-tone of her work, Sarraute renders her texts critically sticky, difficult to swallow.

Taste in mid-twentieth-century France is a precarious affair. Bourdieu describes it as an internalized compass needle that points social players toward the practices and goods that suit their social status. Sarraute, by contrast, is attuned to the disorienting corporeality of taste, which she imagines, in *Do You Hear Them?*, as a round, slimy object that might have fallen out of someone's grotesquely gaping mouth: "la bouche plissée, grotesquement arrondie, il a laissé tomber ça: tout rond, glissant . . . goût."[110] For Bourdieu, the internalized principles of division that subjects exteriorize with their tastes make possible the production of a "common-sense world."[111] Sarraute's texts dramatize the perpetual dissolution (and reconstruction) of this common-sense world. She highlights the instability of its distinctions and partitions, the historical contingency of its terms, and the often dysphoric surges of feeling that accompany everyday acts of aesthetic evaluation.

The collapsed distance between art and cliché in late modernity alters the terms of the game of taste. Is *The Golden Fruits* an intentional or an unintentional copy? An example of artful platitude, or mere "platitude in the raw"? Is the pre-Columbian statuette a piece of junk that should be stashed in the basement, or is it a precious object worthy of display in the Louvre? As Sarraute demonstrates, social subjects continue to stake their worth on aesthetic investments well after any gold standard in aesthetic value has vanished. A provincial reader in *The Golden Fruits* claims that cliché "mastered" in a work of art bears absolutely no resemblance to ordinary, unintended platitude—the "impure" sort that surrounds and infiltrates you like a vague smell.[112] Yet every page of the novel—and of Sarraute's oeuvre— works to spoil this distinction.

Afterword

This book has charted twentieth-century experiments in the aesthetics of the ordinary. In French modernism, I have argued, the aesthetic is bound up in all that it allegedly eschews: quotidian commodity consumption; the labor of making and perceiving; and the vulnerable, finite body, with its unruly pleasures and displeasures, its pointing digits, its trembling tongue.

The authors featured here are keenly aware of how the hunger for distinction shapes mundane acts of seeing and feeling, and each invites us to imagine less exclusive practices of aesthetic perception and production. If Bourdieu teaches us to understand "taste" as a social orienting device rather than simply a gift of nature, Proust, Ponge, and Sarraute teach us to pay attention to the disorienting phenomenology of aesthetic perceptions, which not only solidify social hierarchies, but also unsettle established criteria and habits of classification. At the same time, these authors substitute for the distance and dignity of Kantian "disinterestedness" a variety of non-appropriative, fumbling forms of aesthetic interest. These include Proustian ravishment and the gentler, lateral drift of attention and attachment that Proust calls "dégradation"; the rodent-like laboriousness of poetic making in Ponge; and the moody swell of tropistic feeling in Sarraute. Such unrefined affective orientations give shape to innovative prose styles—a literary language punctuated by the stammers and squawks of aesthetic perceivers who cannot assimilate what they see and feel.

If a single instance of aesthetic beholding could be taken as emblematic of the book as a whole, it is the moment in Proust's "Combray" when the child narrator points pointlessly at a luminous patch of light bouncing between pond and chicken-topped roof. This occasion of wondrous whateverness illuminates an alternative landscape and a different sort of object relation—one that grants the perceiver neither special status nor superior vantage. Instead of standing at a distance, the dazzled beholder is drawn into the luminous scene.

Ponge and Sarraute explore euphoric and dysphoric variations on this vertiginous proximity, this vanishing margin between subject and object. Aesthetic experience for these authors thus involves the spoiling of various distinctions: between sensation and intellection, between speech and gesture, between the raw and the refined, and above all, between the perceiver and the perceived.

As a coda to these lines of reflection, I turn to contemporary playwright Yasmina Reza, whose hit play, *"Art,"* interrogates the shareability of aesthetic experience in late modernity. Examining the fate of the avant-garde once it falls into the clutches of the enthusiastic middle-class collector, *"Art"* asks us to train our eye not on the artwork itself, but on the play of forces that surround it. A play that has itself met with remarkable commercial and critical success, *"Art"* investigates the peculiarities of aesthetic worth: the irrationally high price fixed to works of art, and the strange mix of reverence and revulsion that such objects can provoke.[1]

The play's plot is simple: three friends—Serge, Marc, and Yvan—argue about an expensive minimalist painting that Serge has purchased. The men ultimately come to blows, and the tension is only resolved when Serge invites Marc to ruin the piece by drawing on its white surface with a marker. The play concludes with the friends scrubbing the painting clean. Like Sarraute, Reza presents aesthetic appreciation as a kind of salon warfare: her characters wield art as a weapon of symbolic domination. Yet the play is also about the affective or sensory residue that escapes such schemes, and about the complex and contradictory ways in which one might be "moved" by an inestimable object.

Like Sarraute's *Do You Hear Them?*, *"Art"* examines a particularly unmanageable and contagious form of aesthetic response: laughter. The conflict is sparked when, in the very first scene, Marc laughs at the painting—a work by the fictional artist, Antrios—and is disturbed when Serge does not laugh with him. Marc then bets Yvan that he cannot make Serge laugh either. When Serge and Yvan do subsequently laugh together, Marc is dismissive, arguing that Serge's laughter was merely a ploy to preempt and neutralize his friend's laugh: "if he laughed first, it was to defuse your laughter."[2] Laughter takes many forms in *"Art."* Solitary or collective, defensive or offensive, sign of sympathy or performance of cruelty, sounding too soon or too late, laughter is always significant in this play, but its meaning is never settled.

Serious about art, Serge meets Marc's laughter with cold silence. Audiences, however, have laughed heartily at him and in his place, and with such frequency and gusto that Reza herself complained that they were ruining the play's "subtlety" with their guffaws.[3] In London previews for *"Art,"* audiences began laughing even before any lines were spoken. As Reza frostily puts it: "the white painting showed up on stage; people howled with laughter! No doubt it was funny to see two actors contemplating a white painting for five minutes, but there's no need to howl about it."[4] In 1999, she told a reporter that she would like to see audiences laugh "at the right moments."[5] In her disdain for a response she perceives as "vulgar," Reza sounds like Serge, who resents Marc's lack of respect for his painting, and states with aggravation that he hears a "little smile [. . .] behind every word" his friend utters.[6] Even the playwright Christopher Hampton, who translated *"Art"* into English, could not help laughing in an interview when he explained his decision to set the English version of the play in Paris: "it was my view that three people having an argument about a painting could only happen in France [laughter]."[7]

No doubt a large part of what English and American audiences have found so funny about *"Art"* is the perceived "Frenchness" of its central conflict: the notion that grown men might fight so bitterly about a painting. Yet it is not only a matter of laughing at the French and their attachment to the ghosts of ancien régime distinction. There is something about the very concept of "art"—and note that the play's title keeps the word in quotation marks—that leaves us with little to say. Shaking with laughter—like pointing—is the body's way of speaking to art's strangely full emptiness, its odd mix of contentlessness and overdetermination.

At an earlier historical moment, tears might have seemed a more appropriate response to an artwork that defies explication. (In fact, the clownish Yvan does burst inappropriately into tears at the end of the play, a response he describes as an "uncontrollable, ridiculous convulsion," but he is alone in his weeping.[8]) In 1817, Stendhal experienced dizzying heart palpitations—a sensation he characterized as "a sort of ecstasy"—upon leaving the Basilica Santa Croce in Florence. This swooning response to aesthetic intensity was soon known as the "Stendhal syndrome," and it became a commonplace among middle-class art tourists of the period. According to James Elkins, if people once cried uncontrollably in the presence of art, today we feel very little when we look at paintings. "Few centuries," Elkins argues, are as "determinedly tearless as ours."[9] In explaining their art-provoked tears, Elkins notes, people tended to point to qualities of the artwork itself: it seemed "unbearably *full*," or on the contrary, "unbearably *empty*, dark, painfully vast, cold."[10] In *"Art,"* characters argue about whether the painting is merely white or multicolored, and it is described, alternately, as being scored with fine transversal lines or embellished ("tarted up," in Hampton's translation) with stripes.[11] Yet the most important contradiction here is not really within the painting itself. Instead, the play explores a tension between the perceived emptiness of the (more or less) monochromatic canvas and the excessively full discourses that surround the work—a mismatch that incites audiences to shake with laughter instead of sobs. Their hilarity indexes a non-adequation between the residual, reverential attitude with which the collector approaches the work, and the ordinariness of the object.

This object, of course, is truly ordinary, in the sense that it is no one-of-a-kind avant-garde work, but an approximately four-foot-by-five white canvas

that has been rapidly created by set designers. This is the trick at the heart of
"Art": Reza lures us into being moved not by an expensive "Antrios," but by a
prop among props. The play asks us to suspend our disbelief and imagine that
in looking at this rectangle, we are gazing at something precious and rare. The
painting appears and disappears from the set as do a number of other material things, including a bottle of Perrier, a bowl of olives, and a felt-tipped
pen. Unlike these rapidly consumed commodities, a work of art is made to
endure. Yet as a prop imitating a valuable artwork, the Antrios incites in the
audience—and among the characters—a particular affective response: a mix
of incredulity and suspended disbelief, an oscillation between irony and enchantment. In this regard, Reza is engaged in an experiment similar to the
one Proust undertook with his Lemoine Affair pastiches, Ponge with his glass
of water, and Sarraute with her Pre-Columbian statuette: she is limbing the
boundaries of distinction, testing the line between the world of commonplace
stuff and the sacred realm of art.

Yvan suggests early on (to Marc's disgust) that the painting "has something, it's not nothing," and yet we are never sure if he is right, and if so, what
exactly this "something" might be.[12] Although *"Art"* mocks the amateur collector's pretensions, it also allows the fictional Antrios to resonate with us in
some way. We might suspect, along with Marc and Yvan, that this work is
indeed nothing but "white shit"—but in the end we cannot be so sure.[13] Seemingly devoid of history or depth, object of a dermatologist's "lust," the painting is initially an emblem of bourgeois distinction.[14] It is also metonymically
linked to the other white rectangle that features in the play: Yvan's wedding
invitation. Like an invitation, the avant-garde painting is a marker of group
belonging. It classes and divides, drawing a line between the included and the
excluded—an effect that *"Art"* underscores when Yvan rants at length about
the battles that the choice of names on the front of the invitation has provoked.[15] Yet if the Antrios classifies subjects according to their capacity to
appreciate it, it cannot be entirely reduced to this function. Toward the end of
the play, it appears less as a sign of Serge's distinction than as the structural
double of the unrefined, tragicomic Yvan, the clown who cannot stop weeping: Serge and Marc accidentally strike Yvan in the head and then tend his
wound shortly before they collaborate in vandalizing and repairing the
painting.

Yvan suggests early in the play that the painting represents "the completion of a journey" ("l'accomplissement d'un cheminement"), and by the end
of *"Art,"* the Antrios has indeed undergone a metamorphosis.[16] The object is
transformed when Serge tosses Marc a felt-tipped marker, and Marc slashes
the painting's faint diagonal line into a "slope," then carefully draws in a
"little skier with a woolly hat." Like the collector's laughing children in Sarraute's *Do You Hear Them?* who prettify a sculpture with a cookie box ruff,
Marc liberates the Antrios from its own distinction. Instead of indexing its

owner's good taste, for a moment the valuable painting has all the appeal of a child's scribble. Then, in a collective act of restoration, with the aid of "cleaning products, bottles of white spirit and stain remover, rags, and sponges," the men laboriously wipe the canvas clean.[17] In the final moments of the play, the lighting narrows in on the newly washed Antrios, and Marc reprises his initial monologue. This time, though, he describes the work differently. It is no longer simply "white," but an object that bundles together the visible and the invisible:

> Under the white clouds, the snow is falling. You can't see the white clouds,
> or the snow. Or the cold, or the white glow of the earth.
> A solitary man glides downhill on his skis.
> The snow is falling.
> It falls until the man disappears back into the landscape.[18]

> Sous les nuages blancs, la neige tombe. On ne voit ni les nuages blancs, ni la
> neige. Ni la froideur et l'éclat du sol.
> Un homme seul, à skis, glisse.
> La neige tombe.
> Tombe jusqu'à ce que l'homme disparaisse et retrouve son opacité.[19]

The painting is no longer an emblem of power and sophistication decorating a dermatologist's living room. It even ceases for an instant to signify as a prop in a play. Instead, it has become a dreamscape, a site of virtual apparition and disappearance.

Blotted with Swiss soap and dried with rags, the Antrios may look as blank as ever, but it has undergone an alteration. Only when the painting has been exposed as an ordinary, precarious thing—an object that might be defaced and scrubbed clean with ox gall—can the imagination skip and drift across its surface. Arthur Danto notes the irony of Marc's "conversion" to the modernist painting, which rests on his capacity to preserve his anti-modernist theory of art as imitation.[20] Yet I would suggest that what is fascinating about this play is the way it gradually seduces its audience into seeing multiple layers of meaning and visibility in the Antrios, as if the imaginary painting were a mirror of the theatrical stage itself. Indeed, although the painting is an object of ridicule throughout the play, Danto points out that (in New York, at least), the audience responded to Marc's act of defacement by drawing in its collective breath "the way it would were someone's throat slashed on stage."[21]

"Art" therefore examines the illogic of the art market and the comic self-importance of the connoisseur, but it also invites us to contemplate the phenomenology of blankness, or featurelessness. The Antrios is the lusted-after trophy of a pretentious collector; it is "white shit"; it is a picture of a figure hidden in the snow; it is a prop; but it is also "something, not nothing": a vibrating screen, a space of potentiality. We are asked to see the painting's

empty white expanse as a zone of formation and deformation—as if the canvas were not a vacuum of meaning but a site of permutation and possibility, a space across which any sort of figure might pass, an empty stage on which anything at all might appear and vanish.

Reza's mocked and revered, spoiled and scrubbed stage-prop painting is an appropriate end point to this study of modernist beholding. My objective throughout the book has been to articulate an approach to aesthetics that is alert to the vitality and recalcitrance of the most commonplace aesthetic experiences. From a strictly sociological perspective, twentieth-century French social space can be mapped out in accordance with a set of opposing perceptual schemes: elite/mass, high/low, spiritual/material, light/heavy, free/forced, refined/crude, unique/common, brilliant/dull, and so on. And yet gauging the subtleties of everyday aesthetic attention requires us to suspend such classificatory habits of thought. The cultivation of distinguished taste may uphold principles of social inequality, but as Proust, Ponge, Sarraute, and Reza demonstrate, intensified attention to phenomenality is often incompatible with principles of refinement or decorum: in their work, those who attempt to flaunt their aesthetic competence find themselves behaving in unsophisticated ways.

In Reza and throughout the terrain that this book has charted, "art" indexes a blank spot. Nothing in particular, it is everywhere out of place. A site of inestimable value, a generator of prestige and of embarrassment, and a placeholder for residual meanings and practices, art could be anything, from a plate of asparagus to a perfumed vase of urine, and from a sculptural treasure to an ashtray stand. In French modernism, the work of art is not simply a weapon in the battle for cultural distinction. It is at once something more and something less: remarkably unremarkable, ordinary beyond compare.

{ NOTES }

Introduction

1. Cited in Eric Alliez, *L'Oeil-cerveau: nouvelles histoires de la peinture moderne* (Paris: Vrin, 2007), 150. If, as Thierry de Duve puts it, Manet's first asparagus painting, *A Bunch of Asparagus* (1880), "made room for anything whatever to be represented in painting," the second, much smaller *Asparagus* experiments even more flagrantly with the aesthetics of the ordinary, or "anything whatever." *Kant After Duchamp* (Cambridge, MA: MIT Press, 1996), 327. Underscoring the minorness of its subject, the painting is tiny: just 16.5 by 21.5 centimeters, meaning that the vegetable is rendered more or less to scale. Peter Schjendahl notes that Manet "probably ate the asparagus after he painted it." *The Hydrogen Jukebox: Selected Writings of Peter Schjendahl, 1978–1990*, ed. MaLin Wilson (Berkeley and Los Angeles: University of California Press, 1993), 189.

2. Charles Baudelaire, *Les Fleurs du Mal*, trans. Richard Howard (New York: David R. Godine, 1983), 91, 270, trans. modified.

3. Virginia Woolf, *To the Lighthouse* (New York: Harcourt Brace, 1981), 158.

4. *À la recherche du temps perdu* (Paris: Gallimard, 1989), 4: 231; *In Search of Lost Time*, trans. Scott Moncrieff and Terence Kilmartin, rev. D. J. Enright (New York: Random House, 1992), 5: 884, trans. modified. Hereafter I refer to Proust's novel either as "the *Recherche*" or as *In Search of Lost Time*.

5. Pierre Bourdieu, "Outline of a Sociological Theory of Art Perception," *International Social Science Journal* 20 (November 1968): 608. The commonness of aesthetic pleasure and displeasure poses a problem for the ideology of charisma. John Guillory notes that, to the extent that aesthetic judgment is equivalent to the recognition of cultural capital, it "must deny, as a condition of its exercise, the ubiquity of aesthetic experience." *Cultural Capital: The Problem of Literary Canon Formation* (Chicago: University of Chicago Press, 1993), 336.

6. Peter Bürger, *Theory of the Avant-Garde*, trans. Michael Shaw (Minneapolis: University of Minnesota Press, 1984), 54.

7. I borrow the phrase "high priest" from Leo Bersani, whose work on Proust—and critique of the ideology of redemption, with its concurrent rejection of everyday life—deeply inform this book. I draw in particular on Bersani's suggestion that if the *Recherche* is largely dominated by the fantasy of aesthetic redemption, it also indicates "the possibility of pursuing not an art of truth divorced from experience, but of phenomena liberated from the obsession with truth." *The Culture of Redemption* (Cambridge, MA: Harvard University Press, 1990), 16. My approach to aesthetics differs most from Bersani's in my focus on objects and speech acts, rather than subjectivity.

8. Rei Terada, *Looking Away: Phenomenality and Dissatisfaction, Kant to Adorno* (Cambridge, MA: Harvard University Press, 2009), 4, 22.

9. Terada, *Looking Away*, 8.

10. Catherine Gallagher, "George Eliot: Immanent Victorian," *Representations* 90 (Spring 2005): 61–74; Maurice Blanchot, "La parole quotidienne," in *L'Entretien infini* (Paris: Gallimard, 1969), chapter 11; Anne-Lise François, *Open Secrets: The Literature of Uncounted Experience* (Stanford, CA: Stanford University Press, 2008); Bill Brown, "The Secret Life of Things: Virginia Woolf and the Matter of Modernism," *Modernism/Modernity* 6.2 (1999): 1–28.

11. See, for example, Saikat Majumdar, *Prose of the World: Modernism and the Banality of Empire* (New York: Columbia University Press, 2013); Lisi Schoenbach, *Pragmatic Modernism* (New York: Oxford University Press, 2012); Siobhan Phillips, *The Poetics of the Everyday: Creative Repetition in Modern American Verse* (New York: Columbia University Press, 2010); Liesl Olson, *Modernism and the Ordinary* (New York: Oxford University Press, 2009); Bryony Randall, *Modernism, Daily Time, and Everyday Life* (Cambridge: Cambridge University Press, 2008); Michael Sheringham, *Everyday Life: Theories and Practices from Surrealism to the Present* (New York: Oxford University Press, 2006).

12. Olson, *Modernism and the Ordinary*, 4, original emphasis.

13. Henry James, *Literary Criticism: French Writers, other European Writers, the Prefaces to the New York Edition*, ed. Leon Edel (New York: Library of America, 1984), 543–544.

14. These series were published in album form as *Les Grands Spectacles de la nature. La Vie de Monsieur Quelconque* (Paris: Lith. Belfond & Cie, 1895) and *Les Grands Spectacles de la nature. 2ème série, La Vie de Madame Quelconque* (Paris: Lith. Belfond & Cie, 1895).

15. The *Madame Quelconque* series is comprised of ten prints, titled as follows: *1. Her childhood is happy. 2. She receives the best education. 3. She devotes herself to charitable work. 4. She has success in society. 5. She enjoys the pleasures of her honeymoon. 6. Then the joys of motherhood. 7. And the ecstasies of adultery. 8. After which she returns to the charms of family life. 9. Becomes a grandmother. 10. And dies.* The ten prints of the *Monsieur Quelconque* series are titled: *1. He is born. 2. He undergoes scholarly examinations. 3. He loves for the first time. 4. He pays his debt to the nation. 5. To the ballot boxes!!!! (Aux urnes!!!!) He fulfills his duty as a citizen. 6. He loves for the second time. 7. He is decorated and his friends organize a banquet for him. 8. Called to public service, he appears in official ceremonies. 9. He becomes sick. 10. He dies.*

16. *Camera Lucida: Reflections on Photography*, trans. Richard Howard (New York: Hill and Wang, 1982), 74; *La Chambre claire: note sur la photographie* (Paris, Gallimard: 1980), 119.

17. *Camera Lucida*, 18; *La Chambre claire*, 40–41.

18. *Camera Lucida*, 71, trans. modified; *La Chambre claire*, 115. On photography as a technology that encompasses both the lure of chance and the power of rationalization and abstraction, see Mary Ann Doane, *The Emergence of Cinematic Time: Modernity, Contingency, the Archive* (Cambridge, MA: Harvard University Press, 2002), 10–15.

19. "The Neutral might reside in this nuance (this shimmer): it denies uniqueness but recognizes the incomparable." *The Neutral: Lecture Course at the Collège de France (1977–1978)*, trans. Rosalind E. Krauss and Denis Hollier (New York: Columbia University Press, 2005), 83. "Le Neutre se tiendrait dans cette nuance (cette moire): dénégation de tout unique et cependant reconnaissance de l'incomparable." *Le Neutre: notes de cours au Collège de France, 1977–1978* (Paris: Seuil, 2002), 118.

20. Maurice Blanchot, "Everyday Speech," trans. Susan Hanson, *Yale French Studies* 73 (1987): 13; "La parole quotidienne," 357. When this essay was first published in 1962, it

appeared under the title "L'Homme de la rue." *La Nouvelle Revue française* 114 (June, 1962): 1070–1081.

21. Blanchot, "Everyday Speech," 17–18; "La parole quotidienne," 364.

22. Stéphane Mallarmé, *The Poems in Verse*, trans. Peter Manson (Oxford, OH: Miami University Press, 2013); *Collected Poems and Other Verse*, trans. E. H. Blackmore and A. M. Blackmore (New York: Oxford University Press, 2006).

23. Stéphane Mallarmé, *Oeuvres complètes* (Paris: Gallimard, 1945), 65–66.

24. Mallarmé, *The Poems in Verse*, 152.

25. Blanchot, "Everyday Speech," 13–14. "[L]insignifiant est sans vérité, sans réalité, sans secret, mais est peut-être aussi le lieu de toute signification possible." "La parole quotidienne," 357.

26. Paul Valéry, *Monsieur Teste* (Paris: Gallimard, 1946), 29.

27. "Se dit de l'un des éléments d'une classe en tant qu'il est considéré comme jouissant des mêmes propriétés que tout autre élément de cette classe." *Trésor de la Langue Française informatisé*, s.v. "quelconque," accessed March 29, 2015, http://www.cnrtl.fr/definition/quelconque. Hereafter I refer to this dictionary as *TLFi*.

28. I borrow the term "structure of feeling" from Raymond Williams, for whom it signifies the present-tense sociality of lived experience, or "practical consciousness," not yet fixed into ideological form. "Structures of Feeling," in *Marxism and Literature* (New York: Oxford University Press, 1997), 132. I discuss this term at greater length in chapter 5.

29. Gilles Deleuze, *Cinema 1: The Movement-Image*, trans. Hugh Tomlinson and Barbara Habberjam (Minneapolis: University of Minnesota Press, 1986), 109. "C'est un espace parfaitement singulier, qui a seulement perdu son homogénéité, c'est-à-dire le principe de ses rapports métriques ou la connexion de ses propres parties, si bien que les raccordements peuvent se faire d'une infinité de façons." *Cinéma 1: l'image mouvement* (Paris: Minuit, 1983), 155.

30. Giorgio Agamben, *The Coming Community*, trans. Michael Hardt (Minneapolis: University of Minnesota Press, 1993), 1–2.

31. In Nancy's phrasing, the *quelconque* is a conundrum, signifying "the indeterminateness of being [l'indéterminité d'être] in what is posited and exposed within the strict, determined concretion of a singular thing, and the indeterminateness of its singular existence." "The Heart of Things," in *The Birth to Presence*, trans. Brian Holmes and Rodney Trumble (Stanford, CA: Stanford University Press, 1993), 174; "Le Coeur des choses," in *Une pensée finie* (Paris: Galilée, 1990): 206.

32. Nancy, "The Heart of Things," 174.

33. Rancière often cites eighteenth-century thinkers—Vico, Winckelmann, Kant—when he discusses this historical shift in the organization of the perceptible. Nonetheless, he points to nineteenth-century works (Stendhal's *The Life of Henry Brulard*, for example) when seeking literary evidence of this new way of dividing up the visible world.

34. Jacques Rancière, *Le Partage du sensible: esthétique et politique* (Paris: La Fabrique, 2000), 49; "Why Emma Bovary Had to Be Killed," *Critical Inquiry* 34 (Winter 2008): 237; *Politique de la littérature* (Paris: Galilée, 2007), 64.

35. Rancière, *Le Partage du sensible*, 49, my trans.

36. Rancière, *Aesthetics and Its Discontents*, trans. Steven Corcoran (Cambridge: Polity Press, 2009), 66.

37. Rancière, *Aesthetics and Its Discontents*, 13.

38. Rancière puts it this way: "What is the wrong done by Emma to literature? The answer is that it consists in fusing literature and life and making any source of excitement equal to any other. But those features that define her temper and the allegedly 'democratic'

temper are also the features that define the poetics of her inventor and, more widely, those that define literature as a new regime of the art of writing." "Why Emma Bovary Had to Be Killed," 237–238; *Politique de la littérature*, 64.

39. Bourdieu and Rancière differ significantly in their view of the political consequences of this historical shift. In *Distinction*, especially, Bourdieu focuses on how incorporated schemes of classification work to divide and exclude, while Rancière is interested in aesthetic acts as "configurations of experience that create new modes of sense perception and induce novel forms of political subjectivity." *Politics of Aesthetics*, trans. Gabriel Rockhill (London: Continuum, 2004), 9; *Le Partage du sensible*, 7. Bourdieu attends to the consolidation and persistence of certain habits of perception; Rancière is more attuned to redistributions of such habitual ways of seeing and feeling, and critiques what he sees as the empiricism of Bourdieu's method, arguing, for example, that the sociological questionnaire ignores responses that do not fit into its predetermined schema (intellectual versus popular). As Rancière points out, the sociologist "will judge musical tastes *without having anyone hear music.*" *The Philosopher and His Poor*, trans. John Drury and Corinne Oster (Durham, NC: Duke University Press, 2004), 187, original emphasis.

40. Pierre Bourdieu, *The Rules of Art: Genesis and Structure of the Literary Field*, trans. Susan Emanuel (Stanford, CA: Stanford University Press, 1996), 230; *Les Règles de l'art: genèse et structure du champ littéraire* (Paris, Seuil: 1992), 320.

41. Bourdieu, *Rules of Art*, 63; *Règles de l'art*, 96.

42. Bourdieu, *Rules of Art*, 76; *Règles de l'art*, 115.

43. Bourdieu, *Rules of Art*, 81, 68; *Règles de l'art*, 121, 103.

44. Bourdieu, *Rules of Art*, 68; *Règles de l'art*, 103.

45. Bourdieu, *Rules of Art*, 133; *Règles de l'art*, 191. Philippe Lacoue-Labarthe also gives voice to this modern notion of art as inestimable when he declares that there is nothing "proper" to art: "art has no place of its own . . . without a stable identity, [it is] present everywhere but always elsewhere." *Poetry as Experience*, trans. Andrea Tarnowski (Stanford, CA: Stanford University Press, 1999), 44–45.

46. Antoine Hennion, "Those Things That Hold Us Together: Taste and Sociology," *Cultural Sociology* 1.1 (2007): 104.

47. Bourdieu, *Distinction: A Social Critique of the Judgment of Taste*, trans. Richard Nice (Cambridge, MA: Harvard University Press, 1984), 6. "Le goût classe, et classe celui qui classe: les sujets sociaux se distinguent par les distinctions qu'ils opèrent, entre le beau et le laid, le distingué et le vulgaire, et où s'exprime ou se traduit leur position dans les classements objectifs." *La Distinction: critique sociale du jugement* (Paris: Minuit, 1979), vi.

48. Ibid., 104.

49. Claudio Benzecry, *The Opera Fanatic: Ethnography of an Obsession* (Chicago: University of Chicago Press, 2011).

50. Marielle Macé, "Ways of Reading, Modes of Being," *New Literary History* 44 (2013): 216; *Façons de lire, manières d'être* (Paris: Gallimard, 2011), 15.

51. Kant qualifies the difference between reflecting and determining judgments as follows: "If the universal (the rule, the principle, the law) is given, then the power of judgment, which subsumes the particular under it [. . .] is determining. If, however, only the

particular is given, for which the universal is to be found, then the power of judgment is merely reflecting." *Critique of the Power of Judgment*, trans. Paul Guyer and Eric Matthews (Cambridge: Cambridge University Press, 2000), 66–67. Compelling as I find the theory of "reflecting" judgment, if the Kantian motifs in this book never develop into a dominant theme, it is because I am disloyal to Kant's crucial distinction between "taste of reflection" and "taste of sense," and between "free" and "adherent" beauty. As we see especially in chapter 2, Proust insists upon the material and sensory thickness of aesthetic experience. Even the language of aesthetic judgment in Proust is corporealized: the Proustian aesthete responds to the apparition of ordinary beauty with a stammer, a throaty cry, the caress of a bare foot.

52. On "the aesthetic" as an offshoot of "taste," see Larry Shiner, *The Invention of Art: A Cultural History* (Chicago: University of Chicago Press, 2001), 130–151.

53. Theodor Adorno, *Aesthetic Theory*, trans. Robert Hullot-Kentor (Minneapolis: University of Minnesota Press, 1997), 335.

54. Charles Baudelaire, *Les Fleurs du Mal*, 24.

55. Joseph Litvak, *Strange Gourmets: Sophistication, Theory, and the Novel* (Durham, NC: Duke University Press, 1997); Renu Bora, "Outing Texture," in *Novel Gazing: Queer Readings in Fiction*, ed. Eve Kosofsky Sedgwick (Durham, NC: Duke University Press, 1997); Eve Kosofsky Sedgwick, *Touching Feeling: Affect, Pedagogy, Performativity* (Durham, NC: Duke University Press, 2003); Judith Brown, *Glamour in Six Dimensions: Modernism and the Radiance of Form* (Ithaca, NY: Cornell University Press, 2009); Anne Anlin Cheng, "Shine: On Race, Glamour, and the Modern," *PMLA* 126.4 (October 2011); Sianne Ngai, *Ugly Feelings* (Cambridge, MA: Harvard University Press, 2005); and *Our Aesthetic Categories: Zany, Cute, Interesting* (Cambridge, MA: Harvard University Press, 2012).

56. Ponge, *Mute Objects of Expression*, trans. Lee Fahnestock (New York: Archipelago Books, 2008), 137; *Oeuvres complètes* (Paris: Gallimard, 1999), 1: 415.

57. Nathalie Sarraute, *Oeuvres complètes* (Paris: Gallimard, 1996), 844. This and all further translations of Sarraute are my own.

58. Bourdieu, *Distinction*, 466; *La Distinction*, 544.

Chapter 1

1. A 1905 legal contract refers to the "secret process" by which Lemoine allegedly "discovered (or invented)" a substance "similar in all essential respects to white and colored diamonds." Agreement signed by Henri Lemoine, Wernher Beit & Co, W. Feldenheimer, and Jocelyn Brandon, May 5, 1905, Henri Lemoine Diamond Fraud Collection, Department of Rare Books and Special Collections, Princeton University Library. For a brief synopsis of the story as the newspaper *Le Figaro* presented it, see Jean Milly, *Les Pastiches de Proust* (Paris: Colin, 1970), 16–17. See also Georges Grison's summary: "L'Affaire Lemoine," *Le Figaro*, April 15, 1909. Paul Kanfer offers a dramatic retelling of Lemoine's exploits in *The Last Empire: De Beers, Diamonds, and the World* (New York: Farrar, Straus, Giroux, 1993), 161–165.

2. Lemoine made ambitious claims about this factory's productivity. In an addendum to the May 5, 1905 contract, he promised to prove that his factory could produce "a

quantity of white or colored Diamonds equal to one third of the annual production of all the Diamond Mines of South Africa," and that "the cost of production of the Factory [would] not exceed one fourth of the cost of production of the above Mines." Henri Lemoine Diamond Fraud Collection, Department of Rare Books and Special Collections, Princeton University Library.

3. According to a January 26, 1909 article in *Le Figaro*, a De Beers executive, Sir Julius Wernher, paid 1,575,000 francs, while another investor (a London-based diamond trader named Feldenheimer) was duped into investing 96,488 francs into Lemoine's invention. Wernher states in interviews published in *Le Gaulois* and *Le Figaro* that he went to court to stop Lemoine from publicizing his contract with De Beers; the inventor had begun flaunting the contract as a means of persuading others to invest. See L. de Vignogne, "Trente minutes en taxi-auto avec Sir Julius Wernher: L'affaire des diamants," *Le Gaulois*, January 12, 1908, and the anonymously authored "La Fuite de Lemoine: M. Le Poittevin en disgrâce," *Le Figaro*, June 19, 1908.

4. Lemoine's act was so convincing that the jewelers' syndicate soon came forward with a civil suit of its own, citing the damages the engineer's claims had done to the diamond business. On January 13, 1908, the *Figaro* cites Lemoine's request to replay the spectacle: "en présence des experts, du juge, de toutes les personnes qu'on voudra, je ferai l'expérience définitive." Finally, the judge, Le Poittevin, granted Lemoine's request to be released on bail for two months; the condition was that Lemoine would make a massive synthetic diamond—larger than any on the market—and present it to the court. Lemoine took the opportunity to flee instead. Under the pseudonym Hans Leitner, Lemoine took a long jaunt through Eastern Europe and London before settling into a Paris hotel, where he was apprehended by the police in April of 1909, and eventually sentenced to six years in prison. See Louis Latzarus, "Lemoine à Paris: il est arrêté," *Le Figaro*, April 15, 1909.

5. Georges Grison, "L'Affaire des diamants: Au Parquet," *Le Figaro*, January 15, 1908.

6. "A very curious detail is that it seems the diamonds [. . .] originated from the Jagersfontein mines (State of Orange), and had been bought by M. Haan [a Parisian lapidary testifying against Lemoine] from the De Beers Company, which M. Wernher heads, as we know. This means that Lemoine presented to Wernher, as the product of his own workmanship, diamonds bought from Wernher's company with Wernher's own money." Georges Grison, "La Réponse de Lemoine," *Le Figaro*, February 26, 1908.

7. Proust continued to write Lemoine Affair pastiches throughout the summer of 1908; Milly notes that Proust promised (but never delivered) a Nietzsche pastiche to *Le Figaro* in April 1909. *Les pastiches de Proust*, 19–20. Proust republished his *Figaro* pastiches in *Pastiches et mélanges* in 1919, adding a Saint-Simon imitation to those he had previously completed; these, as well as drafted pastiches of Ruskin, Maeterlinck, and Sainte-Beuve, are now collected in *Contre Sainte-Beuve* (hereafter *CSB*) (Paris: Gallimard, 1971), 7–59, 195–205.

8. A notable exception to this rule is Sara Danius's study of Proust's attraction to modernist technologies of velocity. See her "Aesthetics of the Windshield," in *The Senses of Modernism: Technology, Perception, and Aesthetics* (Ithaca, NY: Cornell University Press, 2002), 91–146. For an overview of scholarship on mass media rhetorics within the "new modernist studies," see Douglas Mao and Rebecca L. Walkowitz, "The New Modernist Studies," *PMLA* 123, no. 3 (2008): 742–745. For details relating to Proust's journalism and the journalistic reception of his novel, see Christine M. Cano, "Journalism," in *Marcel*

Proust in Context, ed. Adam Watt (Cambridge: Cambridge University Press, 2013), 153–159.

9. See, for example, Annick Bouillaguet, *Proust lecteur de Balzac et Flaubert: l'imitation cryptée* (Paris: Honoré Champion, 2000); Michael Finn, *Proust, the Body, and Literary Form* (Cambridge: Cambridge University Press, 1999), chapter 3; Milly, *Les Pastiches de Proust*; and the notes to the Pléiade edition of the pastiches in *CSB*, 690. (The Pléiade editors make the dismally homophobic suggestion that Proust's homosexuality and his inclination toward pastiche are "concordant symptoms of a state of psychosomatic disequilibrium.") In contrast, Gérard Genette suggests that pastiche for Proust is not "an incidental practice, a purely stylistic catharsis, or a simple prenovelistic exercise. It is, along with reminiscence and metaphor, one of the privileged—and in truth, necessary—modes of his relationship to the world and to art." *Palimpsests: Literature in the Second Degree*, trans. Channa Newman and Claude Doubinsky (Lincoln: University of Nebraska Press, 1997), 120. See also Cynthia Gamble, "Finding a Voice: from Ruskin to the Pastiches," in *Marcel Proust in Context*, ed. Adam Watt (Cambridge: Cambridge University Press, 2013), 27–33; and James Austin, *Proust, Pastiche, Postmodernism, or Why Style Matters* (Lewisburg, PA: Bucknell University Press, 2013). Gamble aptly notes that pastiche enabled Proust to develop a "fearless intimate joking relationship" with the authors he took on (32), and Austin focuses on the way in which Proust turned pastiche against its normative function (as a school exercise teaching students to write properly).

10. *CSB*, 23.

11. According to the *Trésor de la Langue Française*, the oldest definition of "prestige" is "illusion produced by magic or a spell," or figuratively, "enchantment, charm, attraction exercised on the mind and the senses by manifestations of artistic or intellectual activity." *TLFi*, s.v. "prestige," accessed March 29, 2015, http://www.cnrtl.fr/definition/prestige.

12. *In Search of Lost Time*, 6: 290; *À la recherche du temps perdu*, 4: 457. Eve Kosofsky Sedgwick refers to this line in Proust as "the story of a successfully consolidated omnipotence." *The Weather in Proust* (Durham, NC: Duke University Press, 2010), 19.

13. It is "materially impossible to believe," Lemoine declared in a January 31, 1908 statement (printed in *Le Figaro*), that "the greatest experts in the world" could have overlooked the jewelers' marks on the diamonds that De Beers was now claiming the engineer had tried to pass off as his own. No one could possibly swallow De Beers's story ("personne ne voudra avaler pareille couleuvre").

14. Marcel Proust, *The Lemoine Affair*, (hereafter *LA*), trans. Charlotte Mandell (NY: Melville, 2008), 35.

15. *CSB*, 23.

16. In a March, 21, 1908, letter to Robert Dreyfus, Proust writes (in reference to his pastiche of Renan): "J'avais réglé mon métronome intérieur à son rythme et j'aurais [pu] écrire dix volumes comme cela." Proust, *Lettres (1879–1922)*, ed. Françoise Leriche (Paris: Plon, 2004), 439.

17. Proust's Michelet declares that contemplating the affair disturbed his mind, making him feel as unwell as he had felt while researching the absolutist reign of Henri XIV: "[P]eculiar headaches every day made me think that I was going to be forced to abandon my history. I didn't really recover my strength until the Tennis Court Oath (20 June 1789). I felt similarly disturbed before this strange realm of crystallization that is the world of the stone." "[D]'étranges maux de tête me faisaient croire chaque jour que j'allais être

obligé d'interrompre mon histoire. Je ne retrouvai vraiment mes forces qu'au serment du Jeu de Paume (20 juin 1789). Pareillement me sentais-je troublé devant cet étrange règne de la cristallisation qu'est le monde de la pierre." *LA*, 28; *CSB*, 45.

18. Although Proust drafted this Lemoine Affair pastiche in June, 1909, it was not published in his lifetime. Jean-Yves Tadié, *Marcel Proust: A Life*, trans. Euan Cameron (New York: Penguin, 2000), 525.

19. *CSB*, 12. Proust added this passage when he expanded the pastiche for publication in *Pastiches et mélanges*. For an interesting analysis of the queer dynamics of this mode of transgression—what Genette terms "narrative metalepsis"—see Michael Lucey, *Never Say I: Sexuality and the First Person in Colette, Gide, and Proust* (Durham, NC: Duke University Press, 2006), 193–214.

20. The Goncourt pastiche is divided into two journal entries. In the first, Goncourt is delighted to hear about Proust's suicide while dining with Proust's friend Lucien Daudet: "Like a bouquet, they brought Lucien the news, presenting me with the denouement of the already sketched play, that their friend Marcel Proust had killed himself after the fall in diamond shares, a collapse that annihilated a part of his fortune." *LA*, 38. "Comme bouquet, on apporte à Lucien la nouvelle, me donnant le dénouement de la pièce déjà ébauchée, que leur ami Marcel Proust se serait tué, à la suite de la baisse des valeurs diamantifères, baisse anéantissant une partie de sa fortune." *CSB*, 24. In the second journal entry, Goncourt awakens to learn that "Marcel Proust has not killed himself, Lemoine has invented nothing at all, is nothing but a conjurer who isn't even very clever, a kind of Robert-Houdin with no hands." *LA*, 40. "Marcel Proust ne s'est pas tué, Lemoine n'a rien inventé du tout, ne serait qu'un escamoteur pas même habile, une espèce de Robert-Houdin manchot." *CSB*, 26.

21. Editorial remarks, *CSB*, 690, 691.

22. "[N]e cherchant pas à 'briller,' je verse généralement dans un pastiche des choses dont un meilleur administrateur de ses biens préférerait avoir l'honneur personnel et la signature." Proust, *Lettres*, 721.

23. Cited in *CSB*, 693.

24. *CSB*, 36.

25. "[S]i vous prenez une pomme de terre cuite au four [. . .] et si ayant déshabillé cette pomme de terre vous la marquez d'encre au dos et précisément sur les points de son relief que quelqu'un qui la tient devant lui ne peut apercevoir sans se casser la tête et une bonne semaine de torticolis, vous avez l'histoire de tout le développement de la peinture murale en Italie, notamment des fresques de Giotto." *CSB*, 204.

26. *Le Figaro*, January 25, 1908.

27. Maurizia Boscagli and Enda Duffy, "Selling Jewels: Modernist Commodification and Disappearance as Style," *Modernism/Modernity* 14.2 (2007): 191.

28. *Rules of Art*, 169; *Règles de l'art*, 240. As Darien Leader points out in his book about the theft of the *Mona Lisa* in 1911, the value of artworks cannot be explained or rationalized in terms of use or exchange: art occupies an invisible, sacred "empty space." This empty space is what makes us perpetually ask the question, "Is this art?" Leader suggests that the *Mona Lisa* case—in which thousands of people flocked to see the blank spot where the stolen painting had hung—reminds us that there is an element of theft in all art: in art, "an object is taken out of the world" and "finds itself in a new place." *Stealing the Mona Lisa: What Art Stops Us from Seeing* (New York: Counterpoint, 2002), 175–176. For a compelling exploration of this intimate relationship between value and nothingness in

modernism, see Anne Anlin Cheng, *Second Skin: Josephine Baker and the Modern Surface* (New York: Oxford University Press, 2010).

29. *Rules of Art*, 169–170; *Règles de l'art*, 240–241, Bourdieu's emphasis.

30. De Duve suggests that Duchamp's urinal (or "fountain") "manifests the magic power of the word 'art.'" Duchamp is therefore playing a game with the notion of aesthetic autonomy: perceiving the urinal as an autonomous artwork requires "an act of faith." *Kant After Duchamp*, 13, 14.

31. For an inspired discussion of the imbricated discourses of enchantment and de-mystification in Proust, see Sedgwick, *The Weather in Proust*, 1–41. On the mixture of belief and disenchantment that characterizes the modern relation to prestige, see James English, *The Economy of Prestige: Prizes, Awards, and the Circulation of Cultural Value* (Cambridge, MA, Harvard University Press, 2005). English argues that our relation to the institutions of cultural prestige is neither one of "perfect lucidity" nor of "radical disillusionment." Rather, at stake is "a kind of suspension between belief and disbelief, between the impulse to see art as a kind of ponzi scheme and the impulse to preserve it as a place for our most trusting investments (118).

32. Joshua Landy notes that the celebrated nineteenth-century "prestidigitateur," Robert-Houdin, acted the role of professor, presenting his own tricks as experiments or miracles of science, and unmasking the tricks of others in volumes such as *Les Tricheries des Grecs dévoilées* (1861) and *Les Secrets de la prestidigitation et de la magie* (1868). As Landy puts it, "Mid-century prestidigitation was a legerdemain in which what was taken away with one hand was, simultaneously, restored with the other." Robert-Houdin's show called for new kind of spectatorship: someone with "mental dexterity equal to his manual dexterity." Robert-Houdin's performances required the spectator's simultaneous conviction and distrust, his or her "aptitude for detached credulity." Hence the ideal spectators would be "ready to don and doff their lucidity repeatedly throughout the show." In this sense, Robert-Houdin provided his audiences with "a model for the construction of a belief system that recognizes itself as illusory." "Modern Magic: Jean-Eugène Robert-Houdin and Stéphane Mallarmé," in *The Re-Enchantment of the World: Secular Magic in a Rational Age*, ed. Joshua Landy and Michael Saler (Stanford, CA: Stanford University Press, 2009), 125, 108, 110. For a broader history of secular magic, see Simon During, *Modern Enchantments: The Cultural Power of Secular Magic* (Cambridge, MA: Harvard University Press, 2002) and James W. Cook, *The Arts of Deception: Playing With Fraud in the Age of Barnum* (Cambridge, MA: Harvard University Press, 2001). Cook notes that in the nineteenth century, magicians began using exposés and how-to manuals as promotional tools. "For the first time, explaining the behind-the-scenes workings of one's magical performance was becoming almost as important and as central to the professional magician's craft as the more conventional work of designing and performing tricks" (178). For a discussion of the relation between the fad for theatrical conjuring and the flourishing of trick cinema in the early twentieth century, see Matthew Solomon, "Up-to-Date Magic: Theatrical Conjuring and the Trick Film," *Theatre Journal* 58, no. 4 (2006): 595–615.

33. "[O]n sait parfaitement que dans le 'pli' déposé dans une banque de Londres il n'y a rien, ou que, s'il y a une formule, elle est sans valeur, on le sait . . . et cependant on aime à s'entendre redire que peut-être il se pourrait qu'il y eût quelque chose."

34. Proust himself was apparently one of the relieved shareholders. In a March 26, 1908 letter to Louis d'Albufera, he references the Goncourt pastiche in which his imagined financial ruin provokes his fictional suicide: "Did you see that in my *Figaro* pastiches I spoke of my failure with De Beers?" ("As-tu vu que, dans mes pastiches du *Figaro*, j'ai parlé de ma déconfiture avec la De Beers?") *Correspondance de Marcel Proust*, ed. Philip Kolb, vol. 8 (Paris: Plon, 1981), 76. The journalist Georges Grison notes that Lemoine's "fantastic discovery" was expected to make diamond prices fall by 80%. "L'Affaire Lemoine," *Le Figaro*, April 15, 1909.

35. According to the *Figaro*, many people wrote to Lemoine in prison, begging him to send them a few diamonds (since making them was so easy for him, or so they imagined): "Détail amusant: Lemoine reçoit à la prison de la Santé des masses de lettres. Beaucoup sont des demandes d'argent, de gens le suppliant de leur venir en aide. Il y a des commerçants menacés de la faillite, des jeunes filles qui ont besoin d'une petite dot pour se marier. . . . 'Il vous serait si facile de faire cinq ou six pauvres diamants dont le prix nous tirerait de peine,' disent-ils." Georges Grison, "L'Affaire des diamants," *Le Figaro*, February 27, 1908.

36. *À la recherche du temps perdu*, 4: 725.

37. For an excellent discussion of Proust's interest in the paradox of a plural singularity, see Chris Eagle's "On 'This' and 'That' in Proust: Deixis and Typologies in *À la recherche du temps perdu*," *MLN* 121.4 (2006). Eagle proposes that the *Recherche* stages a tension between a typological and a particularizing style, playing "the state of generality without substance (thoseness) against the state of phenomenal appearance (thisness, haeccitas)." Suggesting that this text is particularly drawn to the queer zone between particularity and generality, Eagle notes that beyond Proust's repeated Balzacian typologies (marked by plural deixis: "un de ces") and his attention to haecceity ("thisness"), he demonstrates a fascination with "exceptional sets," of which "les hommes-femmes" ("men-women") is a striking example. "On 'This' and 'That,'" 1002, 1008.

38. Kant, *Critique of the Power of Judgment*, 93, 114.

39. Virginia Woolf, "Solid Objects," in *A Haunted House and Other Stories* (New York: Harcourt Brace, 1972), 80.

40. Virginia Woolf, "The Mark on the Wall," in *A Haunted House and Other Stories* (New York : Harcourt Brace, 1972), 38.

41. Henry James, "The Figure in the Carpet," in *Major Stories and Essays* (New York: Penguin, 1999), 276–312.

42. "Quel était son aspect, quelle était sa grosseur, quelle était sa consistance? Était-elle dure ou molle, pulvérulente ou cohésive, amorphe ou cristalline, dense ou légère?" January 15, 1908.

43. Roland Barthes, *The Preparation of the Novel: Lecture Courses and Seminars at the Collège de France (1978–1979 and 1979–1980)*, trans. Kate Briggs (New York: Columbia University Press, 2011), 103; *La Préparation du roman: notes de cours et de séminaires au Collège de France, 1978–1979, 1979–1980* (Paris: Seuil, 2003), 154.

44. Gilles Deleuze, *Proust and Signs*, trans. Richard Howard (Minneapolis: University of Minnesota Press, 2003), 13.

45. *In Search of Lost Time*, 2:68; *À la recherche du temps perdu*, 1: 469.

46. *In Search of Lost Time*, 2: 67.

47. *À la recherche du temps perdu*, 1: 469.

48. *In Search of Lost Time*, 2: 67; *À la recherche du temps perdu*, 1: 469.

49. *Rules of Art*, 148; *Les Règles de l'art*, 211.

50. In a December 1908 letter to Georges de Lauris, Proust writes that he is planning a review article about Sainte-Beuve, which will be framed by a fictional bedside conversation with his mother: "maman viendrait près de mon lit, et je lui raconterais l'article que je veux faire sur Sainte-Beuve, et je le lui développerais." *Lettres,* 465–466. In an early draft of the novel, Proust similarly embeds his narrator's literary ambitions in a newspaper context. The editors of the Pléiade edition paraphrase the passage as follows : "il décrit l'émotion que lui a causée la publication d'un article de lui dans *Le Figaro;* après quoi il s'abandonne à des rêves de voyage; enfin, au cours d'une conversation avec sa mère, il lui annonce son intention d'écrire 'un article' contre la méthode de Sainte-Beuve." *CSB,* 822–823, 830–831, n 217.

51. Dedicating *Swann's Way* to Calmette was surely a savvy move on Proust's part, since it virtually guaranteed that his book would be prominently reviewed in his favorite newspaper. (And indeed, the review was the *Figaro's* cover story on November 27, 1913). As Proust reasoned in a September 1913 letter to the reviewer—his friend Lucien Daudet— "As the book is dedicated to him, if Calmette consented, the most natural [newspaper to publish the review] would be *Le Figaro.*" ("Si Calmette y consentait, le livre lui étant dédié, le plus naturel serait le Figaro.") *Lettres,* 634.

52. *In Search of Lost Time,* 1: 1.

53. *À la recherche du temps perdu,* 1: 3.

54. N.a.Fr. 16641, f. 71 v-f 65, cited in Mireille Naturel, "Le fabuleux destin de l'article dans *Le Figaro,*" in *Marcel Proust 4: Proust au tournant des siècles,* ed. Bernard Brun and Juliette Hassine (Paris: Minard, 2004), 30.

55. *In Search of Lost Time,* 1: 7; *À la recherche du temps perdu,* 1: 7. Thanks to Laurent Jenny for reminding me to include this reference. *Les Débats roses* was the evening issue of the mass daily *Le Journal des débats;* Antoine Compagnon notes that this evening edition began printing in February 1893, and was thus named because it was printed on pink paper. *Preface and Notes to* Du côté de chez Swann (Paris: Gallimard, 1988), 470, n 2. Strangely, Montcrieff translates *Les Débats roses* as "a copy of a children's paper" (1: 7).

56. Like newspaper reading, journalism was closely allied with fantasy for Proust: writing for newspapers and magazines permitted him to experiment with anonymity. His pseudonyms for the printed magazine, "Le Mensuel," included "Étoile Filante" ("Shooting Star"), "De Brabant," "Pierre de Touche," and "Bob"; he published society columns in the *Figaro* under the pseudonyms "Horatio" and "Dominique." Tadié, *Marcel Proust,* 112, 116, 117, 405, 407.

57. On the marketplace-like visual abundance of the late nineteenth-century newspaper, see Kevin G. Barnhurst and John Nerone, *The Form of News: A History* (New York: Guilford Press, 2001), 17.

58. Philip Fisher, "Torn Space: James Joyce's *Ulysses*" in *The Novel,* vol. 2: *Forms and Themes,* ed. Franco Moretti (Princeton, NJ: Princeton University Press, 2006), 667–668.

59. Kevis Goodman, *Georgic Modernity and British Romanticism: Poetry and the Mediation of History* (New York: Cambridge University Press, 2004), 72, 69.

60. Stewart defines reverse ekphrasis as "the visual representation of a confronted—or engaged—verbal representation." Garrett Stewart, *The Look of Reading: Book, Painting, Text* (Chicago: University of Chicago Press, 2006), 81.

61. For an account of this paper's reputation and history, see Claire Blandin, *Le Figaro: Deux Siècles d'histoire* (Paris: Armand Colin, 2007), and Claire Blandin, ed., *Le Figaro: histoire d'un journal* (Paris: Nouveau Monde, 2010).

62. Proust, *Lettres,* 663.

63. Tadié claims that when Flers came through, Proust retracted, and instead pro-posed extracts from volume 2 of his novel ("Odette mariée"), but they were never pub-lished, probably, Tadié notes, because of the war. *Marcel Proust*, 616–617.

64. Ibid., 793.

65. Elisa Tamarkin, "Literature and the News," in *The Oxford Handbook of Nineteenth-Century American Literature*, ed. Russ Castronovo (New York: Oxford University Press, 2012), 313.

66. *In Search of Lost Time*, 5: 788; *À la recherche du temps perdu*, 4: 163.

67. *In Search of Lost Time*, 3: 390; *À la recherche du temps perdu*, 2: 584.

68. *In Search of Lost Time*, 1: 344. "[S]'il lisait dans un journal les noms des personnes qui se trouvaient à un dîner pouvait dire immédiatement la nuance du chic de ce dîner, comme un lettré, à la simple lecture d'une phrase, apprécie exactement la qualité littéraire de son auteur." *À la recherche du temps perdu*, 1: 239.

69. *In Search of Lost Time*, 1: 171; *À la recherche du temps perdu*, 1: 121.

70. *In Search of Lost Time*, 1: 513. "Le nom de Beuzeval l'avait fait penser à celui d'une autre localité de cette région, Beuzeville, qui porte uni à celui-là par un trait d'union, un autre nom, celui de Bréauté, qu'il avait vu souvent sur les cartes, mais dont pour la pre-mière fois il remarquait que c'était le même que celui de son ami M. de Bréauté dont la lettre anonyme disait qu'il avait été l'amant d'Odette." *À la recherche du temps perdu*, 1: 354–355.

71. *In Search of Lost Time*, 5: 731; *À la recherche du temps perdu*, 4: 123.

72. *In Search of Lost Time*, 4: 75; *À la recherche du temps perdu*, 3: 56. The Proustian narrator's point of view is both limited and oddly expansive: he often knows more than a character should, but not as much as a traditional omniscient narrator would. Reading and writing for the *Figaro* likely contributed to shaping this peculiar point of view, as the paper accustomed Proust to seeing himself doubly: sometimes as author, but also fre-quently as a "character" in the society columns. (The paper regularly published news of the comings and goings, parties, funerals, weddings, and celebrations of its subscribers.) The Proustian narrator is also marked by his status as character and author. At once vis-ible and invisible, he exists both inside and outside of the diegesis. On the dynamics of this "double focalization" in Proust, see Genette, *Narrative Discourse*, trans. Jane E. Lewin (Ithaca, NY: Cornell University Press, 1980), 198–211.

73. Erving Goffman, *Behavior in Public Places* (New York: Simon and Schuster, 2008), 52n9.

74. Ibid., 59.

75. *In Search of Lost Time*, 5: 184–185.

76. *À la recherche du temps perdu*, 3: 650.

77. *In Search of Lost Time*, 5: 184–185; *À la recherche du temps perdu*, 3: 650.

78. Walter Benjamin, "On Some Motifs in Baudelaire," in *Selected Writings*: vol. 4, 1938–1940, ed. Howard Eiland and Michael W. Jennings, trans. Harry Zohn (Cambridge, MA: Harvard University Press, 2006), 316.

79. "The Newspaper," in *Selected Writings*: vol. 2, *1931–1934*, ed. Marcus Paul Bullock, Howard Eiland, and Gary Smith, trans. Rodney Livingstone (Cambridge, MA: Harvard University Press, 2005), 740.

80. Ibid., 741.

81. "'Suppose that, every morning, when we tore the wrapper off our paper with fevered hands, a transmutation were to take place, and we were to find inside it—oh! I don't know; shall we say Pascal's *Pensées*?' He articulated the title with an ironic emphasis so as not to appear pedantic. 'And then, in the gilt and tooled volumes which we open once in ten years,' he went on, [. . .] 'we should read that the Queen of the Hellenes had arrived at Cannes, or that the Princesse de Léon had given a fancy dress ball.'" *In Search of Lost Time*, 1: 33–34. "'Du moment que nous déchirons fiévreusement chaque matin la bande du journal, alors on devrait changer les choses et mettre dans le journal, moi je ne sais pas, les . . . Pensées de Pascal! (Il détacha ce mot d'un ton d'emphase ironique pour ne pas avoir l'air pédant.) Et c'est dans le volume doré sur tranches que nous n'ouvrons qu'une fois tous les dix ans, ajouta-t-il [. . .], que nous lirions que la reine de Grèce est allée à Cannes ou que la princesse de Léon a donné un bal costumé.'" *À la recherche du temps perdu*, 1: 26.

82. The narrator recollects these people and places in a state of enchanted disenchantment, recalling how commonplace he had found them, yet wishing that he "could have seen the Cottards again, asked them all sorts of details about Elstir, gone to look at the shop called Little Dunkirk, if it still existed, asked permission to visit the Verdurin mansion where [he] had once dined." *In Search of Lost Time*, 6: 38; *À la recherche du temps perdu*, 4: 295.

83. Frederic Jameson, *Postmodernism, or the Cultural Logic of Late Capitalism* (Durham, NC: Duke University Press, 1991), 17–18.

84. Paul Aron discusses this trend in *Histoire du pastiche: le pastiche littéraire français, de la Renaissance à nos jours* (Paris: Presses Universitaires de France, 2008).

85. Gabriel Tarde, *Les Lois de l'imitation: étude sociologique* (Paris: Félix Alcan, 1890); Marcel Mauss, "The Notion of Bodily Techniques," *Sociology and Psychology: Essays*, trans. Ben Brewster (London: Routledge, 1979), 101–102.

86. Michael Taussig, *Mimesis and Alterity: A Particular History of the Senses* (New York: Routledge, 1993), xi. Taussig notes that for these thinkers, "the wonder of mimesis lies in the copy drawing on the character and power of the original, to the point whereby the representation may even assume that character and that power" (xiii). On the importance of trance, possession, and passivity in the French avant-garde, see also Joyce Cheng's "Mask, Mimicry, Metamorphosis: Roger Caillois, Walter Benjamin and Surrealism in the 1930s," *Modernism/Modernity* (16.1): 61–86.

87. For example, in the 1910 edition, the pastiche of Tolstoy is full of comically unpronounceable names ("Ivan Labibine Ossouzoff, du Gouvernement de Kartimskrasolvitchegosk, district de Vokovosnesensk-Anskrevsantchoursk," etc.). *À la manière de . . .*, ed. Charles Müller and Paul Reboux. (Paris: Grasset, 1910), 33–43.

88. Bourdieu, *Distinction*, 173.

89. "[W]hen I awoke in the middle of the night, not knowing where I was, I could not even be sure at first who I was; I had only the most rudimentary sense of existence, such as may lurk and flicker in the depths of an animal's consciousness; I was more destitute than the cave-dweller; but then the memory—not yet of the place in which I was, but of various other places where I had lived and might now very possibly be—would come like a rope let down from heaven to draw me up out of the abyss of not-being." *In Search of Lost Time*, 1: 4. "[Q]uand je m'éveillais au milieu de la nuit, comme j'ignorais où je me

trouvais, je ne savais même pas au premier instant qui j'étais; j'avais seulement dans sa simplicité première le sentiment de l'existence comme il peut frémir au fond d'un animal; j'étais plus dénué que l'homme des cavernes; mais alors le souvenir—non encore du lieu où j'étais, mais de quelques-un de ceux que j'avais habités et où j'aurais pu être—venait à moi comme un secours d'en haut pour me tirer du néant d'où je n'aurais pu sortir tout seul." *À la recherche du temps perdu*, 1: 5.

90. *In Search of Lost Time*, 2: 670; *À la recherche du temps perdu*, 2: 264.

91. Proust's own love letters to Reynaldo Hahn testify to the notion that pastiche was the very language of intimacy for this author. The letters to Hahn are composed as the pastiche of a foreigner's French: a babbling, pseudo-Germanic invented language Proust called "langasge moschant." For an interesting reading of the "avant-garde" dynamics of this language game, see Rubén Gallo, *Proust's Latin Americans* (Baltimore: Johns Hopkins University Press, 2014), chapter 1.

92. *In Search of Lost Time*, 2: 673 ; *À la recherche du temps perdu*, 2: 266.

93. Genette, *Narrative Discourse*, 183. Malcolm Bowie also highlights Proust's flair for ventriloquism, describing the narrator as "a magpie and a mimic." *Proust among the Stars* (New York: Columbia University Press, 2000), xvi.

94. As the publication of the final volumes of the novel was posthumous, there is some debate over where to place the breaks between volumes. In the 1954 Pléiade edition, *Time Regained (Le Temps retrouvé)* begins with the narrator's statement that he nearly abstained from recounting the return to Combray. The 1987–89 Pléiade edition places this statement at the end of the penultimate volume, *The Fugitive (Albertine disparue)*. The classic Moncrieff/Kilmartin/Enright translation reproduces the original Pléiade volume break.

95. *In Search of Lost Time*, 6: 2; *À la recherche du temps perdu*, 4: 267.

96. The complete *Journal* did not appear until 1956. Jean Milly, *Proust dans le texte et l'avant-texte* (Paris: Flammarion, 1985), 187.

97. *In Search of Lost Time*, 6: 26; *À la recherche du temps perdu*, 4: 286.

98. *In Search of Lost Time*, 6: 36–37; *À la recherche du temps perdu*, 4: 294.

99. *In Search of Lost Time*: 6: 40; *À la recherche du temps perdu*, 4: 297.

100. Ibid.

101. Michael Finn writes, for example, that "there is something of the primordial apparition about the Goncourt pastiche, as though it constituted an earlier form bobbing to the narrative's surface from a time in the writer's life when, with characteristic inarticulation, an imitation of a writing stance that is wrong is presented as a substitute for an explanation of what is right. Proust instinctively juxtaposes mimetism and pastiche with the creative act, and his Narrator/writer is made to live out this juxtaposition, presenting us with an unavowed copy of a famous writer of the day as a prelude to the composition of a novel of his own." *Proust, the Body, and Literary Form*, 141. In contrast, Christopher Prendergast valorizes the pastiche for its capacity to ironically invert Proustian epiphany: Prendergast approvingly notes that Proust "tramples all over the aura of Madeleine as proper name" when his Goncourt claims that Madame Verdurin is the model for Fromentin's *Madeleine*. *Mirages and Mad Beliefs: Proust the Skeptic* (Princeton, NJ: Princeton University Press, 2013), 46, 25.

102. *In Search of Lost Time*, 6: 26–27. "[P]ar une contradiction bizarre, maintenant que ce livre en parlait, j'avais envie de les voir." *À la recherche du temps perdu*, 4: 287. Reading the *Journal* on the eve of his departure for a sanitorium, the narrator will not see these people or places for some years.

Chapter 2

1. Bourdieu, *Distinction*, 474; *La Distinction*, 552.

2. "Le goût, fonctionnant comme une sorte de sens de l'orientation sociale (*sense of one's place*) oriente les occupants d'une place déterminée dans l'espace social vers les positions sociales ajustées à leur propriétés, vers les pratiques ou les biens qui conviennent aux occupants de cette position, qui leur vont." *La Distinction*, 544.

3. Bourdieu, *Distinction*, 499; *La Distinction*, 585.

4. Bourdieu, *Distinction*, 498; *La Distinction*, 584.

5. Bourdieu, *Distinction*, 29; *La Distinction*, 29.

6. Bourdieu, *Distinction*, 54, 32; *La Distinction*, 57, 33

7. Joseph Litvak, *Strange Gourmets: Sophistication, Theory, and the Novel* (Durham, NC: Duke University Press, 1997), 17. Critical approaches that highlight the dynamics of indistinction in Proust are rare; a notable exception is Litvak's brilliant reading of Proust's queer penchant for bad objects. Litvak concentrates on the narrator's education in sophistication, a quality that, it turns out, requires a "highly cultivated taste for waste," and is bound up with an "incorrigible immaturity" (17). According to Litvak, Proust reduces high society to a "dungheap" as part of an elaborate strategy to avoid the merely mediocre, the mundane. The rapidity with which "high" turns into "low" in the *Recherche* can be read, Litvak suggests, "as an ingenious tactic for short-circuiting the middle" and hence for avoiding boredom at all cost (83). It is precisely the return of that short-circuited middle that interests me here. Like Litvak, my focus is the volatility of taste in Proust, but I am interested less in Proustian intelligence (Litvak's vulgar Proust is smarter than ever) than in moments when the ordinariness of things stumps the critical project.

8. "Il pourra se faire qu'une détestable représentation musicale dans un théâtre de province, un bal que les gens de goût trouvent ridicule, soit évoquent en lui des souvenirs, soit se rapportent en lui à un ordre de rêveries et de préoccupations, bien plus qu'une admirable exécution à l'Opéra, qu'une soirée ultra-élégante dans le faubourg Saint-Germain. Le nom de stations dans un indicateur de chemin de fer du Nord, [. . .] un livre insipide pour les gens de goût, [. . .] peuvent avoir pour lui un tout autre prix que de beaux libres de philosophie, et font dire aux gens de goût que pour un homme de talent il a des goûts très bêtes." *Contre Sainte-Beuve*, 215.

9. Ibid.

10. "Je ne sais si je suis bouché à l'émeri, mais je ne comprends pas l'intérêt qu'il peut y avoir à lire trente pages sur la façon dont un Monsieur se retourne dans son lit avant de s'endormir." Cited in Barthes, "Longtemps, je me suis couché de bonne heure," in *Oeuvres complètes*: vol. 5, *1977–1980*, ed. Eric Marty (Paris: Seuil, 2002), 462.

11. Rancière argues that Flaubert "kills" Emma Bovary because her kitsch aesthetics are too close to the author's own doctrine of trans-aestheticization and hence threaten the precarious distinction of art. "Why Emma Bovary Had to Be Killed," 69. See also my discussion of Rancière's reading in the "Aesthetic Indistinction" section of the introduction.

12. "The function and the task of a writer are those of a translator." *In Search of Lost Time*, 6: 291. "Le devoir et la tâche d'un écrivain sont ceux d'un traducteur." *À la recherche du temps perdu*, 4: 469.

13. *In Search of Lost Time*, 6: 290; *À la recherche du temps perdu*, 4: 468.

14. *In Search of Lost Time*, 1: 116–117; *À la recherche du temps perdu*, 1: 84.

15. See *Marcel Proust: The Fictions of Life and of Art* (New York: Oxford University Press, 1965) and *The Culture of Redemption* (Cambridge, MA: Harvard University Press, 1990).

16. Leo Bersani and Ulysse Dutoit, "Beauty's Light," *October* 82 (Autumn, 1997): 24. *In Search of Lost Time*, 6: 290; *À la recherche du temps perdu*, 4: 468.

17. "[B]eneath these signs [a cloud, a triangle, a church spire, a flower, a stone] there lay something of a quite different kind which I must try to discover, some thought which they translated after the fashion of those hieroglyphic characters which at first one must suppose to represent only material objects. No doubt the process of decipherment was difficult, but only by accomplishing it could one arrive at whatever truth there was to read. [. . .] [T]he task was to interpret the given sensations as signs of so many laws and ideas, by trying to think—that is, draw forth from the shadow—what I had merely felt, by trying to convert it into its spiritual equivalent." *In Search of Lost Time*, 6: 273. "[I]l y avait peut-être sous ces signes [un nuage, un triangle, un clocher, une fleur, un caillou] quelque chose de tout autre que je devais tâcher de découvrir, une pensée qu'ils traduisaient à la façon de ces caractères hiéroglyphiques qu'on croirait représenter seulement des objets matériels. Sans doute ce déchiffrage était difficile mais seul il donnait quelque vérité à lire. [. . .] [I]l fallait tâcher d'interpréter les sensations comme les signes d'autant de lois et d'idées, en essayant de penser, c'est-à-dire de faire sortir de la pénombre ce que j'avais senti, de le convertir en un équivalent spirituel." *À la recherche du temps perdu*, 4: 457.

18. As Bersani and Dutoit put it, in this process of "déchiffrage," the self expands in order to possess the secrets of the material world. Ultimately, the subject is "adequately filled" and can "dispense entirely with the external spectacle." "Beauty's Light," *October* 82 (Autumn, 1997): 24. Bersani and Dutoit nonetheless identify an exception to this trend in Proust: an occasional, "non-sadistic" aesthetics of plenitude that illuminates "Being" as pure relationality, or correspondence. Examining the scene in "Combray" in which the narrator beholds a daffodil field, Bersani and Dutoit note that these flowers induce aesthetic pleasure not by being (figuratively) devoured, but precisely because they are inedible. They argue that in this scene, rather than assimilating the world, the perceiver projects his own "useless" pleasure out onto it, and the flowers appear to shine as a result of this displaced narcissism (26–27). Although less appropriative than the Proustian aesthetics of translation or decipherment, the non-sadistic aesthetics that Bersani and Dutoit elaborate here leaves little space for the object. A mere screen for the subject's projections, the daffodils only *appear* to "shine on their own," elevated (or "promoted") to the status of aesthetic objects (27). The perceiver abstains from gobbling up the flowers, and his disinterest is rewarded with a golden treasure. The minor, or occasional aesthetic mode I will investigate throughout this chapter can be distinguished from Bersani and Dutoit's "non-sadistic" aesthetics of plenitude in that it is not grounded in the logic of psychoanalytic compensation, or sublimation, and hence is not only non-sadistic but also non-subject-centered.

19. "[L]e souvenir visuel [. . .] débat trop loin, trop confusément; à peine si je perçois le reflet neutre où se confond l'insaisissable tourbillon des couleurs remuées; mais je ne peux distinguer la forme." *À la recherche du temps perdu*, 1: 45–46.

20. Benjamin seems to invoke precisely this side of the *Recherche* when he writes so enigmatically that Proust's most convincing insights "fasten on their objects as insects fasten on leaves." "On the Image of Proust," in *Selected Writings:* vol. 2, *1927–1930*, ed.

Michael W. Jennings, Howard Eiland, and Gary Smith, trans. Harry Zohn (Cambridge, MA: Harvard University Press, 1999), 242.

21. *In Search of Lost Time*, 1: 218–219.

22. *À la recherche du temps perdu*, 1: 153.

23. According to Jakobson, the first linguistic function acquired by humans (the "phatic") is also the one function shared by birds. Motivated by the simple desire for contact, the phatic is the noisiest—least informative—of all linguistic functions. It refers to messages "serving to establish, to prolong, or to discontinue communication to check whether the channel works ('Hello, do you hear me?'), to attract the attention of the interlocutor or to confirm his continued attention." Roman Jakobson, "Closing Statement: Linguistics and Poetics," in *Style in Language*, ed. Thomas A. Sebeok (Cambridge, MA: MIT, 1960), 355. Jakobson borrows this term from Malinowski, who argues that this type of utterance in "primitive languages" works to signal friendship.

24. Daniel Heller-Roazen, *Echolalias: On the Forgetting of Language* (New York: Zone Books, 2005), 15. The etymology of "zut" is uncertain. The *Trésor de la Langue Française* presents a dizzying array of possible derivations for this exclamation, the first recorded use dating to 1813 (as "z'ut"). One intriguing theory is that "zut" combines two other interjections: "flûte" (an expression of impatience) and "zest" (an expression of suddenness and surprise). Alternatively, "zut" may be a deformation of "ut," which in turn is either onomatopoetic, or derives from the vulgar interjection "foutre" ("damn," "fuck"), or from printers' slang (from the Latin formula "ut tibi prosit meri protio": "may this good pure wine do you much good"). *TLFi*, s.v. "zut," accessed March 29, 2015, http://www.cnrtl.fr/etymologie/zut.

25. Paul Fry, *A Defense of Poetry: Reflections on the Occasion of Writing* (Stanford, CA: Stanford University Press, 1995), 7, 4.

26. "Ravishment" in Proust is allied with the desire to make contact with phenomena, to be *proximate* (rather than dominating). The breaking point of critical language—the point at which judgment gives way to the gasp of astonishment—"ravissement" is also the mood associated with the narrator's very first bit of writing in the novel, the note he sends via Françoise to his mother imploring her to come to him: "my little note, though it would annoy her [. . .], would at least admit me, invisible and enraptured, into the same room as herself." *In Search of Lost Time*, 1: 39, trans. modified. "[M]on petit mot allait, la fâchant sans doute [. . .], me faire du moins entrer invisible et ravi dans la même pièce qu'elle." *À la recherche du temps perdu*, 1: 29–30. Here "ravi" carries the strong sense of rapture or ravishment (literally, the state of being carried away); in his "ravishment," the narrator imagines touching his mother with an outstretched string or line. The note is a "fil délicieux"—"an exquisite thread"—extending the writer's body into another space.

27. "[I]dées confuses qui m'exaltaient et qui n'ont pas atteint le repos dans la lumière." *À la recherche du temps perdu*, 1: 153.

28. *In Search of Lost Time*, 3: 577. "[O]n sentait que la dame allait bientôt se retourner, les bateaux disparaître, l'ombre changer de place, la nuit venir, que le plaisir finit, que la vie passe et que les instants, montrés à la fois par tant de lumières qui y voisinent ensemble, ne se retrouvent pas." *À la recherche du temps perdu*, 2: 714.

29. *In Search of Lost Time*, 6: 290–291; *À la recherche du temps perdu*, 4: 468.

30. Dazzling, yet ultimately inconsequential, this episode might be read as an undistinguished, inarticulate version of the "gratuitous" mode of intervention that Anne-Lise

François theorizes in *Open Secrets: The Literature of Uncounted Experience*. The "open secret" names an act of divulging which is "unwarranted" and "uncompelled," and which makes "no difference," simply making available a significance that one *may* or *may not* take in (119–120, 133). A gift that costs nothing and demands no return, the open secret is "futureless" in that it implies "a knowledge that auditors and speaker alike are meant to continue to overlook rather than exploit" (133).

31. When Bersani argues that the narrator's primary relation to the world is one of anxious appropriation, he points to the bedtime drama as the basis for the narrator's permanent sense of privation. *Marcel Proust: The Fictions of Art and Life* (New York: Oxford University Press, 1965), 42–43. Roger Shattuck describes this scene as "a play within a play enacting [a] ritual of desire and discontent." *Proust's Way: A Field Guide to In Search of Lost Time* (New York: Norton, 2001), 139. Alison Finch notes that the bedtime scene teaches the narrator to associate love with anxiety and to "think of the loved one as enjoying pernicious activities that shut him out." "Love, Sexuality and Friendship," in *The Cambridge Companion to Proust*, ed. Richard Bales (Cambridge: Cambridge University Press, 2001), 172.

32. *Cahier 8:* 37, cited in Edward Hughes, *Marcel Proust, A Study in the Quality of Awareness* (Cambridge: Cambridge University Press, 1983), 89, my translation. "[J]e me levai, je m'assis, j'ouvris les fenêtres, le calme qui résultait de mes angoisses finies, la peur et la soif du danger me mettaient dans une allégresse extraordinaire. J'étais dans une disposition joyeuse, ces paroles insignifiantes que j'entendais [monter] mollement du jardin m'enchantaient. Je me répétais 'Zut! zut! zut! zut! zut! alors!' avec le même accent enivré que si ces mots avaient signifié quelque vérité délicieuse, je sautais seul dans ma chambre, je m'adressai un sourire dans ma glace, et ne sachant sur quoi faire tomber ma tendresse et ma joie, je saisis mon propre bras avec transport et j'y déposai un baiser."

33. *In Search of Lost Time*, 1: 43, trans. modified.

34. *À la recherche du temps perdu*, 3: 692.

35. *In Search of Lost Time*, 1: 58; *À la recherche du temps perdu*, 1: 43.

36. Mieke Bal writes that although "it is generally agreed that this little patch of yellow wall is nowhere to be seen in the painting at La Haye," some critics refer to the patch in the painting "as if its presence were without doubt." They identify it in different parts of the painting, however. *The Mottled Screen: Reading Proust Visually*, trans. Anna-Louise Milne (Stanford, CA: Stanford University Press, 1997), 260. This ambiguity is heightened by the syntax of Bergotte's exclamation: as Didi-Huberman points out, in the phrase "petit pan de mur jaune," it is impossible to determine whether "jaune" ("yellow") qualifies the wall or the patch. He also notes that in colloquial usage, "pan" is an onomatopoetic interjection, translatable as "Bang!" "Thump!" or "Whack!" *Confronting Images: Questioning the Ends of a Certain History of Art*, trans. John Goodman (University Park: Pennsylvania State University Press, 2005), 246, 248.

37. Bal, *The Mottled Screen*, 91.

38. *In Search of Lost Time*, 5: 245.

39. *À la recherche du temps perdu*, 3: 692.

40. *In Search of Lost Time*, 5: 244. Vermeer's *View of Delft* is like the Montjouvain pond scene in its occlusion of iconography or hidden meaning. Svetlana Alpers foregrounds the importance of empiricity in seventeenth-century Dutch painting, arguing that in works like *View of Delft*, "the perceived world *deposits itself* as such—such as it is perceived—in pigments on a picture." *View of Delft* tells no story; it simply makes manifest "the world

staining the surface with color and light, impressing itself upon it [. . .]. Delft is hardly grasped, or taken in—it is just there for the looking." *The Art of Describing: Dutch Art in the Seventeenth Century* (Chicago: University of Chicago Press, 1984), 27.

41. "Étourdi" suggests folly or carelessness, but also a stunning experience that brings the subject close to death: *Littré* cites La Fontaine's fable of the lion and the rat, in which the rat escapes from the lion's paws "assez à l'étourdie." Émile Littré, *Dictionnaire de la langue française (1872-77)*, s.v. "étourdi," accessed May 7, 2015, http://www.littre.org/definition/étourdi.2.

42. *In Search of Lost Time*, 1: 194; *À la recherche du temps perdu*, 1: 136.

43. *In Search of Lost Time*, 1: 195; *À la recherche du temps perdu*, 1: 137.

44. Barthes suggests that if literature tends (in its "perfect moments") to make us cry out, "that's it!" ("c'est ça!"), interpretation makes us say, "that's *not* quite it," and always finds a "shadow" around which to spin a discourse. *La Préparation du roman: notes de cours et de séminaires au Collège de France, 1978-79, 1979-1980* (Paris: Seuil, 2003), 125.

45. Vivasvan Soni, "Communal Narcosis and Sublime Withdrawal: The Problem of Community in Kant's *Critique of Judgment*," *Cultural Critique* 64 (Fall 2006): 5. On the notion that a "certain critical inarticulacy necessarily accompanies the scene of aesthetic judgment," see also Samuel Weber, "The Unraveling of Form," in *Mass Mediauras: Form, Technics, Media*, ed. Alan Cholodenko (Stanford, CA: Stanford University Press, 1996), 29, and "Ambivalence, the Humanities, and the Study of Literature," *Diacritics* 15 (Summer 1985). Weber aptly notes that "Kant's entire philosophical interest in aesthetic judgments [. . .] derives from the peculiar 'perplexity'—or, more properly, the peculiar *embarrassment, Verlegenheit*—that characterizes judgments of beauty or of the sublime, where concepts precisely are not 'given' and where cognition therefore is not a constitutive factor." "Ambivalence, the Humanities, and the Study of Literature," 17. Although he does not reference Kant, Roland Barthes makes the same point in an essay on Cy Twombly, noting that it is "one of language's minor torments" that aesthetic beauty renders the judging subject mute, able only to exclaim "'How beautiful this is!' ["'Comme c'est beau!'"] over and over." *The Responsibility of Forms: Essays on Music, Art, and Representation*, trans. Richard Howard (Berkeley: University of California Press, 1985), 191; *Oeuvres complètes*, vol. 5, 699–700.

46. Peter Collier and J. D. Whiteley, "Proust's Blank Page," *The Modern Language Review* 79.3 (July, 1984): 571.

47. *In Search of Lost Time*, 1: 254. "[L]es deux clochés seraient allés à jamais rejoindre tant d'arbres, de toits, de parfums, de sons, que j'avais distingués des autres à cause de ce plaisir obscur qu'ils m'avaient procuré et que je n'ai jamais approfondi." *À la recherche du temps perdu*, 1: 178.

48. Their shape "tient aussi peu de place, semble aussi épisodique et momentané, que l'arc-en-ciel, la lumière de cinq heures du soir." *CSB*, 64.

49. "Nous n'avons devant les yeux qu'une seconde description [. . .] inutilement plus imagée. Il est vain d'essayer de chercher à travers elle le pourquoi de l'émotion du jeune Marcel, et à cet égard, malgré son apparence descriptive, elle reste aussi opaque que le 'zut' prononcé du côté de Méséglise." Michel Butor, "Les Moments de Marcel Proust," in *Les Critiques de notre temps et Proust*, ed. Jacques Bersani (Paris: Garnier, 1971), 120.

50. Roger Shattuck, "Proust's Stilts," *Yale French Studies* 34 (1965): 91.

51. Offering a different perspective on the defamiliarizing force of everyday perceptions in the *Recherche*, Sara Danius reads this passage as evidence of Proust's fascination with technologies of velocity, or for what she terms "the aesthetics of the windshield." While my reading foregrounds the non-monumentality of the steeples, Danius highlights the thrill of novelty, suggesting that the most important element in the episode is the speed at which the narrator is traveling—a speed that "transforms the surrounding landscape into a phantasmagoria." *The Senses of Modernism*, 131.

52. *In Search of Lost Time*, 1: 257, trans. modified. "[C]omme si j'avais été moi-même une poule et si je venais de pondre un œuf, je me mis à chanter à tue-tête." *À la recherche du temps perdu*, 1: 180.

53. Peter Collier and J. D. Whiteley, "Proust's Blank Page," *The Modern Language Review* 79.3 (July, 1984): 578.

54. Northrop Frye describes cliché as "overused expressions once clever or metaphorical, but now trite and time-worn." *The Harper Handbook to Literature* (New York: Harper & Row, 1985). In De Man's definition, cliché is "a dead or sleeping metaphor which has lost its literal connotations [. . .] and has only kept a proper meaning." *Allegories of Reading* (New Haven, CT: Yale University Press, 1979), 65.

55. Eric Partridge, *A Dictionary of Clichés* (London: Routledge, 1978), 2.

56. Sharon Cameron, *Impersonality* (Chicago: University of Chicago Press, 2007), 97.

57. Cameron, *Impersonality*, 93.

58. As Cameron puts it, "the platitudes that often seem stunning in an Emerson essay—stunning that a writer who displays so much expertise in crafting powerful sentences could also write so vapidly—well serve this goal of voicing words whose particular source is undiscoverable." *Impersonality*, 94.

59. Cameron, *Impersonality*, 93.

60. Bersani and Dutoit, "Beauty's Light," 24.

61. The scene appears in the earliest notebooks of sketches for the *Recherche* (Cahiers 3 and 2). This 1908–1909 sketch opens with the hero tossing in bed as he wonders what has happened to his article on the Martinville steeples: "Je fermai les yeux en attendant le jour; je pensai à un article que j'avais envoyé il y a longtemps déjà au *Figaro*" ("I closed my eyes while waiting for the day, I was thinking about an article that I had long ago sent to the *Figaro*"). In the morning his mother brings him a copy of the newspaper with his front-page article, and he is thrilled to read it as "un quelconque des dix mille lecteurs" ("any ordinary reader out of ten thousand"). *À la recherche du temps perdu*, 4: 671, 673.

62. *In Search of Lost Time*, 5: 766. "[C]e n'était que des journaux. [. . .] J'ouvris 'Le Figaro.' Quel ennui!" *À la recherche du temps perdu*, 4: 147–148.

63. *In Search of Lost Time*, 5: 767. "[P]ain miraculeux, multipliable, qui est à la fois un et dix mille, et reste le même pour chacun tout en pénétrant à la fois, innombrable, dans toutes les maisons." *À la recherche du temps perdu*, 4: 148.

64. *In Search of Lost Time*, 5: 769.

65. *Contra* Benedict Anderson's argument (borrowed from Benjamin) that the newspaper homogenizes time, reducing the fullness and heterogeneity of experience to a flattened "meanwhile," in Proust the newspaper is a volatile text allied with boredom and violence, indifference and extreme concentration. The tonal contradictions allied with the newspaper are particularly striking in a set of early drafts. In those versions of the scene, wildly contrasting moods frame the *Figaro*'s arrival. In the first version, the

narrator's mother puts down the newspaper absentmindedly—"with an air of complete distraction." *À la recherche du temps perdu*, 4: 671, my trans. In the second version, this "distraction" is complicated—her apparent "indifference" conceals an "unaccustomed violence." In this draft, the mother rapidly exits the room "like an anarchist who has planted a bomb." Ibid., 672. A third draft entirely abandons this radical tone, replacing anarchy with a list of mundane excuses for withdrawing—there's an "hour for everything" and this is not the time to chat; one ought not stand around gabbing in one's bathrobe; the cook is waiting for her orders; she must speak with the butcher. Ibid., 672–673.

66. *In Search of Lost Time*, 5: 770; *À la recherche du temps perdu*, 4: 150.

67. "Next time we shall have to try another flavor," she says. *In Search of Lost Time*, 1:45; *À la recherche du temps perdu*, 1: 33.

68. *In Search of Lost Time*, 2: 452, 454; *À la recherche du temps perdu*, 2: 111–112.

69. *À la recherche du temps perdu*, 2: 457–458.

70. Ann Smock, personal communication with the author, April 2006.

71. *In Search of Lost Time*, 5: 770–771. "[A]u moment même où j'essaie d'être un lecteur quelconque, je lis en auteur, mais pas en auteur seulement [. . .]. Et quand je sentais une défaillance trop grande, me réfugiant dans l'âme du lecteur quelconque émerveillé, je me disais, 'Bah!'" *À la recherche du temps perdu*, 4: 150–151.

72. *In Search of Lost Time*, 5: 771, trans. modified. "Mais sapristi, s'ils ne sont pas contents? Il y a assez de jolies choses comme cela, plus qu'ils n'en ont l'habitude." *À la recherche du temps perdu*, 4: 152.

73. The narrator explains that his "relative ruin" is the result of failed speculations: "I had to pay out such considerable sums in brokers' commissions, as well as interest and contango fees, that in a rash moment I decided to sell out everything and found that I now possessed barely a fifth of what I had inherited from my grandmother and still possessed when Albertine was alive." *In Search of Lost Time*, 5: 867; *À la recherche du temps perdu*, 4: 218–219.

74. "In Venice, it is works of art, things of priceless beauty, that are entrusted with the task of giving us our impressions of everyday life." *In Search of Lost Time*, 5: 848. "[À] Venise, ce sont les oeuvres d'art, les choses magnifiques, qui sont chargées de nous donner les impressions familières de la vie." *À la recherche du temps perdu*, 4: 205.

75. Tony Tanner points out that "visiting (the word name) and not-getting to Venice is one of the recurring preoccupations and themes for over five-sixths of the book." *Venice Desired* (Cambridge, MA: Harvard University Press, 1992), 242.

76. Nathalie Mauriac Dyer refers to Proust's "variations on a stereotype," and notes that Proust's intellectual crush, Ruskin, wished to be the "ultimate recorder of [Venice's] collapse." "Genesis of Proust's 'Ruine de Venise,'" in *Proust in Perspective: Visions and Revisions*, ed. Armine Kotin Mortimer and Katherine Kolb (Urbana: University of Illinois Press, 2002), 72, 73.

77. *In Search of Lost Time*, 5: 884; *À la recherche du temps perdu*, 4: 231.

78. *In Search of Lost Time*, 5: 884. "[J]e ne pouvais plus rien lui dire de moi, je ne pouvais rien laisser de moi se poser sur lui." *À la recherche du temps perdu*, 4: 231.

79. "In vain might I fix my mind despairingly upon the beautiful and distinctive curve of the Rialto, it seemed to me, with the mediocrity of the obvious, a bridge not merely inferior to but as alien to the notions I had of it as an actor of whom, in spite of his blond wig and black garments, we know quite well that in his essence he is not Hamlet." *In Search of Lost Time*, 5: 884–885. "J'avais beau raccrocher désespérément ma pensée à la

belle courbe du Rialto, il m'apparaissait avec la médiocrité de l'évidence comme un pont non seulement inférieur, mais aussi étranger à l'idée que j'avais de lui qu'un acteur dont, malgré sa perruque blonde et son vêtement noir, j'aurais su qu'en son essence il n'est pas Hamlet." *À la recherche du temps perdu*, 4: 231.

80. Bourdieu, *Distinction*, 498; Proust, *In Search of Lost Time*, 5: 885. "Tels les palais, le Canal, le Rialto, se trouvaient dévêtus de l'idée qui faisait leur individualité et dissous en leurs vulgaires éléments matériels." *À la recherche du temps perdu*, 4: 232.

81. *À la recherche du temps perdu*, 4: 231.

82. Jameson also describes the Venice episode as a "negative sublime," but for him this means that appearances are stripped away to reveal "the Real" itself: a "zero degree of being" or a "dead extension" beneath the surface. "Joyce or Proust," in *The Modernist Papers* (London: Verso, 2007), 203.

83. Kant, *Critique of the Power of Judgment*, 145.

84. Kant associates the "trivial" with human mortality and physical vulnerability, but also with the activities of everyday existence: "goods, health, and life" and the "spirit of mere commerce." *Critique of the Power of Judgment*, 145–146. Philip Fisher suggests that by privileging the sublime (and its aestheticization of fear), modern thought has neglected more localized (and comparatively small, or trivial) ways of experiencing novelty, such as the feeling of wonder. *Wonder, the Rainbow, and the Aesthetics of Rare Experiences* (Cambridge, MA: Harvard University Press, 1999), 2.

85. *Critique of the Power of Judgment*, 144.

86. *In Search of Lost Time*, 5: 885, trans. modified.

87. *In Search of Lost Time*, 5: 884. "[C]e lieu quelconque était étrange comme un lieu où on vient d'arriver, qui ne vous connaît pas encore, comme un lieu d'où l'on est parti et qui vous a déjà oublié." *À la recherche du temps perdu*, 4 : 232.

88. *À la recherche du temps perdu*, 4: 232.

89. Honoré Daumier illustrates the overcrowding of this supposedly distinguished space in his satirical sketches, "Vue Prise à l'Entrée des Bains Deligny" (1859), which depicts a crush of bathers at the entrance of the baths, and "L'Echelle à quatre heures" (1858), which presents a bathing-suit-clad man thronged by bodies on all sides—and especially by feet and rear ends—as he attempts to descend the bath steps. The Art Institute of Chicago, "Entrance to the Public Baths at Deligny, plate 3 from Croquis D'été," accessed July 2, 2014, http://www.artic.edu/aic/collections/artwork/21590?search_no=1&index=81; "At the Deligny Baths.—The Ladder at 4 p.m., plate 33 from Croquis d'été," accessed July 2, 2014, http://www.artic.edu/aic/collections/artwork/84593.

90. *In Search of Lost Time*, 5: 884.

91. Theodor Adorno, "Opera and the Long-Playing Record," trans. Thomas Y. Levin, *October* 55 (Winter, 1990): 65; Julia Kristeva, *Time & Sense: Proust and the Experience of Literature*, trans. Ross Guberman (New York: Columbia University Press, 1996), 114. Eduardo di Capua composed "O sole mio" in 1898 (the Golden Age of the *canzone napoletana*), and the song became known all over the world after Caruso recorded it for the Victor Talking Machine company in 1916. A popular legend surrounding "O sole mio" is that in 1920 it was played in lieu of the Italian national anthem at the Antwerp Olympics when the conductor failed to locate the appropriate score. Paquito Del Bosco, *O sole mio: Storia della canzona più famosa del mondo* (Rome: Donzelli, 2006), 6. For a chronology of the Venice episode's composition (in 1908 and 1910) and revisions (in 1916, 1919, and 1922), see Dyer, "Genesis of Proust's 'Ruine de Venise,'" 69–72.

92. Malcolm Bowie, "Postlude: Proust and the Art of Brevity," in *The Cambridge Companion to Proust*, ed. Richard Bales (Cambridge: Cambridge University Press, 2001), 227.

93. *In Search of Lost Time*, 5: 886.

94. "[S]ans doute ce chant insignifiant entendu cent fois, ne m'intéressait nullement." *À la recherche du temps perdu*, 4: 232.

95. *In Search of Lost Time*, 5: 887.

96. *In Search of Lost Time*, 5: 887. "[C]haque note que lançait la voix du chanteur avec une force et une ostentation presque musculaires venait me frappait en plein coeur." *À la recherche du temps perdu*, 4: 233.

Chapter 3

1. Maurice Merleau-Ponty, *Phenomenology of Perception*, trans. Colin Smith (London: Routledge, 1962), 204. "On constate d'abord qu'ils le font plus lentement et plus minutieusement qu'un sujet normal: ils rapprochent l'un de l'autre les échantillons à comparer et ne voient pas d'un seul coup d'oeil ceux qui 'vont' ensemble. De plus, après avoir correctement assemblé plusieurs rubans bleus, ils commettent des erreurs incompréhensibles: si par exemple le dernier ruban bleu était d'une nuance pâle, ils poursuivent en joignant au tas de 'bleus' un vert pâle ou un rose pâle,—comme s'il leur était impossible de maintenir le principe de classification proposé et de considérer les échantillons sous le point de vue de la couleur d'un bout à l'autre de l'opération." *Phénoménologie de la perception* (Paris: Gallimard, 2001), 205.

2. Michel Foucault, *The Order of Things: An Archeology of the Human Sciences* (New York: Vintage Books, 1994), xviii; *Les Mots et les choses: une archéologie des sciences humaines* (Paris: Gallimard, 1966), 10. I am grateful to Thangam Ravindranathan for reminding me of this passage.

3. "Even when, at the beginning of the test, they proceed correctly, it is not the conformity of the samples to an idea which guides them, but the experience of an immediate resemblance, and hence it comes about that they can classify the samples only when they have placed them side by side." Merleau-Ponty, *Phenomenology of Perception*, 204. "Même quand, au début de l'épreuve, ils procèdent correctement, ce n'est pas la participation des échantillons à une idée qui les guide, c'est l'expérience d'une ressemblance immédiate, et de là vient qu'ils ne peuvent classer les échantillons qu'après les avoir rapprochés l'un de l'autre." *Phénoménologie de la perception*, 205.

4. Walter Benjamin, "A Child's View of Color," in *Selected Writings:* vol. 1, *1913–1926*, ed. Marcus Bullock and Michael W. Jennings, trans. Rodney Livingstone (Cambridge, MA: Harvard University Press, 1996), 50–51.

5. Benjamin, "A Child's View of Color," 50.

6. Ibid.

7. According to Richard Scholar, "the *je-ne-sais-quoi* enters history as a sign of quality in polite culture." *The Je-ne-sais-quoi in Early Modern Culture: Encounters with a Certain Something* (New York: Oxford University Press, 2005), 182. Index of an indefinable quality shared by artworks and social subjects alike, this concept "defines the way in which [seventeenth-century elite] culture preserves and sustains its sense of distinction" (187).

8. Eleanor Webster Bulatkin, "The French Word Nuance," *PMLA* 70.1 (March 1955): 268.

9. *Distinction*, 70; *La Distinction*, 77.

10. J.-K. Huysmans, *À Rebours* (Paris: Gallimard, 1983), 86.

11. Theodor Adorno, *Minima Moralia: Reflections from a Damaged Life*, trans. E. F. N. Jephcott (London: Verso, 2005), 219.

12. Barthes, *The Preparation of the Novel*, 45; *La Préparation du roman*, 81.

13. For a fascinating discussion of early twentieth-century aesthetic perception as nonstandardized and de-regulating, see chapter 4 of Jonathan Crary's *Suspensions of Perception: Attention, Spectacle, and Modern Culture* (Cambridge, MA: MIT Press, 1999), which investigates Paul Cézanne's resistance to reifying perceptual norms. Crary notes that Cézanne is attentive to the unfolding "intensity" of the animated landscape and seeks to convey "a sustained condition of vibrating instability." As Crary puts it, "the world for Cézanne is conceivable only as an indeterminate series of decenterings." *Suspensions of Perception*, 354.

14. In its concern with the imbrication and mutual determination of perceiver and perceived, this chapter brushes up against the logic of the "new materialism," an emergent critical trend that highlights the unpredictable variation and mutation of matter itself. According to Diana Coole and Samantha Frost, the task of the new materialism is to create "new concepts and images of nature that affirm matter's immanent vitality." *New Materialisms: Ontology, Agency, and Politics*, ed. Diana Coole and Samantha Frost (Durham, NC: Duke University Press, 2010), 8. Similarly, political theorist Jane Bennett advocates for understanding materiality not as inert or even passively resistant but as insistently active and energetic. As Bennett puts it, "worms, or electricity, or various gadgets, or fats, or metals, or stem cells are actants, or what Darwin calls 'small agencies,' that, when in the right confederation with other physical and physiological bodies, can make big things happen." *Vibrant Matter: A Political Ecology of Things* (Durham, NC: Duke University Press, 2010), 94. For these authors, matter is to be valorized for its "restlessness and intransigence" (Coole and Frost, 1). While I am sympathetic to the political aims of the new materialism, this chapter is more concerned with finding a critical language for the peculiar appearance of clouds, flowers, and other nebulous things that thwart the either/or logic of passive availability versus active resistance. I am interested in the challenge of thinking about the smallness of small things that do *not* "make big things happen."

15. "Queer ecology" might be defined as a term for practices of environmental conservation and care that challenge the normative force of what Lee Edelman calls "reproductive futurism." *No Future: Queer Theory and the Death Drive* (Durham, NC: Duke University Press, 2004), 2. For an illuminating discussion of avuncular stewardship as queer ecology, see Sarah Ensor's "Spinster Ecology: Rachel Carson, Sarah Orne Jewett, and Nonreproductive Futurity," *American Literature* 84.2 (2012): 409–435. On queer ecology as a precarious, melancholic bearing toward the world that resists fantasies of inviolable "Nature," see Catriona Mortimer-Sandilands, "Melancholy Natures, Queer Ecologies" in *Queer Ecologies: Sex, Nature, Politics, Desire*, ed. Bruce Erickson and Catriona Mortimer-Sandilands (Bloomington: Indiana University Press, 2010), 331–358. For a fascinating and implicitly queer critique of market-driven industrialized agriculture and the bee colony collapse it has brought about, see Anne-Lise François's "Flower Fisting," *Postmodern Culture* 22, no. 1 (2011), doi: 10.1353/pmc.2012.0004. François demonstrates that outside of the rigid, policed temporal regime of industrial monocultures, bees and flowers are anything but heteronormative, their relations marked instead by "polyamorous insouciance and easy noncommittal." See also the title essay in

Sedgwick's *The Weather in Proust*, which provides particular inspiration for the present chapter. Sedgwick suggests that Proust's de-supernaturalized, meteorological version of reincarnation teaches us to read difference queerly—which is to say, multiply and non-dualistically—rather than according to the either/or, closed-system Oedipal logic that sometimes dominates the *Recherche*.

16. Several critics have recently explored the literary and philosophical resonances of this peculiarly transitory object. For an interesting discussion of the cloud as a figure for an alternative, non-productive modality of Enlightenment thought, see chapter five of Pierre Saint-Amand's *The Pursuit of Laziness: An Idle Interpretation of the Enlightenment*, trans. Jennifer Curtiss Gage (Princeton, NJ: Princeton University Press, 2011). On the "luminous opacity" of the Romantic cloud, which indexes the "constantly shifting relation between perception and feeling," see Mary Jacobus, *Romantic Things: A Tree, a Cloud, a Stone* (Chicago: University of Chicago Press, 2012), 12, 14. And on cloudiness as a diaphanous halo that blurs the edges of poetic form, see Ann Smock's beautiful essay, "Cloudy Roubaud," *Representations* 86 (Spring 2004).

17. Hubert Damisch, *A Theory of /Cloud/: Toward a History of Painting*, trans. Janet Lloyd (Stanford, CA: Stanford University Press, 2002), 31.

18. John Ruskin, *Modern Painters*, vol. 1 (London: Ballantyne, 1883), 216.

19. Ruskin, *Modern Painters*, vol. 6 (London: Ballantyne, 1897), 76–78.

20. Ibid., 216.

21. Pierre Alferi, Regents' Lecture at the University of California, Berkeley (January 27, 2009).

22. Naomi Schor, *Reading in Detail: Aesthetics and the Feminine* (New York: Routledge, 2007), 15.

23. Jean-François Lyotard, *The Inhuman: Reflections on Time*, trans. Geoffrey Bennington and Rachel Bowlby (Stanford, CA: Stanford University Press, 1991), 140.

24. Ibid., 141. As Wayne Koestenbaum puts it, "nuance is not a direct object." "In Defense of Nuance," in *My 1980s and Other Essays* (New York: Macmillan, 2013), 63.

25. "When the sought-after nuance lies halfway between two nuances that are easier to render, the only way is to name both while emphasizing the closer one." ("[L]orsque la nuance cherchée se trouve à mi-chemin entre deux nuances plus faciles à rendre, il n'y a d'autre moyen que de nommer les deux en soulignant la plus proche.") Leo Spitzer, *Études de Style*, trans. Eliane Kaufholz, Alain Coulon, and Michel Foucault (Paris: Gallimard, 1970), 420.

26. Ibid.

27. Ibid., 448–449.

28. Bourdieu, *Distinction*, 2.

29. Jean Baudrillard, *Le Système des objets* (Paris: Gallimard, 1968), 43–44.

30. Barthes, *The Neutral*, 51; *Le Neutre*, 83.

31. Ibid.

32. In his course summary for *The Neutral*, Barthes describes his project as follows: "we have defined as pertaining to the Neutral every inflection that, dodging or baffling the paradigmatic, oppositional structures of meaning, aims at the suspension of the conflictual basis of discourse." *The Neutral*, 211. "[O]n a défini comme relevant du Neutre toute inflexion qui esquive ou déjoue la structure paradigmatique, oppositionnelle, du sens, et vise par conséquent à la suspension des données conflictuelles du discours." *Le*

Neutre, 261. For a helpful discussion of *The Neutral*'s "low-key" utopianism, see Rodolphus Teeuwen, "An Epoch of Rest: Roland Barthes's 'Neutral' and the Utopia of Weariness," *Cultural Critique* 80 (Winter 2012).

33. Barthes, *Oeuvres complètes:* vol. 4, 1972–1976 (Paris: Seuil, 2002), 140.

34. Barthes, *The Preparation of the Novel*, 40; *La Préparation du roman*, 75.

35. Barthes, *The Neutral*, 11, trans. modified; *Le Neutre*, 37.

36. Barthes, *The Preparation of the Novel*, 46; *La Préparation du roman*, 82.

37. Barthes, *The Neutral*, 130; *Le Neutre*, 170.

38. *In Search of Lost Time*, 2: 32, trans. modified; *À la recherche du temps perdu*, 1: 445.

39. *In Search of Lost Time*, 2: 62; *À la recherche du temps perdu*, 1: 465.

40. *In Search of Lost Time*, 2: 25; *À la recherche du temps perdu*, 1: 440.

41. *In Search of Lost Time*, 2: 27; *À la recherche du temps perdu*, 1: 441.

42. *In Search of Lost Time*, 2: 26; *À la recherche du temps perdu*, 1: 440.

43. *In Search of Lost Time*, 2:27; *À la recherche du temps perdu*, 1: 441.

44. *In Search of Lost Time*, 2: 37; *À la recherche du temps perdu*, 1: 448.

45. Bourdieu, *Distinction*, 474; *La Distinction*, 553.

46. "I was told that he had alluded to an evening long ago when he had 'seen the moment in which I was about to kiss his hand'" *In Search of Lost Time*, 2: 68. "[O]n me raconta qu'il avait fait allusion à une soirée d'autrefois dans laquelle il avait 'vu le moment où j'allais lui baiser les mains.'" *À la recherche du temps perdu*, 1: 469.

47. Cited in Christine Cano, *Proust's Deadline* (Urbana: University of Illinois Press, 2006), 58.

48. Jacques Normand [under the pseudonym of Jacques Madeleine], "En somme, qu'est-ce?" in *Les Critiques de notre temps et Proust*, ed. Jacques Bersani (Paris: Garnier, 1971), 20.

49. Ibid., 14. Describing Proust as a "pathological case," Normand is almost as tongue-tied after 712 pages of hyper-nuanced description as the narrator is after his first trip to the theater: "what does all this mean? Where does all this lead? Impossible to know! Impossible to say anything about it!" The critic finds himself reduced to a stammer: "mais pourquoi tout cela ? Mais quel rapport ? Quoi ? Quoi enfin?" ibid., 20, 13.

50. "Une oeuvre de loisir," in *Les Critiques de notre temps et Proust*, ed. Jacques Bersani (Paris: Garnier, 1971), 22.

51. Ibid.

52. Allying intensified attention to detail with a modern "micro-physics of power," Foucault argues that this "mystical calculus of the infinitesimal and the infinite" was elaborated during the classical age in order to make legible and productive a variety of emergent spaces: the school, the barracks, the hospital, the workshop. Michel Foucault, *Discipline and Punish: The Birth of the Prison*, trans. Alan Sheridan. (New York: Vintage, 1977), 139–140. For a discussion of the relation between the detail and positivistic thought, see the final chapter of Didi-Huberman's *Confronting Images*.

53. James Elkins, "On the Impossibility of Close Reading: The Case of Alexander Marshack," *Current Anthropology* 37.2 (April, 1996): 198.

54. Ibid., 199.

55. Susan Stewart, *On Longing: Narratives of the Miniature, the Gigantic, the Souvenir, the Collection* (Durham, NC: Duke University Press, 1996), 28.

56. Deleuze and Guattari use the term "haptic" rather than "tactile" because this word "does not establish an opposition between the two sense organs but rather invites the assumption that the eye itself may fulfill this nonoptical function." Gilles Deleuze and Félix Guattari, *A Thousand Plateaus: Capitalism and Schizophrenia*, trans. Brian Massumi (Minneapolis: University of Minnesota Press, 1987), 492.

57. Deleuze and Guattari, *A Thousand Plateaus*, 493; *Mille plateaux: capitalisme et schizophrénie* (Paris: Minuit, 1980), 615.

58. *A Thousand Plateaus*, 476; *Mille plateaux*, 594.

59. *A Thousand Plateaus*, 477–478; *Mille plateaux*, 596–597.

60. *A Thousand Plateaus*, 478; *Mille plateaux*, 597.

61. *A Thousand Plateaus* 488; *Mille plateaux*, 609.

62. *In Search of Lost Time*, 4: 75–76.

63. *À la recherche du temps perdu*, 3: 56–57.

64. *In Search of Lost Time*, 4: 77; *À la recherche du temps perdu*, 3: 57.

65. *In Search of Lost Time*, 1: 168–169; trans. modified. I borrow the phrase "fairy play" from Lydia Davis's translation. *Swann's Way*, trans. Lydia Davis (New York: Penguin, 2004), 122.

66. *À la recherche du temps perdu*, 1: 119.

67. Michel Riffaterre, "The Intertextual Unconscious," *Critical Inquiry* 13.2 (Winter, 1987): 375.

68. "[P]eindre minutieusement, en revenant souvent à petits coups de brosse ou de pinceau sur des parties déjà faites et en les finissant à l'excès." Littré, *Dictionnaire de la langue française* (1872–77), s.v. "pignocher," accessed May 7, 2015, http://www.littre.org/definition/pignocher. The 1932 edition of the *Dictionnaire de l'Académie Française* defines "pignocher" similarly as an excessively attentive workmanship, "une facture trop soignée." Accessed May 7, 2015, http://www.cnrtl.fr/definition/academie8/pignocher.

69. Barthes, *The Neutral*, 51; *Le Neutre*, 83.

70. Silvan Tomkins, *Shame and Its Sisters: A Silvan Tomkins Reader*, ed. Eve Kosofsky Sedgwick and Adam Frank (Durham, NC: Duke University Press, 1995), 77–78.

71. In a formulation highly relevant to the *Recherche*, a text suffused with depictions of sleeplessness, Tomkins notes that insomnia may be produced by extreme interest or sustained intense excitement. *Shame and Its Sisters*, 76–77.

72. According to Ross Posnock, curiosity is bound up with vulnerability, flexibility, non-identitarian thinking (or the "entwining of self and other") and the "overlap" of "psychological, cultural, critical, and sexual modalities." *The Trial of Curiosity: Henry James, William James, and the Challenge of Modernity* (New York: Oxford University Press, 1991), 20–21.

73. Tomkins, *Shame and Its Sisters*, 79.

74. In thinking about nuance as a phenomenon that requires a particularly light, or "weak" critical touch, I have been inspired by Tomkins's discussion of the difference between "strong" and "weak" affect theories, or modes of organizing perceptual data. According to Tomkins, a strong theory is a theory of wide generality and temporal extension, adept at absorbing a range of particulars into a summary. A weak theoretical strain, on the other hand, attends only to close-by phenomena. It offers "sensitization" to relevant incoming information that might correlate to its interpretation, but its "cognitive antenna" is less anticipatory and far-reaching than that of strong theory. *Shame and Its Sisters*, 166. Eve Kosofsky Sedgwick elaborates on the consequences of "strong" (or "paranoid") and "weak" (or "reparative") theory in *Touching Feeling: Affect, Pedagogy, Performativity*, 123–152. We might also understand the distinction between "strong" and "weak" interpretive modes in

terms of "symptomatic" and "surface" reading. See Stephen Best and Sharon Marcus, "Surface Reading: An Introduction," *Representations* 108 (Fall 2009): 1–21.

75. *In Search of Lost Time*, 1: 158, trans. modified; *À la recherche du temps perdu*, 1: 112. For a compelling phenomenological investigation of this sort of sensory dynamism in Proust, see Anne Simon, *Proust ou le réel retrouvé* (Paris: Presses Universitaires de France, 2000). I share Simon's interest in what she terms "the movement of reversibility between the self and the world," but disagree with her claim that the hawthorn episode exemplifies the "frontal mode of confrontation" that she sees as characterizing the subject-object relation in the early volumes of the novel. *Proust ou le réel retrouvé*, 15, my trans.

76. *In Search of Lost Time*, 1: 193–194.

77. *À la recherche du temps perdu*, 1: 136.

78. *In Search of Lost Time*, 1: 61; *À la recherche du temps perdu*, 1: 45.

79. *In Search of Lost Time*, 1: 61–62; trans. modified; *À la recherche du temps perdu*, 1: 45.

80. *In Search of Lost Time*, 1: 63; *À la recherche du temps perdu*, 1: 46.

81. *In Search of Lost Time*, 1: 194; *À la recherche du temps perdu*, 1: 136–137.

82. *In Search of Lost Time*, 1: 195.

83. *À la recherche du temps perdu*, 1: 137.

84. By contrast, Michel Butor's reading of the hawthorn encounter as a "failure" implicitly heterosexualizes the familiar teleological conversion-to-art plot. According to Butor, the hawthorn flowers are but a harbinger of the women the narrator will vainly pursue throughout the novel—Gilberte, Albertine, and the Duchess of Guermantes. The narrator will only figuratively conquer the flowers and the women by writing a book. "Les Moments de Marcel Proust," 125. According to the logic of this reading, the hawthorn hedge offers a childishly non-productive modality of pleasure—a mere foreshadowing of more productive and virile satisfactions to come. Rather than dismiss the hawthorn scene as incomplete—only an anticipation of future fulfillment—we might understand the narrator's fascination with these ungraspable rhythms and textures as evidence of Proust's interest in multiple forms of desire and modes of enjoyment.

85. Elaine Scarry, *Dreaming by the Book* (Princeton, NJ: Princeton University Press, 1999), 59.

86. *In Search of Lost Time*, 1: 156; trans. modified; *À la recherche du temps perdu*, 1: 111.

87. *In Search of Lost Time*, 1: 194; *À la recherche du temps perdu*, 1: 136.

88. The flowers are not, however, exclusively allied with the narrator's interest in girls. In their association with the peculiar act of hat-stomping, they also point to the narrator's future ambiguous relation to the Baron de Charlus. The scene in which the narrator, like a "princesse de tragédie," stomps on his own hat while saying goodbye to the hawthorn hedge prefigures the scene several volumes later in which he stomps on *Charlus's* hat in a passionate fit of rage—a scene which is apparently choreographed by Charlus for his own pleasure. *In Search of Lost Time*, 1: 204, 3: 766; *À la recherche du temps perdu*, 1: 143, 2: 847.

89. *Critique of the Power of Judgment*, 93. Kant's listing of these objects is a peculiarly vivid moment in the text. It is almost as the flowers and foliage flaunt their own delicate qualities in disregard for the philosopher's insistence that aesthetic (dis)interest is a subjective phenomenon, indifferent to the object's properties.

90. "One must not be in the least biased in favor of the existence of the thing, but must be entirely indifferent in this respect in order to play the judge in matters of taste." *Critique of the Power of Judgment*, 91.

91. "Our past is hidden somewhere outside the realm, beyond the reach of intellect, in some material object (in the sensation which that material object would give us) of which we have no inkling." *In Search of Lost Time*, 1: 59–60, trans. modified. "[Notre passé] est caché hors de son domaine et de sa portée, en quelque objet matériel (en la sensation que nous donnerait cet objet matériel) que nous ne soupçonnons pas." *À la recherche du temps perdu*, 1: 44.

92. Fry, 61, my emphasis.

93. *The Neutral*, 228, n. 25; *Le Neutre*, 107, n. 17. The *Trésor de la Langue Française* defines "cénesthésie" as a non-specifiable feeling of vitality: "Organic sensitivity, emanating from the ensemble of internal sensations, which gives rise to the human being's general feeling of existence, independent of the specific role of the senses." *TLFi*, s.v. "cénesthésie," accessed March 29, 2015, http://www.cnrtl.fr/definition/cénésthesie. For a history of coenesthesis as a medical concept, see Daniel Heller-Roazen, *The Inner Touch: Archeology of a Sensation* (New York: Zone Books, 2007), 237–251.

94. Cornelia Fales, "The Paradox of Timbre," *Ethnomusicology* 46.1 (Winter, 2002): 58.

95. The arrangement of contrasting timbres "moves listeners to different perceptual positions relative to the acoustic world." Ibid., 74.

96. Ibid., 59. Timothy Morton describes the phenomenon of ambiance, including the trope of the timbral, as a "fleeting, dissolving presence that flickers across our perception and cannot be brought front and center." *Ecology Without Nature: Rethinking Environmental Aesthetics* (Cambridge, MA: Harvard University Press, 2007), 51.

97. Fales, "The Paradox of Timbre," 62–63, 77.

98. Ibid., 63. Contributing to this malleability, "timbre" derives from "tympanum," a taut surface that both receives and produces vibrations. For a discussion of the tympanum (*tympan*) as a privileged figure for philosophical deconstruction, see Jacques Derrida, *Marges de la philosophie* (Paris: Minuit, 2003), i–xxv; *Margins of Philosophy*, trans. Alan Bass (Chicago: University of Chicago Press, 1990), ix–xxix. Katherine Bergeron also discusses timbre's resistance to definition and its status as a "queer boundary" in *Voice Lessons: French Mélodie in the Belle Époque* (New York: Oxford University Press, 2010), 135–142.

99. Maurice Merleau-Ponty, *The Visible and the Invisible: Followed by Working Notes*, trans. Alphonso Lingis (Evanston, IL: Northwestern University Press, 1968), 123. "Chaque paysage de ma vie [. . .] est prégnant, en tant que visible, de bien d'autres visions que la mienne." *Le Visible et l'Invisible, suivi de notes de travail* (Paris: Gallimard, 1964), 162. Merleau-Ponty's notion of embodied vision draws significantly on Proust. On the phenomenologist's concept of "shared landscape" as an alternative to an isolated and private vision, see Jacobus, *Romantic Things*, 32–35.

100. *In Search of Lost Time*, 4: 739–740; trans. modified.

101. *À la recherche du temps perdu*, 3: 1445.

102. Barthes, *A Lover's Discourse: Fragments*, trans. Richard Howard (New York: Farrar, Straus, and Giroux, 1978), 169, trans. modified. *Fragments d'un discours amoureux* (Paris: Seuil, 1977), 202.

103. *A Lover's Discourse*, 170, trans. modified; *Fragments d'un discours amoureux*, 202.

104. "Her silences were merely screens, her surface affection merely kept beneath the surface a thousand memories which would have rent my heart." *In Search of Lost Time*,

5: 144. "Ses silences n'étaient donc que des voiles, ses tendresses de surface ne faisaient que retenir au fond mille souvenirs qui m'eussent déchiré." *À la recherche du temps perdu*, 3: 621.

105. *In Search of Lost Time*, 1: 561–562.

106. *À la recherche du temps perdu*, 1: 387, my emphasis.

107. *In Search of Lost Time*, 2: 503–505 (trans. modified), 550; *À la recherche du temps perdu*, 2: 146–148, 180.

108. *In Search of Lost Time*, 2: 728, trans. modified; *À la recherche du temps perdu*, 2: 305.

109. *In Search of Lost Time*, 2: 593; *À la recherche du temps perdu*, 2: 210.

110. *In Search of Lost Time*, 2: 595, trans. modified; *À la recherche du temps perdu*, 2: 212.

111. *In Search of Lost Time*, 5: 744, trans. modified.

112. *À la recherche du temps perdu*, 4: 133–134.

113. *OED*. This painterly meaning is obsolete in English, but alive in French.

Chapter 4

1. *Mute Objects of Expression*, trans. Lee Fahnestock (New York: Archipelago Books, 2008), 153, 144, 151; *Oeuvres complètes* (hereafter *OC*) (Paris: Gallimard, 1999–2002), 1: 424, 419, 423.

2. Francis Ponge, *Selected Poems*, ed. Margaret Guiton, trans. C. K. Williams, John Montague, and Margaret Guiton (Winston-Salem, NC: Wake Forest University Press, 1994), 47; *OC*, 1: 28.

3. On the importance of Kantian aesthetic noninstrumentality to Benjamin and Agamben, see Benjamin Morgan, "Undoing Legal Violence: Walter Benjamin's and Giorgio Agamben's Aesthetics of Pure Means," *Journal of Law and Society* 4 (March 2007), 46–64. As Samuel Weber notes, for Agamben profanation "depends entirely on a notion of 'use' (*usage*) as a practice cut off from a goal or product." *Benjamin's-Abilities* (Cambridge, MA: Harvard University Press, 2008), 314.

4. Giorgio Agamben, *Profanations*, trans. Jeff Fort (Cambridge, MA: Zone Books, 2007), 77.

5. Vincent Kaufmann, *Le Livre et ses adresses: Mallarmé, Ponge, Valéry, Blanchot*. (Paris: Méridiens Klincksieck, 1986), 149.

6. As he puts it in 1941: "From now on, may nothing ever cause me to go back on my resolve: never sacrifice the object of my study in order to enhance some verbal turn discovered on the subject, nor piece together any such discoveries in a poem." *Mute Objects*, 3. "Que rien désormais ne me fasse revenir de ma détermination: ne sacrifier jamais l'objet de mon étude à la mise en valeur de quelque trouvaille verbale que j'aurai faite à son propos, ni à l'arrangement en poème de plusieurs de ces trouvailles." *OC*, 1: 337.

7. "[C]e qu'il a de brut, de *différent*." *The Nature of Things*, trans. Lee Fahnestock (New York: Red Dust, 1995), 3; *OC*, 1: 337, original emphasis.

8. "Mon oeillet ne doit pas être trop grand-chose"; "Tout d'abord, il faut noter que le mimosa ne m'inspire pas du tout." *Mute Objects*, 48, 56; *OC*, 1: 363, 366.

9. This and all unattributed translations of Ponge are my own. *OC*, 1: 215.

10. Jacques Derrida, *Signéponge/Signsponge*, trans. Richard Rand (New York: Columbia University Press, 1994), 88–89, trans. modified. Ponge's sponge-towel, in particular, is for Derrida the "very example" of such worthlessness: "l'exemple même du sans valeur, du

rien ou de si-peu-de-chose, le n'importe quoi de peu de prix, l'anonyme ou presque dans la foule des petits." Ibid.

11. Philippe Met emphasizes the novelty of Ponge's notebook poetry, noting that in his practice of publishing drafts and sketches, Ponge has no predecessor. "Fausses notes: pour une poétique du carnet," *French Forum* 37 (Winter/Spring 2012): 63.

12. Jean-Paul Sartre, *Situations I* (Paris: Gallimard, 1947), 230.

13. *The Nature of Things*, 13–14; *OC* 1: 15–16.

14. "[P]lus tu avances, et plus tu es traversé de choses que tu ne connais pas claire-ment." Paulhan to Ponge, April 13, 1942, in *Correspondance 1923–1968*, ed. Claire Boaretto (Paris: Gallimard, 1986), 272.

15. March 1, 1949, in *The Letters of Samuel Beckett*, vol. 2, trans. George Craig et al. (Cambridge: Cambridge University Press, 2011), 120, 122, trans. modified.

16. Ibid., 122.

17. Barthes, *The Responsibility of Forms*, 165; *Oeuvres complètes*, vol. 5 (Paris: Seuil, 2002), 710.

18. Mary Capello, *Awkward: A Detour* (New York: Bellevue Literary Press, 2007), 115.

19. Ngai, *Our Aesthetic Categories*, 88–93.

20. Ngai also emphasizes an "off" quality in what she sees as the exaggerated cuteness of Ponge's work, but her reading focuses on poetry as an object of consumption, while I argue that Ponge redirects our attention to the pole of production.

21. *The Nature of Things*, 8.

22. *OC*, 1: 38.

23. Michael Thomson, *Rubbish Theory: The Creation and Destruction of Value* (Oxford: Oxford University Press, 1979), 9.

24. Ibid., 671.

25. Gérard Farasse and Bernard Veck, *Guide d'un petit voyage dans l'oeuvre de Francis Ponge* (Villeneuve d'Ascq Nord: Presses Universitaires du Septentrion, 1999), 11.

26. *OC*, 1: LIV.

27. Ibid., 646.

28. *Mute Objects*, 37; *OC*, 1: 356.

29. "Moi ce qui me tient au coeur [. . .] je ne peux guère en parler. Voilà une définition des choses que j'aime: ce sont celles dont je ne parle pas, dont j'ai envie de parler, et dont je n'arrive pas à parler." *OC* 1: 659.

30. *Mute Objects*, 127.

31. *OC*, 1: 356.

32. Ibid., 433. This volume was composed in the early 1940s but not published until 1952.

33. "[J]e travaille *parmi* ou *à travers* le dictionnaire un peu à la façon d'une taupe, re-jetant à droite ou à gauche les mots, les expressions, me frayant mon chemin à travers eux." Ibid., 645, original emphasis.

34. This is how he puts it: "In this way, my expressions appear to me something like cast-out matter, like debris, and the work itself sometimes almost like the tunnel, the gal-lery, or like the chamber I've opened in the rock, rather than like a building, a monument, or a statue." ("Ainsi mes expressions m'apparaissent-elles plutôt comme des matériaux rejetés, comme des déblais et à la limite l'oeuvre elle-même parfois comme le tunnel, la galerie, ou enfin la chambre que j'ai ouverte dans le roc, plutôt que comme une construc-tion, comme un édifice, ou comme une statue.") Ibid., 645.

35. "Il ne fuit donc pas devant le sale, il écrit avec le sale contre le sale, sur le sale, du sale." Jacques Derrida, *Signéponge/Signsponge*, 44–45.

36. The notebook poem exaggerates the jagged edges already on display in the prose poem, a genre Michelle Clayton describes as particularly hospitable to contradiction. Clayton notes that the prose poem tends to "structure itself around a clash of discourses." *Poetry in Pieces: César Vallejo and Lyric Modernity* (Berkeley and Los Angeles: University of California Press, 2011), 201–202.

37. Lois Dahlin, "Entretien avec Francis Ponge: ses rapports avec Camus, Sartre, et d'autres," *The French Review* 54. 2 (December 1980): 278–279.

38. Ponge makes these statements in late August 1941, in a response to Camus's "Myth of Sisyphus." He had been working on *La Mounine* since May. *OC* 1: 207, original emphasis.

39. *OC*, 1: 433.

40. Michel de Certeau, "Vocal Utopias: Glossolalias," trans. Daniel Rosenberg, *Representations* 56 (Autumn 1996): 29–47, 41.

41. *Mute Objects*, 162.

42. Sidney Lévy, "Mutisme pongéen et chose mallarméenne," *Dalhousie French Studies* 25 (Winter-Fall 1993): 82.

43. *Mute Objects*, 136, original ellipses.

44. *OC*, 1: 414.

45. *Mute Objects*, 136.

46. Ibid., 133, 134, 158.

47. "Qui se manifeste ou se fait sentir avec une importance particulière mais non susceptible de mesure directe." *TLFi*, s.v. "intense," accessed March 29, 2015, http://www.cnrtl.fr/definition/intense.

48. *Mute Objects*, 430; *OC*, 1: 430.

49. Ibid., 163; Ibid., 430.

50. Monique David-Ménard, "Must One Seek the Universal in Beauty?" *Umbr(a): Aesthetics & Sublimation* (1999): 55–56.

51. Ibid., 57.

52. *OC*, 1: 438.

53. Ibid., 438.

54. *OC*, 1: 1013.

55. *Mute Objects*, 163; *OC*, 1: 431, original emphasis.

56. *Mute Objects* 165; *OC*, 1: 432.

57. *OC*, 1: 675.

58. Ibid., 777. *Rédhibition* is etymologically derived from *redhibere*: "faire reprendre une chose vendue" ("to take back something sold"). *TLFi*, s.v. "rédhibition," accessed March 29, 2015, http://www.cnrtl.fr/etymologie/redhibition.

59. Francis Ponge, *Le Savon* (Paris: Gallimard, 1967), 55.

60. *OC*, 2: 469.

61. For an illuminating discussion of imperfectionism as a "democratic ethos," see Leela Gandhi, *The Common Cause: Postcolonial Ethics and the Practice of Democracy, 1900 to 1955* (Chicago: University of Chicago Press, 2014). See also Anahid Nersessian's *Utopia, Limited: Romanticism and Adjustment* (Cambridge, MA: Harvard University Press, 2015), which theorizes the ecological import of a utopianism "peel[ed] away from perfection" (17).

62. "Comment qualifier cette perfection qui se dispense ainsi sans compter, que tout le monde peut cueillir?" *OC*, 1: 585.

63. *OC*, 1: 585.

64. Ibid., 592.

65. Ibid., 585, original ellipses.

66. This and the preceding two citations are from *OC*, 1: 592.

67. Adam Smith, *The Wealth of Nations, Books 1–3* (London: Penguin, 2003), 131–132.

68. *OC*, 1: 584–585.

69. Ibid., 595. The second set of ellipses are Ponge's.

70. Ibid., 592.

71. Ibid., 596.

72. "Pour vous, qui que vous soyez, dans quelque état que vous vous trouviez, un verre d'eau. Ce livre soit un verre d'eau." Ibid., 596.

73. "Cette fois, on ne m'ennuiera plus avec la poésie." Ibid., 591.

74. "[I]l faut que cela passe d'un trait, presque sans conséquence." Ibid., 591.

75. "Rendre autre, changer, modifier"; "modifier en mal, détériorer, dénaturer, dégrader"; "changer la vraie nature d'une chose, falsifier." *TLFi*, s.v. "altérer," accessed March 29, 2015, http://www.cnrtl.fr/definition/alterer.

76. As Ponge puts it, punning on "désalterer," "ce manque de qualités fait qu'elle n'altère en aucune façon celui que d'abord elle désaltère." *OC*, 1: 590.

77. Ibid., 583.

78. Ibid., 596.

79. Ibid., 594.

80. Ibid., 591.

81. Ibid.

82. "[I]l ne lui manque rien [. . .]. Il s'affirme comme tel, sans plus." Ibid., 597.

83. Ibid., 602.

84. As he puts it, it quenches (dis-alters) you, which is to say, returns you to yourself ("elle vous désaltère, c'est-à-dire vous restitue en votre identité, votre moi"). Ibid., 588.

85. Ibid., 586.

86. Explaining why he was drawn to this relatively unknown artist, Ponge notes that even twenty-five years later, Kermadec's work provokes in him a "happy surprise" and a "blessed 'incomprehension.'" *OC*, 2: 723.

87. On this contrast, see Madeline Pampel, *Francis Ponge et Eugene de Kermadec, histoire d'un compagnonnage* (Villeneuve d'Ascq: Presses Universitaires du Septentrion, 2011), 201–205.

88. *OC*, 1: 589.

89. Bach's *Well-Tempered Clavier* comprises forty-eight prelude-and-fugue pairs, which cover all the keys of the complete tonal system. Valorizing regularity and equality of tones and semitones, the *Well-Tempered Clavier* puts the modern chromatic cycle of tones and semitones to the test. Richard Teruskin, *Music in the Seventeenth and Eighteenth Centuries: The Oxford History of Western Music* (New York: Oxford University Press, 2009), 249.

90. *OC*, 1: 589.

Chapter 5

1. Bourdieu, *Distinction*, 6; *La Distinction*, vi.

2. *Oeuvres complètes* (hereafter *OC*) (Paris: Gallimard, 1996), 1602; 1603–1604.

3. Ibid., 89–90.

4. Sianne Ngai defines "feeling-tone" as a "global or organizing affect, [a text's] general disposition or orientation toward its audience and the world." *Ugly Feelings*, 28.

5. Among the many recent critical works on affect, I have been particularly inspired by Sianne Ngai's *Ugly Feelings*, an Adorno-inflected study of "minor" or "unprestigious" aesthetic emotions in American literature, and Eve Kosofsky Sedgwick's *Touching Feeling: Affect, Pedagogy, Performativity*, which draws on performance studies, the writings of Henry James, and the work of psychologist Silvan Tomkins in order to develop a non-moralistic theory of shame. Kevis Goodman's writing on nostalgia has also helped me to see how interesting the history of emotion can be; see her "Uncertain Disease: Nostalgia, Pathologies of Motion, Practices of Reading," *Studies in Romanticism* 49 (Summer 2010). Jonathan Flatley provides a useful glossary of terms related to affect studies in *Affective Mapping: Melancholia and the Politics of Modernism* (Cambridge, MA: Harvard University Press, 2008), 11–27.

6. *OC*, 1705.

7. Ibid., 1153.

8. Ibid., 1761.

9. "[I]l fallait décomposer ces mouvements et les faire se déployer dans la conscience du lecteur à la manière d'un film au ralenti." *OC*, 1154.

10. Sarraute describes her difference from her contemporaries this way: "Linguistics was supposed to serve as a model for writers. Nothing existed outside of words. Nothing preexisted them. Those who ventured to timidly affirm—as I myself did—that in all of our minds there were representations, immediate and global perceptions, sensations [. . .], were instantly snubbed." ("[L]a linguistique devait servir de modèle aux écrivains. Rien n'existait hors de mots. Rien ne leur préexistait. Ceux qui s'aventuraient, comme je l'ai fait moi-même, à affirmer timidement qu'il y avait dans l'esprit de chacun de nous des représentations, des perceptions immédiates et globales, des sensations . . . que quelque chose donc existe hors des mots, se faisaient aussitôt rabrouer.") *OC*, 1699. On the "neutral and combinational," anti-phenomenological style characteristic of the *nouveau roman*, see Jameson, *Postmodernism, or, the Cultural Logic of Late Capitalism*, 133, 135.

11. Williams, "Structures of Feeling," 134.

12. Ibid., 132.

13. Flatley, *Affective Mapping*, 25. For an illuminating discussion of the structure of feeling as the "affective residue" of history-in-the-present, see Goodman's *Georgic Modernity and British Romanticism*, 3, 5–9.

14. Williams, "Structures of Feeling," 132.

15. J. L. Austin distinguishes between two types of statements (an opposition that ultimately proves to be untenable, since each relies parasitically on the other): the *constative* (descriptive statements, or statements of fact, which can be either true or false) and the *performative* (forceful, event-producing, successful or unsuccessful, "happy" or "unhappy"). Taking the marriage vow as paradigmatic of the performative utterance, Austin investigates the force of certain verbs when spoken in the first person, present, indicative, active voice: "I promise," "I apologize," "I bet," and so on. Such statements do what they say; in speaking them, one accomplishes an act. "In these examples it seems clear that to utter the sentence (in, of course, the appropriate circumstances) is not to *describe* my doing of what I should be said in so uttering to be doing or to state that I am doing it: it is to do it. [. . .] When I say, before the registrar or alter, etc., 'I do,' I am not

reporting on a marriage: I am indulging in it." *How to Do Things with Words* (Cambridge, MA: Harvard University Press, 1975), 6. The declaration of an object's aesthetic value—as in the statement, "this is beautiful"—might seem like a constative statement or proposition, judgeable according to a true-false criteria, rather than as felicitous or infelicitous. But because aesthetic objects in modernity are defined, precisely, by their lack of proper subject matter or attributes, a statement of aesthetic worth cannot be determined to be true or false. Instead, as Bourdieu demonstrates, aesthetic judgments (including the act of selecting particular objects for display in a museum or on one's mantle) legitimate the object as worthy of a certain kind of suspended attention (a gaze attentive to its formal aspect). They also generate and reproduce social hierarchies, reinforcing the dividing line between those with and without the cultural authority to make such judgments. Art does not exist independently of the appreciation practices of museum-goers, collectors, and critics. Unlike a judge's act of calling the court to order, or a priest's legitimation of marriage vows, however, it is difficult to determine whether an aesthetic judgment is "felicitous" or not, and a judgment that is felicitous in one context will inevitably fall flat in the next.

16. In *Distinction*, members of the dominant class master the discourse of aesthetic judgment, controlling even the rhetoric of the sociological interview. Bourdieu notes their capacity to turn lacunas into disdainful refusals and confusion into seeming absentmindedness; the bourgeois subjects have mastered the art of masking and deflecting. *Distinction*, 174; *La Distinction*, 194. Working-class subjects, on the other hand, expose the awkwardness of the aesthetic encounter by uttering ambivalent performatives such as "it's beautiful but [. . .] it's not my cup of tea." ("Oui c'est très beau, mais [. . .] ce n'est pas mon genre.") Bourdieu notes that, among working-class interviewees, three-fourths of aesthetic judgments begin with "if." *Distinction*, 41–42; *La Distinction*, 42–43.

17. Austin, *How to Do Things with Words*, 52, 148.

18. Kant, *Critique of the Power of Judgment*, 98.

19. In fact, tempering his description of the aesthetic judgment's forceful universality, Kant suggests (in §19) that the judgment of taste not only "ascribes assent to everyone," but in fact "*solicits* assent from everyone." *Critique of the Power of Judgment*, 121, my emphasis. (In Meredith's translation: "We are suitors for agreement from everyone else.") In this one regard, Sarraute's representation of aesthetic judgment is closer to Kant's than to Bourdieu's.

20. *OC*, 1453, original ellipses. Throughout this chapter, all unbracketed ellipses are Sarraute's.

21. *OC*, 1587. Aesthetic taste is a particularly irritating subject in Sarraute's world: a number of her works feature scenes in which one speaker verbally pokes or chafes another in speaking about taste. In *Tropisms*, for example, an anonymous "she" tries to pull away "gently" ("doucement") while an anonymous "he" verbally prods her: "There was no way of escaping. No way to stop it. [. . .] He would continue, without pity, without respite: 'Dover, Dover, Dover? Eh? Eh? Thackeray? Eh? Thackeray? England? Dickens? Shakespeare? Eh? Eh? Dover? Shakespeare? Dover?'" *OC*, 22. Similarly, in *Portrait of a Man Unknown*, a character references artworks, museums, the Uffizi, and Rembrandt ("eh?") only to surreptitiously mock and provoke the narrator. *OC*, 88. A negative affect Ngai describes as a "strangely aggressive kind of weakness," irritation combines "hyperresponsiveness" to one's external surroundings with a disengagement from vehement emotion or expressiveness. *Ugly Feelings*, 182, 190–91.

22. Erving Goffman, *Interaction Ritual: Essays in Face to Face Behavior* (New York: Anchor Books, 1967), 100.

23. Ibid., 102, 99.

24. Ibid., 106. As Sarraute puts it, certain words provoke minor flusterings or irritations, which in turn incite a play of action and reaction: words enter into a subject, where "they swell, they explode, they make waves and ripples around them which, in turn, rise, touch the surface, and spread out into words" ("elles enflent, elles explosent, elles provoquent autour d'elles des ondes et des remous qui, à leur tour, montent, affleurent et se déploient au-dehors en paroles"). *OC*, 1598.

25. Ibid., 529.

26. Ibid., 576.

27. Ibid., 590.

28. Ibid., 592.

29. Ibid., 592.

30. Ibid., 605.

31. Austin lists six conditions for the "felicity" (the "smooth" or "happy" functioning) of a performative: (1) "there must exist an accepted conventional procedure having a certain conventional effect, that procedure to include the uttering of certain words by certain persons in certain circumstances"; (2) "the particular persons and circumstances in a given case must be appropriate for the invocation of the particular procedure invoked"; (3) "the procedure must be executed by all participants correctly"; (4) and "completely"; (5) "where, as often, the procedure is designed for use by persons having certain thoughts or feelings, or for the inauguration of certain consequential conduct on the part of any participant, then a person participating in and so invoking the procedure must in fact have those thoughts or feelings, and the participants must intend so to conduct themselves"; (6) and "must actually so conduct themselves subsequently." *How to Do Things with Words*, 14–15. Despite the precision of these qualifications, *How to Do Things with Words* is largely a list of all the possible ways a performative can fail, and the dichotomy of performatives and constatives is eventually abandoned "in favour of more general *families* of related and overlapping speech acts." Ibid., 150.

32. Ibid., 16, Austin's ellipses.

33. *OC*, 84.

34. In foregrounding Sarraute's interest in performative noise, I am countering Ann Jefferson's claim that Sarraute's sentences "all tend toward [a] pattern of repetition—phonetic, semantic and syntactic—which has the effect of drawing the world and all its manifestations of difference into a vortex—or a haven—of equivalences." *Nathalie Sarraute, Fiction and Theory: Questions of Difference* (Cambridge: Cambridge University Press, 2000), 34. While Jefferson sees Sarraute's "clusters" of images as "equivalent," I suggest that Sarraute is drawing our attention not to an engulfing sameness, but to extremely slight, minor, or unqualifiable distinctions and dissonances—the difference between "oui" and "si . . . si . . . ," for example.

35. Austin, *How to Do Things with Words*, 81.

36. Ibid., 99–100; 121.

37. Ibid., 126.

38. As Stanley Cavell puts it, Austin imagines the illocutionary act as a temporally precise "offer of participation in the order of law." *Philosophy the Day after Tomorrow*

(Cambridge, MA: Harvard University Press, 2005), 185. The perlocutionary act, on the other hand, is not an explicit citation of convention, and hence its successes and failures may be difficult to gauge: "there is no final word, no uptake or downturn, until a line is drawn, a withdrawal is effected, perhaps in order to be revoked." Cavell notes that while illocutionary acts "must be executed by all participants both correctly and completely," there is no analogue for perlocutionary acts, "there being no antecedent procedure in effect." Ibid., 183, 181.

39. Sedgwick, *Touching Feeling*, 68.

40. Ibid., 79.

41. Ibid., 73.

42. Ibid., 69.

43. Ibid., 70.

44. Ibid.

45. Ibid., 75.

46. *OC*, 746. On laughter as a bumping, jolting, "blank citation," see Kevin Newmark, "Traumatic Poetry: Charles Baudelaire and the Shock of Laughter," in *Trauma: Explorations in Memory*, ed. Cathy Caruth (Baltimore: Johns Hopkins University Press, 1995), 251.

47. *OC*, 739.

48. Ibid., 756.

49. "Il est pareil à un acteur qui continue à jouer dans une salle d'où les spectateurs se sont retirés, à un conférencier qui s'efforce de parler comme si de rien n'était devant des chaises vides." Ibid., 756.

50. *Distinction*, 92; *La Distinction*, 100.

51. *OC*, 343–344.

52. Ibid., 344.

53. Ibid., 516.

54. The Duc is particularly unmoved by an asparagus still-life that Swann has urged him to purchase: "I refused to swallow M. Elstir's asparagus. He wanted three hundred francs for them. Three hundred francs for a bundle of asparagus! A louis, that's as much as they're worth, even early in the season. I thought it a bit stiff." *In Search of Lost Time*, 3: 686. "[M]oi, je me suis refusé à avaler les asperges de M. Elstir. Il en demandait trois cents francs. Trois cents francs, une botte d'asperges! Un louis, voilà ce que ça vaut, même en primeurs! Je l'ai trouvée roide." *À la recherche du temps perdu*, 2: 791.

55. What counts as "high" and what as "low" depends on context, so that sometimes "heavy" signifies as petit bourgeois, sometimes as intellectual. Nonetheless, according to Bourdieu, the dualistic structure coheres. *Distinction*, 469–470; *La Distinction*, 546–547.

56. *Distinction*, 282; *La Distinction*, 320–321.

57. We do not know for certain how the owner's father acquired the piece, but it reminds the neighbor of his own colonialist "finds" abroad: "You have a superb piece here. . . . Yes, such strokes of chance, such strokes of luck do happen. . . . Once, I remember, I was on a mission in Cambodia, and in the shop of a little bric-a-brac trader . . . at first I thought . . . and then, imagine, when I looked more closely. . . ." ("Vraiment, vous avez là une pièce superbe. . . . Oui, il y a de ces coups de hasard, de ces coups de chance. . . . Une fois, je me rappelle, j'étais en mission au Cambodge, et chez un petit brocanteur . . . au premier abord j'ai pensé . . . et puis, figurez-vous, en y regardant de plus près. . . .") *OC*, 738–739.

58. In 1928, Georges Rivière organized the first exhibition of pre-Columbian art ("Les arts anciens d'Amérique") at the Musée des arts décoratifs in Paris. One of Bataille's first published texts was a piece written for this exhibition—an essay titled "L'Amérique dispa-rue," celebrating the sacred violence of Aztec civilization. See Georges Bataille, *Oeuvres complètes*, vol. 1 (Paris: Gallimard, 1970), 152–158; Georges Henri Rivière, "My Experience at the Musee D'Ethnologie," Proceedings of the Royal Anthropological Institute of Great Britain and Ireland (1968), 17–21; and James Clifford, "On Ethnographic Surrealism," in *The Predicament of Culture: Twentieth-Century Ethnography, Literature, and Art* (Cambridge, MA: Harvard University Press, 1988), 117–151.

59. *OC*, 739.

60. Ibid., 754.

61. *Distinction*, 281; *La Distinction*, 320.

62. *Distinction*, 279. "Par la maîtrise d'un *langage d'accompagnement*, de préférence technique, archaïque et ésotérique, qui sépare la dégustation savante de la simple con-sommation désarmée et passive, enfermée dans l'instantanéité du plaisir, le *connaisseur* s'affirme digne de s'approprier symboliquement les biens rares qu'il a les moyens matéri-els d'acquérir." *La Distinction*, 318.

63. *Distinction*, 281. "Les objets qui sont dotés du plus haut pouvoir distinctif sont ceux qui témoignent le mieux de la *qualité de l'appropriation*, donc de la qualité du proprié-taire." *La Distinction*, 320.

64. Malraux temporarily loaned out two of France's most precious museum treasures: the *Mona Lisa* was sent to the United States in 1963, and the *Venus de Milo* went to Tokyo in 1964. On the cultural politics of these loans, see Herman Lebovics, *Mona Lisa's Escort: André Malraux and the Reinvention of French Culture* (Ithaca, NY: Cornell University Press, 1999), 9–26.

65. Cited in David L. Looseley, *The Politics of Fun: Cultural Policy and Debate in Con-temporary France* (New York: Berg Publishers, 1995), 37.

66. Lebovics, *Mona Lisa's Escort*, 5.

67. Ibid., 3, 132.

68. Cited in Looseley, *The Politics of Fun*, 36.

69. Ibid., 40.

70. Cited in Looseley, *The Politics of Fun*, 41.

71. Michel Beaujour, "Culture," in *A New History of French Literature*, ed. Denis Hol-lier (Cambridge: Harvard University Press, 1989), 184. Malraux elaborated his fantasy of a democratized high culture in a series of essays published in 1947, 1951, and 1963, which celebrate a concept he termed *le musée imaginaire* (the "museum without walls"). The *musée imaginaire* is essentially the corpus of consecrated works of art, available across the globe thanks to photographic reproduction. A number of Malraux's contemporaries took aim at this fantasy. Bourdieu's early sociological work, for example, seems to be motivated by annoyance toward Malraux's ideology of "Art" as universal essence, the codes of which are supposedly legible without any special training or initiation. Other outspoken critics of the *musée imaginaire* include the art historian Georges Duthuit, who criticized the imperialist logic implicit in Malraux's project in *Le musée inimaginable* (Paris: Corti, 1956). Jean Dubuffet, inventor of the category of "art brut," also attacks Malraux's concep-tion of culture in a book first published in 1968, *Asphyxiante culture* (Paris: Minuit, 1986). Dubuffet argues that state (mono-)culture works like an "antibiotic," flattening all strains of expression except those it officially stamps as legitimate. On the "museum without

walls" and its critics, see Rosalind Krauss, "The Ministry of Fate," in *A New History of French Literature*, ed. Denis Hollier (Cambridge, MA: Harvard University Press, 1989), 1000–1006, and "Postmodernism's Museum without Walls," in *Thinking about Exhibitions*, ed. Reesa Greenberg, Bruce W. Ferguson, and Sandy Nairne (New York: Routledge, 1996), 341–348.

72. *OC*, 792.

73. Ibid., 793.

74. Ibid., 802.

75. Ibid., 829.

76. Ibid., 834.

77. Ibid., 584.

78. Ibid., 540.

79. Ibid., 560.

80. Ibid., 571.

81. Each of these adjectives appears in quotation marks in the original. It is notable that Bourdieu insists on the feminine association of "easiness" here: good taste is founded on the refusal of the facile, not only as a stylistic effect, but also the "easiness [. . .] of a woman or of her lifestyle" ("d'une femme ou de ses mœurs"). *La Distinction*, 566. Bourdieu's explicit gendering of the facile is slightly downplayed in translation; Richard Nice renders this passage as "the refusal of [. . .] 'easy virtue' or an 'easy-lay.'" *Distinction*, 486.

82. Ngai, *Ugly Feelings*, 22.

83. Jameson, *Postmodernism*, 158.

84. *OC*, 1759.

85. *TLFi*. The passage is from *The Age of Suspicion* (1956): "A danger is dissimulated in these *douceâtre* phrases, murderous impulses insinuate themselves within affectionate worry, a tender expression suddenly distills into subtle venom." ("Un danger se dissimule dans ces phrases douceâtres, des impulsions meurtrières s'insinuent dans l'inquiétude affectueuse, une expression de tendresse distille tout à coup un subtil venin.")

86. Ngai, *Ugly Feelings*, 179.

87. Annette Baier, "What Emotions Are About," *Philosophical Perspectives* 4 (1990): 3. On the objectlessness of mood, see also Flatley, *Affective Mapping*, 19.

88. *OC*, 1718.

89. Ibid., 16.

90. Ibid., 31.

91. Ibid., 14.

92. Ibid., 4.

93. Ibid., 3, 14, 15.

94. Ibid., 12.

95. Ibid., 173.

96. Denis Hollier, *Absent without Leave: French Literature under the Threat of War*, trans. Catherine Porter (Cambridge, MA: Harvard University Press, 1997), 96.

97. For a discussion of Bellmer's "tumescent" mutilated dolls, see Rosalind Krauss, "Corpus Delecti," *October* 33 (Summer 1985): 31–72.

98. *OC*, 994.

99. Ibid., 1013.

100. Ibid.

101. Kant, *Critique of the Power of Judgment*, 155.

102. M. Chaouli, "Van Gogh's Ear: Toward a Theory of Disgust," in *Modern Art and the Grotesque*, ed. Frances S. Connelly (Cambridge: Cambridge University Press, 2003), 61; Jacques Derrida, "Economimesis," trans. R. Klein, *Diacritics* 11 (Summer 1981): 22.

103. *OC*, 511–512.

104. Christopher Ricks, *Force of Poetry* (Oxford: Clarendon Press, 1984), 361; Daniel Smith, *Essays on Deleuze* (Edinburgh: Edinburgh University Press, 2012), 232.

105. Ricks, *Force of Poetry*, 361.

106. *OC*, 1759.

107. Ibid., 1040.

108. Ibid., 811.

109. Ibid., 812.

110. Ibid., 810.

111. *Distinction*, 468; *La Distinction*, 546.

112. *OC*, 584.

Afterword

1. *"Art"* itself has provoked conflicting responses. The play premiered in Paris in 1994, went on to sell out for six years in London, and to run for six hundred shows on Broadway. It won Reza a Molière, an Olivier, and a Tony. By 2008 *"Art"* had been translated into thirty-five languages and had grossed two hundred million dollars. Still—or perhaps because of this box office success—some critics have derided the play as "big ideas lite" and "little black dress theatre," and have dismissed Reza as middlebrow, or even, intriguingly, as a "mini-Proust." Agnès Poirier, "Please Stop Laughing at Me," *The Independent*, March 16, 2008; Caryn James, "High School Reunion," *The New York Times*, March 4, 2007. For an intelligent defense and analysis of Reza's work, see Denis Guénoun, *Avez-vous lu Reza?* (Paris: Albin Michel, 2005).

2. Reza, *"Art,"* trans. Christopher Hampton (London: Faber and Faber, 1996), 16; *Théâtre* (Paris: A. Michel, 1998), 209.

3. Bruno Villien, "L'Oeil de Yasmina Reza: l'art au-delà des mots et du spectacle." *L'Oeil* 513 (February 2000), 6, cited in Hélène Jaccomard, "Serge, un peu d'humour! Homo ridens et 'Art' de Yasmina Reza," *Australian Journal of French Studies* 48.2 (2012): 191.

4. "Le tableau blanc arrivait sur scène, les gens hurlaient de rire! C'était sans doute amusant de voir deux acteurs contemplant un tableau blanc pendant cinq minutes, mais il n'y avait pas de quoi hurler." Ibid.

5. Poirier, "Please Stop Laughing at Me."

6. Lakis Proguidis, "Entretien avec Yasmina Reza," cited in Jaccomard, 191. Reza, *"Art,"* 26; *Théâtre*, 218.

7. Christopher Hampton, Alexander St. Press Interview, in the L.A. Theatre Works audio reproduction of *"Art,"* directed by Peter Levin, performed by Bob Balaban, Brian Cox, and Jeff Perry, recorded January 1, 2009, accessed August 21, 2014, http://search.alexanderstreet.com/view/work/895409.

8. Reza, *Théâtre*, 250.

9. James Elkins, *Pictures & Tears: A History of People Who Have Cried in Front of Paintings* (New York: Routledge, 2001), x.

10. Ibid., xi.

11. Reza, *"Art,"* 1, 8 ; *Théâtre*, 195, 201.

12. *"Art,"* 17; *Théâtre*, 210.

13. *"Art,"* 5, 59; *Théâtre*, 199, 248.

14. *"Art,"* 1; *Théâtre*, 195.

15. *"Art,"* 27–30; *Théâtre*, 219–221.

16. *"Art,"* 18; *Théâtre*, 210.

17. *"Art,"* 61; *Théâtre*, 250.

18. *"Art,"* 63.

19. *Théâtre*, 251.

20. Arthur Danto, "Yasmina Reza's *Art*," in *The Madonna of the Future: Essays in a Pluralistic Art World* (New York: Farrar, Straus and Giroux, 2000), 307.

21. Ibid., 309.

{ REFERENCES }

Adorno, Theodor. *Aesthetic Theory*. Translated by Robert Hullot-Kentor. Minneapolis: University of Minnesota Press, 1998.

———. *Minima Moralia: Reflections from a Damaged Life*. Translated by E.F.N. Jephcott. London: Verso, 2005.

———. "Opera and the Long-Playing Record." Translated by Thomas Y. Levin. *October* 55 (Winter 1990): 62–66.

Agamben, Giorgio. *The Coming Community*. Translated by Michael Hardt. Minneapolis: University of Minnesota Press, 1993.

———. *Profanations*. Translated by Jeff Fort. New York: Zone, 2007.

Alliez, Eric. *L'Oeil-cerveau: nouvelles histoires de la peinture moderne*. Paris: Vrin, 2007.

Alpers, Svetlana. *The Art of Describing: Dutch Art in the Seventeenth Century*. Chicago: University of Chicago Press, 1984.

Aron, Paul. *Histoire du pastiche: le pastiche littéraire français, de la Renaissance à nos jours*. Paris: Presses Universitaires de France, 2008.

Austin, James. *Pastiche, Proust, Postmodernism, or Why Style Matters*. Lewisburg, PA: Bucknell University Press, 2013.

Austin, J. L. *How to Do Things with Words*. Cambridge, MA: Harvard University Press, 1975.

Baier, Annette. "What Emotions Are About." *Philosophical Perspectives* 4 (1990): 1–29.

Bal, Mieke. *The Mottled Screen: Reading Proust Visually*. Translated by Anna-Louise Milne. Stanford, CA: Stanford University Press, 1997.

Barnhurst, Kevin G., and John Nerone. *The Form of News: A History*. New York: Guilford Press, 2001.

Barthes, Roland. *Camera Lucida: Reflections on Photography*. Translated by Richard Howard. New York: Hill and Wang, 1982.

———. *La Chambre claire: note sur la photographie*. Paris: Gallimard, 1980.

———. *Fragments d'un discours amoureux*. Paris: Seuil, 1977.

———. *A Lover's Discourse: Fragments*. Translated by Richard Howard. New York: Farrar, Straus, and Giroux, 1978.

———. *The Neutral: Lecture Course at the Collège de France (1977–1978)*. Translated by Rosalind E. Krauss and Denis Hollier. New York: Columbia University Press, 2005.

———. *Le Neutre: notes de cours au Collège de France, 1977–1978*. Paris: Seuil, 2002.

———. *Oeuvres complètes*. Vol. 4, 1972–1976. Edited by Éric Marty. Paris: Seuil, 2002.

———. *Oeuvres complètes*. Vol. 5, 1977–1980. Edited by Éric Marty. Paris: Seuil, 2002.

———. *La Préparation du roman: notes de cours et de séminaires au Collège de France, 1978–1979, 1979–1980*. Paris: Seuil, 2003.

———. *The Preparation of the Novel: Lecture Courses and Séminars at the Collège de France (1978–1979 and 1979–1980)*. Translated by Kate Briggs. New York: Columbia University Press, 2011.

———. *The Responsibility of Forms: Essays on Music, Art, and Representation*. Translated by Richard Howard. Berkeley: University of California Press, 1985.

Bataille, Georges. *Oeuvres complètes*. Vol. 1, 1922–1940. Paris: Gallimard [Bibliothèque de la Pléiade], 1970.

Baudelaire, Charles. *Les Fleurs du Mal*. Translated by Richard Howard. New York: David R. Godine, 1983.

Baudrillard, Jean. *Le Système des objets*. Paris: Gallimard, 1968.

Beaujour, Michel. "Culture." In *A New History of French Literature*, edited by Denis Hollier, 181–185. Cambridge, MA: Harvard University Press, 1989.

Beckett, Samuel. *The Letters of Samuel Beckett*. Vol. 2. Translated by George Craig et al. Cambridge: Cambridge University Press, 2011.

Benjamin, Walter. *The Arcades Project*. Translated by Howard Eiland and Kevin McLaughlin. Cambridge, MA: Harvard University Press, 1999.

——. "A Child's View of Color." In *Selected Writings*. Vol. 1, *1913–1926*, edited by Marcus Bullock and Michael W. Jennings, translated by Rodney Livingstone, 50–51. Cambridge, MA: Harvard University Press, 1996.

——. "The Newspaper." In *Selected Writings*. Vol. 2, *1931–1934*, edited by Marcus Paul Bullock, Howard Eiland, and Gary Smith, translated by Rodney Livingstone, 741–742. Cambridge, MA: Harvard University Press, 2005.

——. "On the Image of Proust." In *Selected Writings*. Vol. 2, *1927–1930*, edited by Howard Eiland, Michael W. Jennings, and Gary Smith, translated by Harry Zohn, 237–247. Cambridge, MA: Harvard University Press, 1999.

——. "On Some Motifs in Baudelaire." In *Selected Writings*. Vol. 4, 1938–1940, edited by Howard Eiland and Michael W. Jennings, translated by Harry Zohn, 313–355. Cambridge, MA: Harvard University Press, 2006.

Bennett, Jane. *Vibrant Matter: A Political Ecology of Things*. Durham, NC: Duke University Press, 2010.

Benzecry, Claudio. *The Opera Fanatic: Ethnography of an Obsession*. Chicago: University of Chicago Press, 2011.

Bergeron, Katherine. *Voice Lessons: French Mélodie in the Belle Époque*. New York: Oxford University Press, 2010.

Bersani, Leo. *The Culture of Redemption*. Cambridge, MA: Harvard University Press, 1990.

——. *Marcel Proust: The Fictions of Art and Life*. New York: Oxford University Press, 1965.

Bersani, Leo, and Ulysse Dutoit. "Beauty's Light." *October* 82 (Autumn, 1997): 17–29.

Best, Stephen, and Sharon Marcus. "Surface Reading: An Introduction." *Representations* 108 (Fall 2009): 1–21.

Blanchot, Maurice. "Everyday Speech." Translated by Susan Hanson. *Yale French Studies* 73 (1987): 12–20.

——. "L'Homme de la rue." *La Nouvelle Revue française* 114 (June 1962): 1070–1081.

—— "La parole quotidienne." In *L'Entretien infini*, 355–366. Paris: Gallimard, 1969.

Blandin, Claire. *Le Figaro: deux siècles d'histoire*. Paris: Armand Colin, 2007.

——, ed. *Le Figaro: histoire d'un journal*. Paris: Nouveau Monde, 2010.

Bora, Renu. "Outing Texture." In *Novel Gazing: Queer Readings in Fiction*, edited by Eve Kosofsky Sedgwick, 94-127. Durham: Duke University Press, 1997.

Boscagli, Maurizia, and Enda Duffy. "Selling Jewels: Modernist Commodification and Disappearance as Style." *Modernism/modernity* 14.2 (2007): 189–207.

Bouillaguet, Annick. *Proust lecteur de Balzac et Flaubert: l'imitation cryptée*. Paris: Honoré Champion, 2000.

Bourdieu, Pierre. *Distinction: A Social Critique of the Judgment of Taste*. Translated by Richard Nice. Cambridge, MA: Harvard University Press, 1984.
——. *La Distinction: critique sociale du jugement*. Paris: Minuit, 1979.
——. "Outline of a Sociological Theory of Art Perception." *International Social Science Journal*, 20 (November 1968): 589–612.
——. *Les Règles de l'art: genèse et structure du champ littéraire*. Paris, Seuil: 1992.
——. *The Rules of Art: Genesis and Structure of the Literary Field*. Translated by Susan Emanuel. Stanford, CA: Stanford University Press, 1996.
Bowie, Malcolm. "Postlude: Proust and the Art of Brevity." In *The Cambridge Companion to Proust*, edited by Richard Bales, 216–229. Cambridge: Cambridge University Press, 2001.
——. *Proust Among the Stars*. New York: Columbia University Press, 2000.
Brown, Bill. "The Secret Life of Things: Virginia Woolf and the Matter of Modernism." *Modernism/Modernity* 6.2 (1999): 1–28.
Brown, Judith. *Glamour in Six Dimensions: Modernism and the Radiance of Form*. Ithaca, NY: Cornell University Press, 2009.
Bulatkin, Eleanor Webster. "The French Word Nuance." *PMLA* 70.1 (March 1955): 244–273.
Bürger, Peter. *Theory of the Avant-Garde*. Translated by Michael Shaw. Minneapolis: Minnesota University Press, 1984.
Butor, Michel. "Les Moments de Marcel Proust." In *Les Critiques de notre temps et Proust*, edited by Jacques Bersani, 116–128. Paris: Garnier, 1971.
Cameron, Sharon. *Impersonality*. Chicago: University of Chicago Press, 2007.
Cano, Christine M. "Journalism." In *Marcel Proust in Context*, edited by Adam Watt, 153–159. Cambridge: Cambridge University Press, 2013.
——. *Proust's Deadline*. Urbana: University of Illinois Press, 2006.
Capello, Mary. *Awkward: A Detour*. New York: Bellevue Literary Press, 2007.
Cavell, Stanley. *Philosophy the Day after Tomorrow*. Cambridge, MA: Harvard University Press, 2005.
Chaouli, M. "Van Gogh's Ear: Toward a Theory of Disgust." In *Modern Art and the Grotesque*, edited by Frances S. Connelly, 47–62. Cambridge: Cambridge University Press, 2003.
Cheng, Anne Anlin. *Second Skin: Josephine Baker and the Modern Surface*. New York: Oxford University Press, 2010.
——. "Shine: On Race, Glamour, and the Modern." *PMLA* 1026.4 (October 2011): 1022–1041.
Cheng, Joyce. "Mask, Mimicry, Metamorphosis: Roger Caillois, Walter Benjamin and Surrealism in the 1930s." *Modernism/Modernity* 16.1 (January 2009): 61–86.
Clayton, Michelle. *Poetry in Piece: César Vallejo and Lyric Modernity*. Berkeley: University of California Press, 2011.
Clifford, James. *The Predicament of Culture: Twentieth-Century Ethnography, Literature, and Art*. Cambridge, MA: Harvard University Press, 1988.
Collier, Peter, and J. D. Whiteley. "Proust's Blank Page." *The Modern Language Review* 79.3 (July 1984): 570–578.
Compagnon, Antoine. Préface and Notes to *Du côté de chez Swann*. Paris: Gallimard, 1988.
Coole, Diana, and Samantha Frost, eds. *New Materialisms: Ontology, Agency, and Politics*. Durham, NC: Duke University Press, 2010.
Cook, James W. *The Arts of Deception: Playing with Fraud in the Age of Barnum*. Cambridge, MA: Harvard University Press, 2001.

Crary, Jonathan. *Suspensions of Perception: Attention, Spectacle, and Modern Culture.* Cambridge, MA: MIT Press, 1999.

Crimp, Douglas. "On the Museum's Ruins." In *The Anti-Aesthetic: Essays on Postmodern Culture,* edited by Hal Foster, 49–64. New York: The New Press, 1998.

Dahlin, Lois. "Entretien avec Francis Ponge: ses rapports avec Camus, Sartre, et d'autres." *The French Review* 54.2 (December 1980): 271–281.

Damisch, Hubert. *A Theory of /Cloud/: Toward a History of Painting.* Translated by Janet Lloyd. Stanford, CA: Stanford University Press, 2002.

Danius, Sara. *The Senses of Modernism: Technology, Perception, and Aesthetics.* Ithaca, NY: Cornell University Press, 2002.

Danto, Arthur. "Yasmina Reza's Art." In *The Madonna of the Future: Essays in a Pluralistic Art World,* 304–311. New York: Farrar, Straus and Giroux, 2000.

David-Ménard, Monique. "Must One Seek the Universal in Beauty?" *Umbr(a): Aesthetics & Sublimation* (1999): 45–60.

De Duve, Thierry. *Kant after Duchamp.* Cambridge, MA: MIT Press, 1996.

Del Bosco, Paquito. *O sole mio: Storia della canzona più famosa del mondo.* Rome: Donzelli, 2006.

Deleuze, Gilles. *Cinéma 1: l'image mouvement.* Paris: Minuit, 1983.

———. *Cinema 1: The Movement-Image.* Translated by Hugh Tomlinson and Barbara Habberjam. Minneapolis: University of Minnesota Press, 1986.

———. *Francis Bacon: The Logic of Sensation.* Translated by Daniel W. Smith. Minneapolis: University of Minnesota Press, 2003.

———. *Proust and Signs.* Translated by Richard Howard. Minneapolis: University of Minnesota Press, 2003.

———. *Proust et les signes.* Paris: Presses Universitaires de France, 1976.

Deleuze, Gilles, and Félix Guattari. *Mille plateaux. Capitalisme et schizophrénie.* Paris: Minuit, 1980.

———. *A Thousand Plateaus: Capitalism and Schizophrenia.* Translated by Brian Massumi. Minneapolis: University of Minnesota Press, 1987.

De Man, Paul. *Allegories of Reading.* New Haven, CT: Yale University Press, 1979.

Derrida, Jacques. "Economimesis." Translated by R. Klein. *Diacritics* 11.2 (Summer 1981): 3–25.

———. *Marges de la philosophie.* Paris: Minuit, 2003.

———. *Margins of Philosophy.* Translated by Alan Bass. Chicago: University of Chicago Press, 2003.

———. *Signéponge/Signsponge.* Translated by Richard Rand. New York: Columbia University Press, 1984.

Didi-Huberman, Georges. *Confronting Images: Questioning the Ends of a Certain History of Art.* Translated by John Goodman. University Park: Pennsylvania State University Press, 2005.

Doane, Mary Ann. *The Emergence of Cinematic Time: Modernity, Contingency, the Archive.* Cambridge, MA: Harvard University Press, 2002.

Dubuffet, Jean. *Asphyxiante culture.* Paris: Minuit, 1986.

Duthuit, Georges. *Le musée inimaginable.* Paris: Corti, 1956.

Dyer, Nathalie Mauriac. "Genesis of Proust's 'Ruine de Venise.'" In *Proust in Perspective: Visions and Revisions,* edited by Armine Kotin Mortimer and Katherine Kolb, 67–84. Urbana: University of Illinois Press, 2002.

Eagle, Christopher. "On 'This' and 'That' in Proust: Deixis and Typologies in *A la recherche du temps perdu.*" *MLN* 121.4 (2006): 989–1008.

Edelman, Lee. *No Future: Queer Theory and the Death Drive.* Durham, NC: Duke University Press, 2004.

Elkins, James. "On the Impossibility of Close Reading: The Case of Alexander Marshack." *Current Anthropology* 37.2 (April 1996): 185–226.

———. *Pictures & Tears: A History of People Who Have Cried in Front of Paintings.* New York: Routledge, 2001.

English, James. *The Economy of Prestige: Prizes, Awards, and the Circulation of Cultural Value.* Cambridge, MA: Harvard University Press, 2005.

Ensor, Sarah. "Spinster Ecology: Rachel Carson, Sarah Orne Jewett, and Nonreproductive Futurity." *American Literature* 84.2 (2012): 409–435.

Fales, Cornelia. "The Paradox of Timbre." *Ethnomusicology* 46.1 (Winter, 2002): 56–95.

Farasse, Gérard, and Bernard Veck. *Guide d'un petit voyage dans l'oeuvre de Francis Ponge.* Villeneuve d'Ascq Nord: Presses universitaires du Septentrion, 1999.

Finch, Alison. "Love, Sexuality and Friendship." In *The Cambridge Companion to Proust,* edited by Richard Bales, 168–182. Cambridge: Cambridge University Press, 2001.

Finn, Michael. *Proust, the Body, and Literary Form.* Cambridge: Cambridge University Press, 1999.

Fisher, Philip. "Torn Space: James Joyce's *Ulysses.*" In *The Novel.* Vol. 2, *Forms and Themes,* edited by Franco Moretti, 667–686. Princeton, NJ: Princeton University Press, 2006.

———. *Wonder, the Rainbow, and the Aesthetics of Rare Experiences.* Cambridge, MA: Harvard University Press, 1999.

Flatley, Jonathan. *Affective Mapping: Melancholia and the Politics of Modernism.* Cambridge, MA: Harvard University Press, 2008.

Foucault, Michel. *Discipline and Punish: The Birth of the Prison.* Translated by Alan Sheridan. New York: Vintage, 1977.

———. *Les Mots et les choses: une archéologie des sciences humaines.* Paris: Gallimard, 1966.

———. *The Order of Things: An Archeology of the Human Sciences.* New York: Vintage Books, 1994.

François, Anne-Lise. "Flower Fisting." *Postmodern Culture* 22, no. 1 (2011). doi:10.1353/pnc.2012.0004.

———. *Open Secrets: The Literature of Uncounted Experience.* Stanford, CA: Stanford University Press, 2008.

Freud, Sigmund. "Fetishism." In *Sexuality and the Psychology of Love,* edited by Philip Rieff, 204–209. New York: Touchtone, 1997.

Fry, Paul H. *A Defense of Poetry: Reflections on the Occasion of Writing.* Stanford, CA: Stanford University Press, 1995.

Frye, Northrop. *The Harper Handbook to Literature.* New York: Harper & Row, 1985.

Gallagher, Catherine. "George Eliot: Immanent Victorian." *Representations* 90 (Spring 2005): 61–74.

Gallo, Rubén. *Proust's Latin Americans.* Baltimore: Johns Hopkins University Press, 2014.

Gamble, Cynthia. "Finding a Voice: from Ruskin to the Pastiches." In *Marcel Proust in Context,* edited by Adam Watt, 27–33. Cambridge: Cambridge University Press, 2013.

Gandhi, Leela. *The Common Cause: Postcolonial Ethics and the Practice of Democracy, 1900 to 1955.* Chicago: University of Chicago Press, 2014.

Genette, Gérard. *Narrative Discourse.* Translated by Jane E. Lewin. Ithaca, NY: Cornell University Press, 1980.

———. *Palimpsests: Literature in the Second Degree.* Translated by Channa Newman and Claude Doubinsky. Lincoln: University of Nebraska Press, 1997.

Ghéon, Henri. "Une oeuvre de loisir." In *Les Critiques de notre temps et Proust,* edited by Jacques Bersani, 20–25. Paris: Garnier, 1971.

Goffman, Erving. *Behavior in Public Places.* New York: Simon and Schuster, 2008.

———. *Interaction Ritual: Essays in Face to Face Behavior.* New York: Anchor Books, 1967.

Goodman, Kevis. *Georgic Modernity and British Romanticism: Poetry and the Mediation of History.* New York: Cambridge University Press, 2004.

———. "Uncertain Disease: Nostalgia, Pathologies of Motion, Practices of Reading." *Studies in Romanticism* 49 (Summer 2010): 197–227.

Guénoun, Denis. *Avez-vous lu Reza?* Paris: Albin Michel, 2005.

Guillory, John. *Cultural Capital: The Problem of Literary Canon Formation.* Chicago: University of Chicago Press, 1993.

Heller-Roazen, Daniel. *Echolalias: On the Forgetting of Language.* New York: Zone Books, 2005.

———. *The Inner Touch: Archeology of a Sensation.* New York: Zone Books, 2007.

Hennion, Antoine. "Those Things That Hold Us Together: Taste and Sociology." *Cultural Sociology* 1.1 (2007): 97–114.

Hermann-Paul [pseudonym of René Georges Hermann Paul]. *Les Grands Spectacles de la nature. La Vie de Monsieur Quelconque.* Paris: Lith. Belfond & Cie, 1895.

———. *Les Grands Spectacles de la nature. 2ème série, La Vie de Madame Quelconque.* Paris: Lith. Belfond & Cie, 1895.

Hollier, Denis. *Absent without Leave: French Literature under the Threat of War.* Translated by Catherine Porter. Cambridge, MA: Harvard University Press, 1997.

Hughes, Edward. *Marcel Proust, A Study in the Quality of Awareness.* Cambridge: Cambridge University Press, 1983.

Huysmans, J.-K. *À Rebours.* Paris: Gallimard, 1983.

Jaccomard, Hélène. "Serge, un peu d'humour! Homo ridens et 'Art' de Yasmina Reza." *Australian Journal of French Studies* 48.2 (2012): 183–195.

Jacobus, Mary. *Romantic Things: A Tree, A Cloud, A Stone.* Chicago: University of Chicago Press, 2012.

Jakobson, Roman. "Closing Statement: Linguistics and Poetics." In *Style in Language,* edited by Thomas A. Sebeok, 350–377. Cambridge, MA: MIT, 1960.

James, Henry. "The Figure in the Carpet." In *Major Stories and Essays,* 276–312. New York: Penguin, 1999.

———. *Literary Criticism: French Writers, Other European Writers, Prefaces to the New York Edition.* Edited by Leon Edel. New York: Library of America, 1984.

Jameson, Frederic. "Joyce or Proust." In *The Modernist Papers,* 171–203. London: Verso, 2007.

———. *Postmodernism, or the Cultural Logic of Late Capitalism.* Durham, NC: Duke University Press, 1991.

Jefferson, Ann. *Nathalie Sarraute, Fiction and Theory: Questions of Difference.* Cambridge: Cambridge University Press, 2000.

Kanfer, Paul. *The Last Empire: De Beers, Diamonds, and the World.* New York: Farrar, Straus, Giroux, 1993.

Kant, Immanuel. *Critique of the Power of Judgment.* Translated by Paul Guyer and Eric Matthews. Cambridge: Cambridge University Press, 2000.

Kaufmann, Vincent. *Le Livre et ses adresses: Mallarmé, Ponge, Valéry, Blanchot.* Paris: Méridiens Klincksieck, 1986.

Koestenbaum, Wayne. "In Defense of Nuance." In *My 1980s and Other Essays*, 51–64. New York: Macmillan, 2013.

Krauss, Rosalind. "Corpus Delecti." *October* 33 (Summer 1985): 31–72.

———. "The Ministry of Fate." In *A New History of French Literature*, edited by Denis Hollier, 1000–1006. Cambridge, MA: Harvard University Press, 1989.

———. "Postmodernism's Museum without Walls." In *Thinking about Exhibitions*, edited by Reesa Greenberg, Bruce W. Ferguson, and Sandy Nairne, 341–348. New York: Routledge, 1996.

Kristev, Julia. *Time & Sense: Proust and the Experience of Literature.* Translated by Ross Guberman. New York: Columbia University Press, 1996.

Lacoue-Labarthe, Philippe. *Poetry as Experience.* Translated by Andrea Tarnowski. Stanford, CA: Stanford University Press, 1999.

Landy, Joshua. "Modern Magic: Jean-Eugène Robert-Houdin and Stéphane Mallarmé." In *The Re-Enchantment of the World: Secular Magic in a Rational Age*, edited by Joshua Landy and Michael Saler, 102–129. Stanford, CA: Stanford University Press, 2009.

Leader, Darian. *Stealing the Mona Lisa: What Art Stops Us from Seeing.* New York: Counterpoint, 2002.

Lebovics, Herman. *Mona Lisa's Escort: André Malraux and the Reinvention of French Culture.* Ithaca, NY: Cornell University Press, 1999.

Lévy, Sidney. "Mutisme pongéen et chose mallarméenne." *Dalhousie French Studies* 25 (Fall-Winter 1993), 79–88.

Litvak, Joseph. *Strange Gourmets: Sophistication, Theory and the Novel.* Durham, NC: Duke University Press, 1997.

Looseley, David L. *The Politics of Fun: Cultural Policy and Debate in Contemporary France.* New York: Berg Publishers, 1995.

Lucey, Michael. *Never Say I: Sexuality and the First Person in Colette, Gide, and Proust.* Durham, NC: Duke University Press, 2006.

Lyotard, François. *The Inhuman: Reflections on Time.* Translated by Geoffrey Bennington and Rachel Bowlby. Stanford, CA: Stanford University Press, 1991.

———. *L'inhumain: causeries sur le temps.* Paris: Galilée, 1988.

Macé, Marielle. *Façons de lire, manières d'être.* Paris: Gallimard, 2011.

———. "Ways of Reading, Modes of Being." Translated by Marlon Jones. *New Literary History* 44.2 (2013): 213–229.

Majumdar, Saikat. *Prose of the World: Modernism and the Banality of Empire.* New York: Columbia University Press, 2013.

Mallarmé, Stéphane. *Collected Poems and Other Verse.* Translated by E. H. Blackmore and A. M. Blackmore. New York: Oxford University Press, 2006.

———. *Oeuvres complètes.* Paris: Gallimard [Bibliothèque de la Pléiade], 1945.

———. *The Poems in Verse.* Translated by Peter Manson. Oxford, OH: Miami University Press, 2013.

Mao, Douglas, and Rebecca L. Walkowitz. "The New Modernist Studies." *PMLA* 123. 3 (2008): 742–745.

Marx, Karl. *Capital*. Vol. 1. Translated by Ben Fowkes. New York: Penguin, 1976.

Mauss, Marcel. "The Notion of Bodily Techniques." In *Sociology and Psychology: Essays*, translated by Ben Brewster, 97–105. London: Routledge, 1979.

Merleau-Ponty, Maurice. *Phénoménologie de la perception*. Paris: Gallimard, 2001.

———. *Phenomenology of Perception*. Translated by Colin Smith. London: Routledge, 1962.

———. *The Visible and the Invisible: Followed by Working Notes*. Translated by Alphonso Lingis. Evanston, IL: Northwestern University Press, 1968.

———. *Le Visible et l'Invisible, suivi de notes de travail*. Paris: Gallimard, 1964.

Met, Philippe. "Fausses notes: pour une poétique du carnet." *French Forum* 37 (Winter/ Spring 2012), 53–67.

Milly, Jean. *Les Pastiches de Proust*. Paris: Colin, 1970.

———. *Proust dans le texte et l'avant-texte*. Paris: Flammarion, 1985.

Morgan, Benjamin. "Undoing Legal Violence: Walter Benjamin's and Giorgio Agamben's Aesthetics of Pure Means." *Journal of Law and Society* 4 (March 2007): 46–64.

Mortimer-Sandilands, Catriona. "Melancholy Natures, Queer Ecologies." In *Queer Ecologies: Sex, Nature, Politics, Desire*, edited by Bruce Erikson and Catriona Mortimer-Sandilands, 331–358. Bloomington: Indiana University Press, 2010.

Morton, Timothy. *Ecology without Nature: Rethinking Environmental Aesthetics*. Cambridge, MA: Harvard University Press, 2007.

Müller, Charles, and Paul Reboux, eds. *À la manière de. . . .* Paris: Grasset, 1910.

Nancy, Jean-Luc. "Le Coeur des choses." In *Une pensée finie*, 197–223. Paris: Galilée, 1990.

———. "The Heart of Things." In *The Birth to Presence*, translated by Brian Holmes and Rodney Trumble, 167–188. Stanford, CA: Stanford University Press, 1993.

Natural, Mireille. "Le fabuleux destin de l'article dans *Le Figaro*." In *Marcel Proust 4: Proust au tournant des siècles*, edited by Bernard Brun and Juliette Hassine, 23–39. Paris: Minard, 2004.

Nersessian, Anahid. *Utopia, Limited: Romanticism and Adjustment*. Cambridge, MA: Harvard University Press, 2015.

Newmark, Kevin. "Traumatic Poetry: Charles Baudelaire and the Shock of Laughter." In *Trauma: Explorations in Memory*, edited by Cathy Caruth, 236–255. Baltimore: Johns Hopkins University Press, 1995.

Ngai, Sianne. *Our Aesthetic Categories: Zany, Cute, Interesting*. Cambridge, MA: Harvard University Press, 2012.

———. *Ugly Feelings*. Cambridge, MA: Harvard University Press, 2005.

Normand, Jacques [under the pseudonym of Jacques Madeleine]. "En somme, qu'est-ce?" In *Les Critiques de notre temps et Proust*, edited by Jacques Bersani, 13–20. Paris: Garnier, 1971.

Olson, Liesl. *Modernism and the Ordinary*. New York: Oxford University Press, 2009.

Pampel, Madeline. *Francis Ponge et Eugene de Kermadec, histoire d'un compagnonnage*. Villeneuve d'Ascq: Presses Universitaires du Septentrion, 2011.

Partridge, Eric. *A Dictionary of Clichés*. London: Routledge, 1978.

Paulhan, Jean, and Francis Ponge. *Correspondance 1923–1968*. Edited by Claire Boaretto. Paris: Gallimard, 1986.

Phillips, Siobhan. *The Poetics of the Everyday: Creative Repetition in Modern American Verse*. New York: Columbia University Press, 2010.

Ponge, Francis. *Mute Objects of Expression*. Translated by Lee Fahnestock. New York: Archipelago Books, 2008.

———. *Oeuvres complètes.* 2 vols. Paris: Gallimard [Bibliothèque de la Pléiade], 1999–2002.

———. *Le Savon.* Paris: Gallimard, 1967.

———. *Selected Poems.* Translated by Margeret Guiton, John Montague, and C. K. Williams. Winston-Salem, NC: Wake Forest University Press, 1994.

Posnock, Ross. *The Trial of Curiosity: Henry James, William James, and the Challenge of Modernity.* New York: Oxford University Press, 1991.

Prendergast, Christopher. *Mirages and Mad Beliefs: Proust the Skeptic.* Princeton, NJ: Princeton University Press, 2013.

Proust, Marcel. *À la recherche du temps perdu.* 4 vols. Paris: Gallimard [Bibliothèque de la Pléiade], 1987–1989.

———. *Contre Sainte-Beuve.* Paris: Gallimard [Bibliothèque de la Pléiade], 1971.

———. *Correspondance de Marcel Proust.* Edited by Philip Kolb. 21 Vols. Pari: Plon, 1970–1993.

———. *In Search of Lost Time.* Translated by Scott Moncrieff and Terence Kilmartin. Rev. D. J. Enright. 6 vols. New York: Random House, 1992.

———. *The Lemoine Affair.* Translated by Charlotte Mandell. New York: Melville, 2008.

———. *Lettres (1879–1922).* Edited by Françoise Leriche. Paris: Plon, 2004.

———. *Swann's Way.* Translated by Lydia Davis. New York: Penguin, 2004.

Rancière, Jacques. *Aesthetics and Its Discontents.* Translated by Steven Corcoran. Cambridge: Polity Press, 2009.

———. *Le Partage du sensible: esthétique et politique.* Paris: La Fabrique, 2000.

———. *The Philosopher and His Poor.* Translated by John Drury and Corinne Oster. Durham, NC: Duke University Press, 2004.

———. *Le Philosophe et ses pauvres.* Paris: Flammarion, 2007.

———. *Politique de la littérature.* Paris: Galilée, 2007.

———. *The Politics of Aesthetics.* Translated by Gabriel Rockhill. London: Continuum, 2004.

———. "Why Emma Bovary Had to Be Killed." *Critical Inquiry* 34 (Winter 2008): 233–248.

Randall, Bryony. *Modernism, Daily Time, and Everyday Life.* Cambridge: Cambridge University Press, 2008.

Reza, Yasmina. *"Art."* Translated by Christopher Hampton. London: Faber and Faber, 1996.

———. *Théatre.* Paris: A. Michel, 1998.

Ricks, Christopher. *Force of Poetry.* Oxford: Clarendon Press, 1984.

Riffaterre, Michel. "The Intertextual Unconscious." *Critical Inquiry* 13.2 (Winter 1987): 371–385.

Rivière, Georges Henri. "My Experience at the Musee D'Ethnologie." *Proceedings of the Royal Anthropological Institute of Great Britain and Ireland* (1968): 17–21.

Ruskin, John. *Modern Painters.* Vol. 1. London: Ballantyne, 1883.

———. *Modern Painters.* Vol. 6. London: Ballantyne, 1897.

Saint-Amand, Pierre. *The Pursuit of Laziness: An Idle Interpretation of the Enlightenment.* Translated by Jennifer Curtiss Gage. Princeton, NJ: Princeton University Press, 2011.

Sarraute, Nathalie. *Oeuvres complètes.* Paris: Gallimard [Bibliothèque de la Pléiade], 1996.

Sartre, Jean-Paul. *La Nausée.* Paris: Gallimard, 1972.

———. *Situations I.* Paris: Gallimard, 1947.

Scarry, Elaine. *Dreaming by the Book.* Princeton, NJ: Princeton University Press, 1999.

Schjendahl, Peter. *The Hydrogen Jukebox: Selected Writings of Peter Schjendahl, 1978–1990*. Edited by MaLin Wilson. Berkeley and Los Angeles: University of California Press, 1993.

Schoenbach, Lisi. *Pragmatic Modernism*. New York: Oxford University Press, 2011.

Scholar, Richard. *The Je-Ne-Sais-Quoi in Early Modern Europe: Encounters with a Certain Something*. New York: Oxford University Press, 2005.

Sedgwick, Eve Kosovsky. *Touching Feeling: Affect, Pedagogy, Performativity*. Durham, NC: Duke University Press, 2003.

———. *The Weather in Proust*. Durham, NC: Duke University Press, 2011.

Shattuck, Roger. "Proust's Stilts." *Yale French Studies* 34 (1965): 91–98.

———. *Proust's Way: A Field Guide to In Search of Lost Time*. New York: Norton, 2001.

Sheringham, Michael. *Everyday Life: Theories and Practices from Surrealism to the Present*. New York: Oxford University Press, 2006.

Shiner, Larry. *The Invention of Art: A Cultural History*. Chicago: University of Chicago Press, 2001.

Simon, Anne. *Proust ou le réel retrouvé*. Paris: Presses Universitaires de France, 2000.

Smith, Adam. *The Wealth of Nations, Books 1–3*. London: Penguin, 2003.

Smith, Daniel. *Essays on Deleuze*. Edinburgh: Edinburgh University Press, 2012.

Smock, Ann. "Cloudy Roubaud." *Representations* 86 (Spring 2004): 141–174.

Solomon, Matthew. "Upto-Date Magic: Theatrical Conjuring and the Trick Film." *Theatre Journal* 58 (2006): 595–615.

Soni, Vivasvan. "Communal Narcosis and Sublime Withdrawal: The Problem of Community in Kant's *Critique of Judgment*." *Cultural Critique* 64 (Fall 2006): 1–39.

Spitzer, Leo. *Études de style*. Translated by Eliane Kaufholz, Alain Coulon, and Michel Foucault. Paris: Gallimard, 1970.

Stewart, Garrett. *The Look of Reading: Book, Painting, Text*. Chicago: University of Chicago Press, 2006.

Stewart, Susan. *On Longing: Narratives of the Miniature, the Gigantic, the Souvenir, the Collection*. Durham, NC: Duke University Press, 1996.

Tadié, Jean-Yves. *Marcel Proust: A Life*. Translated by Euan Cameron. New York: Penguin, 2000.

Tamarkin, Elisa. "Literature and the News." In *The Oxford Handbook of Nineteenth-Century American Literature*, edited by Russ Castronovo, 309–326. New York: Oxford University Press, 2012.

Tanner, Tony. *Venice Desired*. Cambridge, MA: Harvard University Press, 1992.

Tarde, Gabriel. *Les Lois de l'imitation: étude sociologique*. Paris: Félix Alcan, 1890.

Taussig, Michael. *Mimesis and Alterity: A Particular History of the Senses*. New York: Routledge, 1993.

Teeuwen, Rodolphus. "An Epoch of Rest: Roland Barthes's 'Neutral' and the Utopia of Weariness." *Cultural Critique* 80 (Winter 2012): 1–26.

Terada, Rei. *Looking Away: Phenomenality and Dissatisfaction, Kant to Adorno*. Cambridge, MA: Harvard University Press, 2009.

Teruskin, Richard. *Music in the Seventeenth and Eighteenth Centuries: The Oxford History of Western Music*. Oxford: Oxford University Press, 2009.

Thomson, Michael. *Rubbish Theory: The Creation and Destruction of Value*. Oxford: Oxford University Press, 1979.

Tomkins, Silvan. *Shame and Its Sisters: A Silvan Tomkins Reader.* Edited by Eve Kosofsky Sedgwick and Adam Frank. Durham, NC: Duke University Press, 1995.

Valéry, Paul. *Monsieur Teste.* Paris: Gallimard, 1946.

Weber, Samuel. "Ambivalence, the Humanities, and the Study of Literature." *Diacritics* 15 (Summer 1985): 11–25.

———. *Benjamin's -Abilities.* Cambridge, MA: Harvard University Press, 2008.

———. "The Unraveling of Form." In *Mass Mediauras: Form, Technics, Media*, edited by Alan Cholodenko, 9–35. Stanford, CA: Stanford University Press, 1996.

Williams, Raymond. "Structures of Feeling." In *Marxism and Literature*, 128–135. New York: Oxford University Press, 1977.

Woolf, Virginia. *A Haunted House and Other Stories.* New York: Harcourt Brace, 1972.

———. *To the Lighthouse.* New York: Harcourt Brace, 1981.

{ INDEX }

Note: Locators followed by the letter 'n' refer to notes.